NER
press

The Tongue is Also a Fire

The Tongue is Also a Fire

Essays on Conversation, Rhetoric and the Transmission of Culture
...and on C. S. Lewis

James Como

Published by New English Review Press
a subsidiary of World Encounter Institute
PO Box 158397
Nashville, Tennessee 37215
&
27 Old Gloucester Street
London, England, WC1N 3AX

Cover Art & Design by Kendra Mallock

ISBN: 978-1-943003-04-4

Second Printing

NER press NEW ENGLISH REVIEW PRESS
newenglishreview.org

Copyright Acknowledgments

The titles below are listed chronologically according to their dates of publication. These form the bases of ten essays in this book, each numbered (as in the table of contents) to the left of its original source. All are reproduced here by permission.

(12) "Elitism at the Core: Dare We Call it 'Rhetoric'?" *The Core and the Curriculum*, University of North Texas Press, 1993, pp. 54-59.

(10) "The Hero Storyteller [Mario Vargas Llosa and Peruvian Political Culture]," *National Review*, April 17, 1995, pp. 53-56 (conc. 72). © 1995 National Review, Inc. Reprinted by permission.

(15) "Thornton Wilder & the Gods," *The New Criterion*, 29:9 (May 2011), pp. 78-80.

(14) "True Minds" [a review of Reyes, ed., C. S. Lewis's Lost 'Aeneid'], *The New Criterion*, 30:1 (September 2011: thirtieth anniversary issue), pp. 136-138.

(13) "C. S. Lewis's Quantum Church," in *C.S. Lewis and the Church: Essays in Honour of Walter Hooper*, edd. Brendan Wolfe and Judith Tonning. T&T Clark: London, 2011.

(16) "His Fugitive Voice: After Fifty Years," *CSL*, 44:6 (November 2013), pp. 1-10, 12.

(19) "The Salon: Restoring Conversation," *Arion: A Journal of the Humanities and the Classics*, 22:1 (spring/summer 2014), pp. 33-49.

(7) "Obama's Self-Organizing Rhetoric," *New English Review* (online), March 2015.

(18) "The Mick: In Memoriam," *New English Review* (online), April 2015.

(6) "'The Tongue is Also a Fire'," *New English Review* (online), May 2015.

to James Emil,
Helen Alexandra,
And to their mother, our Xandrita,
heart of our heart

Contents

PREFACE

THIS BOOK is a collection of free-standing, loosely-sequenced essays (which someone has astutely told us should be "assertive, intimate, polemical, whimsical . . . but always open and reflective"). They are associated, sometimes explicitly at other times implicitly, with my pivotal theme, conversation, as trees are to each other in a single wood. My hope is that by way of this stand there will emerge a fully foliated image: how cultures can grow from fertile soil.

Thus if the book-as-a-whole has a point-of-view, a fundamental premise, it is this: conversation is both recreative (that is, not merely "recreational") and helps build culture, whether high or popular. In our private, social and civic lives I believe nothing matters more. The movie producer (*e.g.* of *Splash* and *A Beautiful Mind*) Michael Grazer demonstrates as much in his engaging and useful book *A Curious Mind: The Secret to a Bigger Life*, in which he describes not only the uses of curiosity but the value of "curiosity conversations." Bravo, Mr. Grazos, and welcome to the club.

I also hope to encourage an appreciation of the rhetorical scaffolding that goes with our various conversations. My vocation over nearly five decades has been the effective transmission of a healthy culture, the prosecution of which, in my case, is achieved by rhetoric beyond all other means. Exploring and upholding that belief is my agenda. But the book *per se* is not an argument, even though it contains arguments about certain points-of-culture that merit robust conversation. May they provoke, not quarrels but further argument.

The subtitle of this book might have been "essays selected from a lifetime of teaching, reading, talking, and traveling" because these essays reflect my career as a professor, scholar, foreign correspondent, and compulsive critic (of books, social and public communication, movies, boxing, baseball . . . the analytical impulse is irrestistable). It's all conversaton, and in that I have found—and I'm told—that I'm unrelenting. Moreover I am one of very many people whose interior life has been significantly influenced by both the apologetic and scholarly work of C. S. Lewis. (Among other things he has been to me what the great dialectician and tutor W. T. Kirkpatrick was to him.) That is why the temptation here is to chronicle my engagement with him, but I've written or edited three books on my earthly master, so I will resist. On the other hand, Peru (my wife's *patria*) is always calling, so for a brief spell now I will yield to that Siren.

For the past nearly-five decades I've traveled through and lived in that unutterably diverse, mysterious, and variously beguiling country. I have family there, of course, and my wife and I have made sure that our (now grown) children are virtually bi-cultural. So I was excited when *National Review* commissioned me to cover the landmark presidential elections of 1990: the renowned and wealthy novelist Mario Vargas Llosa (now a Nobelist) versus the completely unknown and eventual winner (and now criminally convicted) Alberto Fujimori.

Every journalist from abroad had to be fully-credentialed as a foreign correspondent, which required a trip to the Ministry of Exterior Relations (the Peruvian State Department), and that meant a re-enactment of Kafka's *The Castle*. When my photo was snapped, the photographer slightly turned the knot of my tie to the right, which I later learned was code for "American." Thereafter I roamed at will, including to Fujimori's campaign headquarters, where I was almost alone. The one other person present was Mrs. Fujimori, dressed on stage in full, old-school Japanese garb. (She would turn out to be a force to be reckoned with, and not a happy one for her husband.)

I was able to get a room at the Hilton, Vargas Llosa's headquarters located across the street from the primary polling place, The Ministry of Justice. The line on election day was a kilometer long (voting in Peru is mandatory), and the Hilton was only madness. When Fujimori finished a close-enough second to warrant a run-off—and left with a glum Vargas Llosa after refusing to withdraw—pandemonium was loosed upon the grand ballroom. Indelible. (My thoughts on Peru, including memories of other memorable incidents, are gathered in essay #11)

I've emphasized culture. Conversation matters because it in building both personal relationships and whole cultures; it ties the past to the present and both to the future, articulating custom and convention, iterating pieties, and giving rise to collective identities of varying scope. Conversation is also unavoidable, either directly (that is, face-to-face, same time, same place) or by proxy (*e.g.* telephone, email, social media). It is our first medium of maturing and mature human interanimation and quickly becomes indispensable to our communal good health. Unfortunately—and for all the talk of "having a conversation," national or otherwise about this or that—conversation is also often brutally twisted, its terms too-often dictated or (just as dangerous) taken for granted.

This was not always the case, at least not commonly. Until the present age (the last hundred years or so) we were educated to culture, making, recording, molding and enjoying both its methods and manners. We studied rhetoric. For example, we knew the difference between argument and quarrel and were instructed in the arts of expression. We read well, thought carefully, and we spoke civilly, amusingly if we could, and persuasively, or at least we believed we ought so to read, think and speak. Whether or not we knew the word *rhetoric* (and more likely than not we did) we at least intuited the importance of it to building good cultures. In short, we understood the nature and application of the rhetorical scaffolding to the arts of seeing, knowing, thinking, saying and making.

Dr. Samuel Johnson once told us that people need to be reminded more often than instructed, and since I agree, I offer that reminding—as personal reflection, history, instruction, and criticism—in light of this admonition: the best conception of conversation is certainly broad, from what is called the Great Conversation (*e.g.* of Western Civilization) to daily—even intimate—life. (It includes these essays.) No, not trivial, *phatic* exchanges ("high how ya doin'?"), but just about all others, no matter their form or format. (However, as we shall see within, face-to-face conversation, for which all other media of exchange are surrogates, matters most—and by far.)

The sequence joining the three big concepts of Conversation, Rhetoric and Education (the means whereby culture is transmitted) are mostly straight-forward. Education, the enterprise that "leads forth" (*educare*), trains us in rhetoric, the art of persuasion (meaning, at its root, *per+suase*, "by sweetness"). From that simple notion rhetoric grows into the art that designs, builds, and guides our conversations, teaching us at least the nuts and bolts of private, social, and public discourse, from the bedroom and the "parlor" (where we *parler*, or parley), to civil groupings and schools, on to parliaments of various kinds, and always to the arts of literature, history, philosophy, the sciences, and social service of one form or another. In short, it becomes an instrument of cultivation: we use rhetoric to enrich (or, alas, to poison) the soil from which robust conversation, and thereby culture, might grow.

Some of the essays were written expressly for this book, some not; some have already been published (*e.g.* in *The New Criterion, National Review, The New English Review*), others not; a few are scholarly, most, though, are not (and—full disclosure—there is some overlapping among them). The essays are loosely grouped: 1-5, 6-10, 11-13, 14-18, 19 and 20. But these groupings are merely suggestive; the essays can be read in any order. I wish there were others here, for example, on the novelists Sigrid Undset, William Kennedy, Walker Percy, Robertson Davies, Mark Helprin, and Emily Bronte (*Wuthering Heights* is not about love but revenge!); or on the nineteenth-century American actress Ada Rehan (the greatest shrew ever tamed); or on Roberto Duran ("Mucho Mas," *National Review,* March 6, 1995), the greatest pound-for-pound boxer (for a time) since the very greatest of all time, Sugar Ray Robinson; or on the Bush-Clinton debates of 1992 ("Debates, Debates, and Showbiz," *National Review,* November 16, 1992), or—well, you get the idea, I'm sure. There simply is no such thing as too much conversation.

That is so because conversation and its rhetoric—their artfulness and efficacy, fun and pure distinctiveness—are the fundamental faculties of our species. They are also how our individuated social selves begin.

It is with genuine glee that I thank Rebecca Bynum, publisher and managing editor of the *New English Review*, for her judgment, her generous stewardship, and for her unmatchable assiduousness.

ONE

Apologia
Reflections of a Rhetoric Professor

HAVING BEEN formally laboring in the rhetorical vineyard—as student, practitioner, and especially as teacher—for fifty years, I wonder: whence my own distinctive rhetorical urge? I say "distinctive" because although all of us have that pressing urge (though very few people know it as rhetorical) each of us manifests it differently, my own presenting as lecturing, writing and compulsive conversing. Having recently retired from nearly five decades of teaching rhetoric to college students—in the spring semester of 2014, I taught Rhetorical Theory and Criticism for what promises to be my last time—I decided to ponder the question seriously.

1.

I've always liked to see how things work, including how language and ideas work when put together and piled up. I found that when I applied this curiosity it came out as argument. A passion blossomed. Still, the greater need to know—from movies and baseball to literature, history, religion and even cosmology—was bigger than my appetite for the clash of ideas, as a galaxy is bigger than a solar system.

Thus my urge to read, and getting books mattered not only to read but to have them at the ready. That's why in my early adolescence I spent what money I had to address that urge, and around the ninth or tenth grade I intuited that some system for arranging my books would be helpful, so I became orderly. I stacked and re-stacked my ten, then twenty, and thereafter hundreds (and now a thousand or so) books with great care, often according to categorical principles so complex that no one but I could have figured them out. I even drew a diagram of the ideal personal library. I had become, and have remained, one of those people who could easily live in a library.

And yet I had not grown up among many books. Instead I grew up among readers and talkers, especially my father. Raconteur, living room debater, versatile conversationalist, salesman, and most of all a respecter of language properly spoken ("try not to say 'yeah', son"), he did not exhort or scold but rather encouraged and taught by example. Before I hit my teens he told me and others I would be a writer, which he cloaked in a joke (as was his custom): "my son already writes the best letter you've ever read, but he'll have trouble mailing it."

I find that talk of my father brings to mind several teachers I've had. A man named Herbert Schwartzberg, given the many wonderful teachers I am about to name, should be dispatched early. As my fifth grade teacher he was competent, I suppose, but also a bigot. The class was strong and amiable, I one of the stronger and more amiable pupils of the twenty-five or so. I was also one of only two Gentiles, the very two pupils not promoted by Mr. Schwartzberg to the fast-track sixth grade class which fed into the Special Progress Track (so-called by the New York City Board of Education) that eliminated the eighth grade.

I was devastated, so much so that my father—a widower raising my older brother and me virtually alone—took the unusual step of visiting Mr. Schwartzberg, who told him that I lacked the advantages of other students whose parents, after all, were largely college graduates who could provide for their offspring a "domestic environment more conducive to accelerated learning." He might have known that my father had dropped out of high school, earning his G.E.D. after serving in World War Two. But did Schwartzberg know that Pop averaged a book a week (he would often read all through the night and at red lights)? Or maybe the sonofabitch was compensating for his own hereditary inadequacy: could his grandfather, like mine, quote Dante, Petrarch and the Orlando Furioso from memory, for an hour? In the event, I would skip the eighth grade.

On the other hand . . . A nasty, but very constructive, lesson began with my own stupid refutation of corrections made on an essay I had submitted to my Freshman Composition professor. Dr. Gilmore's response, one closely-written page, and a classic, began "Dear Mr. Como, to call you an idiot would be a compliment" and went downhill from there. Herbert Schwartzberg may have been civil, mean-spirited and wrong, but Gilmore—rude and ill-humored—was right, and effective. For a while I persisted, until my father simply instructed me to do exactly as Gilmore required. That is precisely when I began to learn how to write.

A bit later, as an English literature major and a speech-communication minor (that indecisive abomination is what rhetoric was called in those days), I was bothered by what seemed to be an arbitrary division within one thing—the effective deployment of words—as though it were two. Then I discovered the One Thing formally, and it was Rhetoric. At the same time I came under the influence of my first academic and best boss, my first and best mentor, and my first and best teacher of rhetoric, all the same man, Forbes Iverson Hill, who would also become a friend (and on whom more later).

I had had great teachers before Forbes and after. Margaret O'Dea in the first grade, at P.S. 57 in East Harlem, was the first person (outside my family) to see me as smart, and as a gentleman: most of the boys wore white shirts and ties and carried clean handkerchiefs every school day—in first grade. In the seventh grade Mrs. Burrows was a homeroom teacher who handled my first crush with exquisite sensitivity. Ado Bolles, my seventh-grade English teacher, taught me to love both *Don Quixote* and *Julius Caesar* and not to obsess over writing the flawless essay; he was personally and intellectually respectful of his very young pupils. Miss Harris, my first African American teacher, was short and fat and had lumps on one side of her face, and she wantonly jubilated over the teaching of science and over our ability to learn it. I was very fond of her, as she was of me, and I worked extraordinarily hard just to see how happy she became when I had learned what she had to teach. Mr. Balish, my twelfth-grade English teacher, when he caught me reading *Compulsion* (the novel of the Loeb-Leopold-Franks murder case) that I was holding under my desktop, did not ask me to stop but instead suggested that when I finished with that I should try *An American Tragedy* which, at age fifteen, turned me into Clyde Griffiths for a good six months; there are vestiges of him in me still.

Another man stands as high in my personal pantheon as any teacher I've ever had. I have hoped to do for my students what my eleventh grade American history teacher, the unrelenting Dr. Leonard Gelber, did for me. Dr. Gelber was severe, uncompromising, unpatronizing. We would stand when we answered in his class, and there was no leaning on the desk or slouching. He welcomed any opinion, but woe unto the student who could not back it up. Dr. Gelber spoke many an opinion of his own, candidly—no worming about for him—and I always disagreed. In short order the daily dose of learning-is-fun for my classmates became the inevitable Gelber-Como confrontation, which would last for as long as twenty minutes. I always lost, of course, but I got in my licks. I still marvel at what he allowed: I would cross-examine him! Yet, being as callow as I was, from time-to-time I actually felt unfairly put upon rather than privileged, often muttering vows of polemical revenge. How utterly abashed and greatly gratified was I when I saw that my yearbook inscription from him was as high as any compliment I have ever received. He had known all along what he was doing, and he had read me just right. A great, a very great, teacher was Leonard Gelber. He knew what I continue to learn. Whenever we speak, whenever we so perform *this* action, it is *never about us*.

As an undergraduate at Queens College of the City University of New York, there was Robert Towers, a low-key Southern gentleman who, when teaching Eighteenth-Century English literature as something to be taken from the inside, took us all seriously as students and gentlepersons, probing, suggesting, reading evocatively and having us do the same, and asking questions as though he really did care to know what we thought. Dorothy Jones, a literary critic as straight-laced as they came, encouraged and guided my burgeoning interest in C. S. Lewis with exactly the severity I needed. Wilbur Gilman, strictly old-school, like Towers and Jones, addressed me almost as though I were a colleague. There were others of course; some bad ones too. But they did not mar me anywhere near as much as the finest ones cultivated me.

Later at Fordham University, where as a graduate student I studied Medieval English literature, Paul Memmo's frenetic zeal was at once absurd and riveting; and at Columbia (Teachers College) there was the brilliant Jonas Soltis, a philosopher's philosopher for whom conceptual thinking was an art and who let me know that I could be an artist. Paul Kozelka brought to life medieval mystery plays, taught acting as though it were recreation, and allowed me to believe that I was teaching myself (though those of us who were already teaching knew better). James Andrews was that rare oxymoron, a generous ideologue; he helped win for me a small (but-oh-so-essential) scholarship. And Maxine Greene, another literary critic of enormous capaciousness and sympathy, paid us the compliment of seeming to confer—and was more than a friendly face during my dissertation defense. These all had a genius for teaching.

Yet it was Professor Forbes Hill, my first graduate school professor and the director of the Basic Course in Speech at Queens College and thus my boss when I was a teaching assistant, who with great intellectual and personal elegance set very high standards of scholarship and hard work and simply expected us to satisfy them, as if there were no question of our interest in doing so, or of our ability. He not only tolerated but encouraged one to think broadly: for example, no one else in Speech in the City University of New York was contending with Wayne Booths' *The Rhetoric of Fiction*, a landmark book that would add to as well as greatly rearrange my conceptual furniture.

His tastes and tolerances were both catholic. A supporter of the hard-Left Henry Wallace for president in 1948, and a supporter of both Hubert Humphrey and George McGovern against Richard Nixon, he wrote a perfectly objective analysis of Richard Nixon's Viet Nam Address to the Nation. I was deeply flattered when he asked me (his ideological opposite) to vet the article for biases. My antennae were tuned, but I found none, and I was very pleased, and proud, to have been asked, not least when a dogmatic hard-Left critic lambasted Forbes for his Right-Wing biases which, she said, must have deep roots in his past! We all had a great laugh at that.) Forbes answered, elegantly of course.

2.

It was while I worked under Forbes nearly fifty years ago that I entered a college classroom as a teacher for the first time. I was that graduate teaching assistant, twenty years old, assisting no one and getting virtually no assistance myself, and cannot remember being more frightened before or since. Most of the students were seniors; they and most of the juniors were older than I; some of them had been my classmates the semester before. I spent the fifty-minute hour seated—almost for the last time until late in my career when arthritis would make its claims—looking out of the window, looking anywhere, in fact, rather than at them. I knew the material well enough, and I had a plan. I have that plan, as well as the roster from that class, to this day.

It was an admirably complete plan, containing such cues as "stand now," "write on board," and "tell joke here." Coming at midpoint, that last is followed in my notes by the actual joke, which I told: "Welcome back to Queens College, class. We were going to have the annual Parade of the Virgins, but one got sick and the other refused to march alone." The silence was broken by a groan—not a stage groan but a spontaneous expression of genuine pain. I sat, looked out of the window, lost myself briefly in the polychromatic foliage beyond, and then crawled back into my clammy, sagging skin. One thing more I remember: I carried on. When I left that room I knew I would never allow fear in that place again. The next day, I decided, I would at least *act* like a teacher.

Within the month any ambition I had of going to law school was gone and I knew that teaching college would be it for me. How, exactly, did I know? These are guesses at best: I could talk, perform, influence, satisfy my ego in the way it seemed most to be satisfied, and continually work my mind. I could do some good. What I have learned since, really, is that the decision had little to do with me. I believe now that Providence stepped in, making the college classroom, the lecture hall and the seminar table my small worlds to this day.

But seven years earlier, at age thirteen, as an expression of my curiosity about argument, I had begun a year of reading books about great lawyers. Among these were Earl Rogers (*The Final Verdict*, by his daughter Adela), Louis Nizer (*My Life in Court*), the unscrupulous William Fallon (*The Great Mouthpiece*), and Sam Leibowitz (*Court-room*), the book that made Leibowitz a hero to me. In 1933 he had accepted the invitation of a Communist Front organization to defend the nine boys and young men—The Scottsboro Boys, so called—accused of raping two white women in the South, than which there could be no tougher, unfair, or (there and then) more dangerous job. He would stay with the case for four years, finally taking it the Supreme Court—in spite of violent Ku Klux Klan mobs that threatened his and his wife's lives, a Communist Party attempt to hijack the case, and a judge so bigoted that he explicitly mocked the defendants and their lawyer in open court. Later when arguing before the Supreme Court, he was allowed the unprecedented right of introducing evidence; registration lists showed that Negroes had been systematically excluded from jury rolls. The end of that exclusion began then and there. For all of this he never accepted a penny, neither as a fee nor in reimbursement of his own expenses.

Nine years after reading Reynolds' book—I was twenty-two and in my second year of teaching full-time at York College, where I would spend the next forty-two full-time years—something happened that influenced me more deeply than I realized at the time. Sam Leibowitz came to York College. I was team-teaching a course in American Social Change, a topic being the Scottsboro case (which I had suggested). One of the team, an active member of the Democratic Party in Brooklyn, wondered if we would care to have Judge Leibowitz visit. "Sure," I said, containing myself. Some days later my colleague told me that, indeed, the judge was expecting a call—from me. A few days later I made the call. I had rehearsed my spiel to the gatekeeper-secretary. After two rings the judge himself answered the phone, so I stammered—and hung up! I called back immediately and heard an angry growl: "did you just hang up on me?" So I . . . lied. "I lost the connection, your Honor." "Uh huh," I heard. "What's on your mind?" A few days later we welcomed Samuel Leibowitz to the College. The deal was that we would buy him lunch—a tuna sandwich—and give him a lift to LaGuardia Airport.

Our room was packed with some fifty people, half of them young black men. Many of the male students were bare-chested, with their belts worn across their chests and their Che berets prominent: it was an angry time, and (for reasons I still cannot fathom) black anti-Semitism, especially among militant blacks, was already on the rise. They were astonished at what they saw. Leibowitz, seventy-five years old, balding and dapper, was no more than five-feet-ten-inches tall. His voice was strong and commanding, his self-assurance palpable, his manner at first temperate. But slowly that changed. As he began to recall the details of the events he began to relive them, and this man who never lost his temper in a courtroom began to do so in front of our very eyes.

He began with "those racist bastards," went on to "the Commie sons-of-bitches"—by now the class is dead silent and some of the students are actually on their feet—and rose to. . . language not heard in either courtrooms or college classrooms (we profs were stupefied). And all the while he was cutting the air with open hands and throwing punches as he moved about the front of the room, never taking his eyes off the class, as though it were a jury convened in a back alley. After nearly an hour the judge, his jacket now off, was soaked with sweat, and so were most of us. The students gave him a standing ovation, not least for his sheer authenticity.

As it happened, I would join him for lunch and provide the lift. Our conversation was desultory, and I realized only too late that I had been too diffident. But I did ask where he was headed. "To Cornell," he said. "They want me to discuss the Scottsboro Case. And"—here a chuckle—"they're paying me $3000!" And, I thought, and continue to think, "priceless."

How did this riveting first-hand account influence me? Leibowitz, along with my experience of Paul Memmo (who would have seemed an utter fool but for his authenticity, good will, and sheer teaching effectiveness), formed in me a different explicit conception of teaching than that of the pedant reading from notes (I had had my share of those, alas). Good teaching was a performing art, not unlike litigation. Yet only for the last thirty years have I had a concrete idea of what I am doing and only for the last twenty-five or so have acted upon it.

3.

The urgent epiphany catalyzing the change was that I must begin at the beginning. So on the first day of almost every class I've taught, my students hear the opening of St. John's Gospel; and immediately upon hearing that everything started with the Word they hear that John, using Greek, wrote *Logos*, evoking a concept far richer than anything indicated by our spare *word* (or the common Latin option, verbum).

I do not cite Isaiah ("So shall my word be . . . . It shall not return me to void, but shall do my will" [55.11]) and Jeremiah (the resonant "Is not my word like fire, says the Lord, like a hammer shattering rocks?" [23:29]). Sometimes, though, I do go on to say that its origin is in *lego* (literally "I say" and implying computation, measure and proportion), or that it took on real steam in Heraclitus (fl. 500 B.C.), who considered it the creative power permeating creation. Often I point out that John, a learned man, would have known the fundamental and pervasive application of it by Philo the Jew (30? B.C. – 45? A.D.), who considered Logos the divine pattern of the cosmos, a sort of mediator between God and humanity. In the event, the effect on me of beginning those classes as I do has been simple, the way a scalpel cutting away a small, but deadly, tumor is simple, and the impact on my students has been routinely dynamic, the way dynamite is dynamic.

Here, however, a necessary caveat arises against a superstitious allegiance to a sort of communication magic. For at least the last forty years our therapeutic-cum-narcissistic culture has regarded the slightest personal, familial, social, or even historical discomfort as a "dysfunction" to be treated. Well, "meaningful communication" does not always make the booboo go away; all communication has meaning, we are meaning machines after all, and often it makes things worse. Sometimes it must.

I had already learned earlier that unsettling students ought to be a goal of any legitimate college course and—no small point—makes for much fun. This matters. "What is learning?" I would catechize my children. "Learning is fun," they would drone, like body-snatched pod people. When my students have refused to play along, well, then I have invoked my hard rule: "at least one person in this class is going to have fun," meaning me of course. However, since teaching at its best is a performing art compelling engagement, the unsettler may be himself unsettled, and so my lessons continued.

For example, about forty years ago I learned that I could lighten up; a few years thereafter, that I should; several years after that, how not to. In a nutshell: it is much easier to lighten up than to tighten up; easier for Mussolini to become St. Francis than vice versa. And I learned to lie; that is, I learned to attribute some of my useful ideas to past students: it adds a suasory luster to the point and detoxifies an otherwise-deadly whiff of narcissism. (Whatever genius said there's no telling how much you can accomplish if you're willing to forgo credit was right.) Alas, I also learned, along the way and with accumulating misery, that dynamiting a desert does not necessarily alter the lay of the land in any important way.

Here is another lesson learned. Worrying over my slowness of progress towards a doctorate, tenure, and promotion, a driven dean (not always a redundancy, and, for the record, the decanal heart was not in the right place) asked if I cared to move things along by writing a textbook. She had . . . "connections." I had been teaching for a mere five years and was astonished. I knew the only textbook I could write would be one that rearranged other textbooks. Later I would learn that such is largely the way of the textbook world, but in the event I said no, thanks. That was one lesson learned.

And finally this, from my friend and colleague of over forty-five years, Samuel Hux. Older than I by nearly a half a generation, he described a sea change in American higher education. Imagine two circles next to each other, a very large one representing Knowledge and a much smaller one a Pupil. Until about thirty years ago the pupil expected the university to lead him into the larger circle, allowing him to grow into it as much as he could; since then, however, the pupil has demanded that knowledge be shrunk, or sliced into bits small enough to fit the pre-existing—and fixed—size of the pupil who, not so incidentally, selects the bits he prefers or thinks he needs. Thus we have the very worst of both the educational worlds that John Dewey described as Traditional education and his own Progressive response: higher learning now deals in "product," neither liberal nor educational. It is not a "leading out or forth" (the original meaning of "educate") but merely a "stuffing in" (Traditional), with the stuff itself selected and manipulated by pupils as they please ("the freedom of the learner"—Progressive).

Along the way I have heard, commented upon, and graded some 20,000 student-speeches; coached dozens of debaters and judged scores of debates; mediated, resolved, and reported upon conflicts in English and in Spanish across the Americas, within venues private and public; advised, counseled, and cajoled thousands of people, not only to think clearly and to speak authentically, but to do so eagerly and knowledgeably. And from the stinking hallways and menacing playgrounds of the James Weldon Johnson Housing Projects on Lexington Avenue and 112th Street in Harlem, to the minefield of the Long Island City High School yard, and on to the privacy of my own office when threatened by either a looming thug (I jumped Crazier-Than-Thou, a technique common in the projects) or an even-more-looming, fetchingly-displayed co-ed oozing in favor of a non-existent "oral option" to a term paper (here the Van Helsing-hold-up-a-Cross-to-Dracula response proved useful)—for that duration I have argued, persuaded, postured and otherwise *rhetorized* my way out of (and certainly into) trouble. All this, as well as the throbbing pulse of conversation, disputation, musings both silent and aloud, as well as prayer, have animated me. (Still I would not write a textbook.)

"What we have here is a failure to communicate," moans the chilling Strother Martin in that wonderful and savagely cynical movie *Cool Hand Luke*. The captain really would prefer not to beat his helpless convicts and wouldn't, if only they would stifle their passion for *utterance*; but that passion, like any *eros*, cannot be stifled. Rather, it must be mined, refined, and appropriately guided. Our very Personhood—we really cannot be reminded of this often enough—derives from that cognizant *Self*, a person's irreducible axiom; the most satisfying, treacherous, and promising of ambivalent challenges; the most elusive of the many elusive ambiguities in all God's creation: an image, perhaps, certainly an instrument, a switching board, if you will, for turning mere creatures into His actual progeny.

In short, speech is about our *Logos* at its greatest reach, about not just being but about *human* being. To attempt less than that fullness is to squander a gift. We are Homo sapiens, which entails a burden of accountability and the privilege of being voluble: discovering, knowing, choosing, designing, examining, arguing, judging, making and demanding sense, and finally performing—as though something were at stake, as though others mattered greatly and we owed them our best. These have been my subjects. So I must ask, How *not* unsettled?

At the end of the day this is what my father knew and what I've lent myself to teaching for almost five decades. When we speak *we cannot not perform*, cannot *not* blow things up a bit. There is no opting out. Do it badly, sporadically, thoughtlessly, indirectly, or by way of surrogates: but do it we must. The alternatives are sleep, coma, death, or removal to a desert cave. You see, we really *are* Meaning Machines, and that machinery runs on *Logos*, that is, on all kinds of conversations—personal, social, public, direct, or mediated. We have no choice, even as the disease of confusion courses through our individual and collective veins. "*Do you care?*" I have asked my students. And I say, if not, then listen no further, merely watch your Personhood shrink.

After all, the widening divide of our culture-in-conflict runs through every human heart, as the great writer and Soviet dissident Solzhenitsyn reminded us in his historic Harvard address, and the implications are grave. Nevertheless, we must try to reconstitute meaning, quiet Pandemonium, build genuine community, and become bigger on the inside than on the outside. And of course it is personal—because we are persons who matter absolutely. In that light have I hoped to educe students into the spontaneity, rigors, exhilaration, satisfactions, and a mastery of a *rhetoric* of human being, of performing in the present tense. That is the way of *eros,* and *that*—we are told by, for example, Plato, Dante and Petrarch—is the way of rhetoric: a tale for another time. For now, though, in what has been a personal reflection, a higher truth is fitting, an insight from a writer who has come to mean a very great deal to me. In his *The Will to Meaning,* the great Viktor Frankl (1905-97) reminds us that Einstein said, "mere thinking cannot reveal to us the highest purpose." Frankl then adds:

> I would say that the ultimate meaning, or as I prefer to call it, the supra-meaning is no longer a matter of thinking but rather a matter of believing. We do not catch hold of it on intellectual grounds but on existential grounds, out of our whole being, *i.e.,* through faith.

TWO

EDUCTION

educate: from educare, "to lead forth"

A LL DIRECT human communication is a performance, but teaching is a performing art. Its tactics may be calculated, improvised, abandoned, recovered or utterly ignored, but success or failure originates in the teacher. Whether in the classroom, lecture hall, laboratory, studio or at the seminar table, the teacher's effusion of presence—that "movement of the air," that "turning of space into place"—may at least assure attention, even arouse curiosity, or better yet win engagement. That teacher's conviction, vitality, command, and, above all, attentiveness to the students themselves can secure learning beyond what otherwise would be the case. Teachers get what they give, more or less. Moreover, I've learned, after forty-seven years before the mast that such engagement is often in spite of certain institutional landmines—and even in spite of many students. In that light there follow here a bouquet of ruminations, complaints, diagnoses, and prescriptions. Please keep in mind that every now and then we need a Jeremiah, especially if that geezer still has some hope.

1.

This we ought know. A mindless neophilia is rampant in current college curricula: gender this, identity that, and the likes of "Themes of Discovery in Contemporary Soap Opera," instead of Shakespeare (even for English majors)—all of it entirely politicized, racialized, ethnicized and juvenalized. Thanks Frankfurt School of Cultural Criticism and the Marxist bastards who have corrupted two generations of simple-minded wannabe inellectual *sansculottes*. Among these are the professorial children

26

of certain baby boomers who long for the Woodstock ways of their mamas and papas, dressing down, slouching low, and, pathetically, trying to stay *au courant* in order to "relate."

Layered on top of this morass is a micro-managing upper-level administration (along with acquiescent faculty senates refusing to govern) who obsess over "outcomes" and make everyone else share that obsession. What, you ask, is an outcome? Well, we used to say, "we will teach this, this, and that." Then we had to say, "students will learn that, that, and this." Now we must say, "students will learn this, etc., so that . . ." and you are sunk if you presume to complete that sentence with, "the person will be bigger on the inside than on the outside," or "students will fill leisure time with activity suited to free persons instead of to slaves." Ask typical students what kind of institution they are attending and why and you simply will not get an answer: they are genuinely flummoxed. For all many of them know, they may as well be attending the Apex School of Refrigeration and Cooling, where after six weeks you get a certificate and get to keep your tools.

Consider these three statements. The first is from John Henry Newman (theologian, historian, Catholic apologist, educator), the second from a review of a book about him, the third from a *bright* student thirty years ago. 1/ "A cultivated intellect, a delicate taste, a candid, equitable, dispassionate mind," these are the objectives of higher education. 2/ "[Such a person], surely, is *still* the central aim of preprofessional undergraduate education." 3/ "Can you give me just the *gist* of the French Revolution?" The first two tell how we were and how some of us dream. The third tells how we are in fact, except that most students would likely not bother to ask. They copy what we write on the blackboard, while others try to sneak a phone-text or Google the state of Beyonce's marriage.

I've suggested "cheating" (of a sort) to certain students, taking shortcuts not on the internet (students already know those). Hirsch's *Dictionary of Cultural Literacy* (they come at various levels) has awakened, and alarmed, some students: "I should have known that!" More selective is Jones' and Wilson's *An Incomplete Education*, which has amused students. Kenneth Rexroth's *Classics Revisited* and *More Classics Revisited* have done more than that. Waldhorn's, Weber's and Zeiger's *Good Reading: A Guide for Serious Readers* is more bibliographical than the others, but a reading of its short annotations will vindicate its title. Finally there is the incomparable Charles Van Doren. His *The Joy of Reading* is both a joy to read in and of itself and will, if you act upon it, remake you in ways that greatly matter. The same is true of his and Mortimer Adler's classic reference work,

The Great Treasury of Western Thought. These aren't for everyone, of course; rather they are only for those who like to browse the old-fashioned way and who know, curiously, that there's no such thing as too many dots to connect.

This, too, we know. Most students have already limited themselves to some occupational (technical, vocational or professional) interest, so that anything not directly pertaining to that interest is undertaken merely for the sake of gaining a credential. They would be processed rather than led forth. In short, *there is a cataclysmic loss of curiosity, especially respecting the learning that most marks our humanity.* All learning must, for them, be instrumental, and rather quickly so. But, I ask, What about their souls? Historical identity, interpretive adroitness, expressive suppleness and efficacy, deductive and inferential skill, the command of concepts and a knowledge of how both to build and to discover them, cultural literacy, linguistic range, refined taste, "natural philosophy" (that is, science and its application to the world both concretely, as with geography, or abstractly, as with mathematics and physics)—these orders of learning expand our consciousness more richly and enduringly than any drug. They are *therapeutic.*

So I am one of those who bemoans the fact that higher education is becoming ever lower. (Most college profs who claim otherwise are either delusional or lying.) I believe that the highness of higher education must be recovered (even as the number of students and of colleges and universities therefore decreases), and that vocational and technical training (along with the old-fashioned apprenticeship system) be brought back to its proper place, which is not an institution of higher liberal learning, a position now gaining adherents. Regard a sampling: Kevin Carey's "College for All?" in the August 2011 issue of *The Wilson Quarterly,* James Pierson's "What's wrong with our universities?" in the September 2011 issue of *The New Criterion*), Craig Brandon's *The Five-Year Party,* Naomi Schaefer Riley's *The Faculty Lounges, and Other Reasons Why You Won't Get the College Education You Paid For,* Mark Taylor's *Crisis on Campus,* Hacker and Dreifus's *Higher Education?,* and Arum and Roksa's *Academically Adrift: Limited Learning on College Campuses.* These are not quite of-a-piece, but they do constitute a sort of chorus.

What follows was my local part in that chorus. I posted it some years ago to our faculty email list. This most of us know but will not say.

Dear Colleagues,

I fear I'm about to belabor the obvious. Or am I? I actually do not know. My claims: A cluster of foundational deficiencies is a substantial cause of the non-performance or dangerously weak performances of our weakest students. This set, in the concentration we experience it here, is (as in American higher education generally) relatively new and unacknowledged. Our silence respecting this cluster has given rise to a virtual sub-culture of deficiency and enablement. Withal, the students seem to me more naïve—monumentally so—than blameworthy. Consider the following.

Every semester for the past several semesters, tutoring for the Speech 101 final exam has been available: free, without the necessity of an appointment, at a great variety of times throughout the nearly two-week tutoring period, and for as many encounters as a student cares to have. That is, the tutoring is as user-friendly as possible. In that light consider:

1. We know positively that this tutoring not only helps but has been dispositive in many cases: students who would have failed the course have passed; others have raised their grades by one, even by two, whole grades.

2. Each semester some 275 students take Speech 101.

3. Each semester I've told all of them these very same things.

4. Alas, in any one semester only as many as thirty students (and that many only last semester, when I cajoled, supplicated, exhorted and remonstrated, the prior high being a dozen or so) have ever come for this tutoring.

Of course, this experience could be atypical. But if it is not, then over the decades, in the face of this and other sorts of inertness, we have tended towards indulgence: sentimentalizing, or, more accurately, patronizing, or, most alarmingly, exploiting our variously deficient students (yes, exploited, but that is a separate discussion). So that the cliché, facile and largely false, that "we are failing our students" has come to bear some ironic truth.

The following five deficiencies are, I believe, among the most damaging and persistent. I call them 'foundational' because, like a foundation, they are underlying, strong, and largely ignored in favor of the more visible structure they support.

1. *Reading, not writing, is the fundamental intellectual challenge to the students in question.* Many simply cannot, others simply will not, read. People who do not read cannot write (let

alone write well). A corollary: I'm told by both students and faculty that *English instructors in composition classes no longer formally teach grammar, usage and the mechanics of writing* (and yet call for even more required courses in composition).

2. This second deficiency is probably among the causes of the first and the most liable to misunderstanding: *the students in question tend to be linguistically compromised in English in various ways and to varying degrees.* English is often their second (third?) language, or may as well be. I happen to see this most in their performances as speakers, but this deficiency seriously compromises their comprehension of both spoken and written English.

3. *The 13th Grade Syndrome.* For many, intellectual and academic maturity come very late; and many of our students see college as an extension of high school, cluelessly squandering at least one semester, usually more. They are perfunctory, happy to build a Yugo (remember that car? The doors would actually fall off) rather than the Caddy, and are largely impassive.

4. *Calling ourselves "student-centered" (rather than "learning-centered") was and remains a great mistake.* As a result of this focus and to a wide extent the College is tending towards a state which I call the Hotel Syndrome, with us as its concierges. Hyperbole? Most of us have heard the same innumerable anecdotes. Student-centeredness is among those factors that permits insouciance ("whatever"), perpetuates inertness, and even invites an often-cynical finger-pointing that justifies non-performance: like hotel guests who are never accountable for their messes or forgetfulness. Worse: the *hotelier* is disposed to think that the customer is (almost) always right.

5. *Our students generally have little conception of the sort of institution they attend.* I mean a liberal arts institution and the entire conceptual penumbra thereunto appertaining. Many would shrink the great sphere of knowledge rather than labor to grow so as to take into themselves as much of that sphere as possible.

A few years ago our valedictorian came close to summarizing these when he told his graduating class the Three Secrets of Student Success. He did so because he had witnessed certain routine protocols ignored so routinely that he inferred they *must*, in fact, *be* secrets. The three are: show up and on time, do your work, follow instructions. Lamentable. If the valedictorian is right, and we care to address the problem—and who among us would not? Our students deserve no less—we should begin by discussing it, by fostering not only an engagement with learning but a culture thereof.

In the event, my missive dropped like a stone in a shallow puddle—except unlike the stone this made not even a ripple. It elicited absolutely no conversation whatsoever: institutional entropy at its worst.

We have been left with the very worst of both the educational worlds that John Dewey described as Traditional education and his own Progressive response: Higher Learning now deals in "product," neither liberal nor educational, not a "leading out or forth" (the original meaning of "educate") but merely a "stuffing in" (Traditional), with the stuff itself selected and manipulated by pupils as they please ("the freedom of the learner"—Progressive).

2.

Though *sometimes* practiced by students, absolute silence has never been quite the *rule* among them. Some I've led forth, of others I'm not so sure. During my full-time career as a college professor (at the same college) I have spent thousands of hours—perhaps as many as three thousand — conversing with them in class, on campus outside of class and, in fact, outside my official capacity as an academic advisor or tutor, sometimes in my home. Over the years I reckon that nearly sixty students had become close: dropping in when they pleased long after they were enrolled in any class I taught. Of those, a dozen or so became friends off campus, with a handful remaining in close touch decades after the fact. (And a couple of dozen re-established contact decades after their undergraduate years.) Many of our conversations have deeply embedded themselves in my memory.

Often these conversations were mutually satisfying: smart students talking ideas. The debaters were the most fun. More often the interaction was therapeutic. They were young people wanting contact: paternal, or avuncular—a sort of mentoring. Very many times they wanted advice about problems to solve or choices to be made, even very intimate ones. Ms. Z, a very bright young Muslim women, was performing badly in class: defensively, angrily. In my office I made inquiries and told her how offended people were to hear that they mistrusted her, people whom she did not know. When I told here to address her listeners as though they were guests in her home she responded that she didn't know how to do that. Could I give her an example? Sure, I said. So with a smile I offered her a lozenge and told her I'd be pleased if she would accept; I then suggested she do the same for me. Her response stunned me. She broke down weeping. I waited. I did not ask if she were okay. I did ask why—if she cared to say— she had had that response. "Because," she said, "no one has ever been this nice to me before." Now, how can that not break your heart? The result was trust: she returned to practice her speech, took advice, and wound up doing very well: she was a different person, really. She wrote an exceedingly kind email to thank me, and we have remained friends since.

An unhappy exchange was with a student who visited to complain about a grade. He was a truculent young black man whose first play was always race. In those days my office was isolated and remote. It was late. Standing in front of my desk (I was seated) he began, first to imply violence and then to make threats. His hands were in his pockets. He was tall, thin and fit. Finally I decided to bring this to an end one way or another, so I applied the almost-always-reliable Crazier-Than-Thou trick. "If you take those hands out of your pockets," I said, "no matter what's in them or if they're empty . . . I'll break your arm and throw you out of the mother-f___ing window." He then used a trick of his own: "Why are you getting so upset professor, using that language? Haven't I been a gentleman?" I told him he had to the count of three to leave; he left. I didn't see him again until registration next semester. There he complained that he was being treated unfairly and drew a knife. Our chief of security (a former Marine captain) disarmed him with one move and hauled him away. Was he dismissed from the college? No—at least not until he walked into the secretarial pool, completely disrobed, and displayed himself to each of the women there one by one.

One the other hand some students seem aggressive but turn out . . . well, take Raymond. He is the only student I've ever had who stood every time he answered ("because I am Jamaican," he nearly chanted in a Jamaican accent), always from the back of the room and at the farthest reach from the door. Already pushing thirty when he took his first course with me, Raymond was wise beyond even those years, and a wise-guy to boot.

Very early in that first semester I pointed to him and asked his name. He had already heard me refer to students by their surnames, but he, rising slowly and sort of settling in, answered "my name is Raymond," spoken in what was very close to a Southern drawl. "Very well Raymond," said I, "and your central idea?" After the briefest pause, the better to cement eye-contact, this man-of-many-accents again drawled "prostitution should be legalized." The class watched him, then looked at me, wondering if

I meant it when I had said they could choose any topic they pleased. "Good," I said. "Real good," he said. Then, after taking a beat of my own, "but just one thing Raymond. In this instance just what do you mean by 'prostitution'?"

His answer was a pearl; I haven't heard it's like since. "Oh come come, professor," with a smile of impatient resignation, "we *are* both men of the world now, are we not?" The class laughed, albeit guardedly, and I must confess it was hard not to. "Well Raymond," I answered with a straight face, "perhaps you've seen more of the world than I have. Please humor me, won't you?" Raymond: "Of course professor. You know; she's got it, you want it, you pay, *she gives!* Prostitution." The dam broke. I waited, of course not having any choice, then, "I see. You mean the sale of sexual favors." "Oh," said Raymond, "that's good. That's very good, professor. Yes. The sale of sexual favors. I believe I'm going to use that." "Be my guest, Raymond. Very well: the sale of sexual favors should be legalized. Is that all?" "Yes," he said. "Are you sure?" I asked. "Yes," he said. He sat down.

My very favorite quotation from Martin Luther King, Jr., is this one: "Rarely do we find men who willingly engage in hard, solid thinking. There is an almost universal quest for easy answers and half-baked solutions." He concluded, "nothing pains some people more than having to think." Pure gold. Had he met Raymond?

I turned to the class and asked if the matter were clear to them. Now, the Rev. King aside for a moment, students generally do not like being drawn into discussions that might put a classmate on the spot, especially if that student is pulling more than his weight on the learning-is-fun front. So they mumbled their customary assent. "Good," I said, "then you all understand that Raymond would legalize juvenile prostitution." Raymond was on his feet in a heartbeat.

"I said nothing about little children, professor." Raymond was not smiling.

"Oh. I'm sorry Raymond. Did you say 'adult' and I missed it?" Sometimes I like dressing up like Big Bird.

"No."

"Well, would you like to?"

"Yes."

"Fine. Is that all?"

"It is."

"Are you sure?"

"I am, professor," and Raymond sat.

So again I turned to the class and asked if *now* the thesis were clear.

Stares. Mumbles. Nods. "Then," I took my time, "you all understand that Raymond would legalize homosexual prostitution." And Raymond—it matters that he was Jamaican, and I knew it—was not only on his feet before "-tion" hit the air but a step or two closer to me. "Professor, I didn't say anything"—he hastened now, loud, very impatient but no longer re-signed—"about faggots." Me: "We won't tolerate insults here, Raymond, as I'm sure you understand, being Jamaican, but I ask: Did you say 'het-erosexual' and I missed it? Because, if so, once again I must say how sorry I am to have mistaken you."

"No. I didn't."

"Would you care to include it?"

"Yes, I certainly would."

"Is that all?" I asked.

And Raymond . . . hesitated. "I *think* so," he said, slowly and not without a faint smile. By the time we were done Raymond had finally said what he meant: "The sale of adult, heterosexual sexual favors, limited to certain specially-designated red-light districts, taxed by the city, and under medical supervision, should be legalized."

There was nothing insouciant about Raymond; nothing perfunctory. Best of all, when on the spot and genuinely put upon, he nevertheless intuited what I was up to *and lent himself to it*. "You *see*," I said finally, "it's easy to say what you mean and to mean what you say—*if* you know what *you* mean in the first place. Which most of us do not . . . at first." He understood that healthy speech—*conversation*—is people standing togeth-er with words, skillfully or not, on small scales and large, revving up and *maximizing personhood*: thinking—hard, long, as clearly as possible, and eagerly—and speaking, feelingly, purposefully, directly, confidently and joyfully, in all settings that either permit, invite, or compel conversation. A fine student, Raymond.

The closest to personal danger I've ever come in the classroom hap-pened in the spring of 1970. It was the semester of the student killings on the campuses of Kent State and Jackson State Universities. We were a country deeply divided. At York College, some students formed The Rainbow Committee and called for a campus-wide strike: classes would be suspended. This in good conscience I could not do; I simply cannot abide bullying. So I taught, in room thirteen. As a young woman spoke in front of the room, where the door was, I sat in the back making notes.

About halfway through the speech a band of some half dozen stu-dents—mostly bare-chested, belts drawn diagonally from one shoulder to the opposite side of their waists, Che Guevara berets jauntily arrayed—

burst into the room shouting, "we're liberating room thirteen. There will be no more teaching" and left. The girl was petrified, but the whole scene had happened so quickly that I told her to just keep going, which she did. Back came the liberators, this time sauntering. The leader was a black chap who said, slowly and deliberately, "I said, this room been liberated." The girl, now literally trembling, stopped once again. I rose and said, "if you want to liberate this room, you'll have to liberate me with it." "Then that," said Baby Che, "is just what I'll do."

Before I had time to wonder about my sanity, I heard a voice from directly behind me. Mike Wilson, a black student who was the center on our basketball team, had stood. He put his hand on my shoulder and said to the bossman, "well, if you liberate him, you'll have to liberate me, too." "Awright, awright brother. Be cool," said Wannabe Che, "we're cool," and he and his band backed out of the door. At that point Mike said, "you keep teaching us, prof. You're doing real good." I thanked him and we carried on. I would see Michael Wilson from time-to-time, but we never made mention of the incident. He would fulfill his ambition to become a New York City high school history teacher. A stand-up guy if ever there was one.

Thirty years ago I asked students to complete this phrase: "Communication is like ____." K. answered, "garbage." She was bitter, and we would wind up talking for hundreds of hours. She now has her Ph.D. *in communication* and, as a professor, chairs her Department of Communication in a small liberal arts college, where I'm sure she is accumulating her own "Ks." Does it get better than that for a teacher? I've been privileged to receive cards signed by entire classes at the end of semesters and to receive rounds of applause: no, still not better than knowing how K. has turned out and what role I played in that.

3.

Any essay is a still photo, and no photo can convey the teeming variations of humanity that some ten thousand students have provided for forty-five years. In that light, I know that any ending must be arbitrary, otherwise the photo would become a never-ending film. But it is that film that runs steadily in the mind. Here is a snippet that has stayed with me for nearly two decades. Early of a semester, another Wilson rose in my class to inform his classmates on the origin and subsequent history of "the middle finger curse," as it has been called (and as he called it). Now, it matters to the story to know that students often ask ahead of time if they may do this or that. My answer is always the same: you may do anything you please within the bounds of the law and of common courtesy—but *it had better work!* In this instance, Wilson came to me before his speech and gave me a heads up: he would be rolling the dice (so to speak) and asked that I not interrupt.

Wilson, sitting in the front row, was in position quickly after I called his name, smiling as he gazed around the room, then nodding as he fixed his gaze on me. His classmates, too, looked at me, puzzled. What was up? After a beat or two, Wilson said, "by now all of us have given a short speech. We've seen the professor, Professor Como, right there"—he pointed—"taking his little notes so that he could make his little comments." The students were palpably nervous: they are generally willing to go along with almost anything but this . . . was this *prudent?* "And I know what you're all thinking as he does it, too. Professor Mr. Picky, scribble, scribble, scribble, pick, pick. pick." By now some students were looking down, hiding a snigger or two, others were sneaking peaks at me; I was smiling mutedly. "And I know that you don't like it! You don't," he almost shouted. "But you say nothing. Nothing." Some nods. "Well, that's why I'm here. I'm here to express to Mr. Professor Picky back there what all of you want to say." He turned to me. "Are you watching, professor? Well then, this is from all of us." And at that he gave me an emphatic Middle Finger Salute.

It's the only time I've heard a class gasp collectively. Wide-eyed they turned first to me, then back to Wilson, then to me, and finally back to Wilson, who continued. "Do you see? Watch." And at that he gave the salute with both hands, not merely hold his fingers up but jabbing the air with them—straight up, side-to-side, and finally *directly* at me, all the while wiggling his hips! Throwing caution to the winds, the class went wild. I confess to never having been more astonished and amused by a student in my life. Wilson, having withdrawn his fingers, raised one hand as though to call for silence; the class obeyed. "Do you see?" he intoned. "Professor Como is helpless. Absolutely *helpless!* It's as though I've cast a magic spell that surrounds me, protecting me even from—from *him*." Here he merely nodded towards me. "So I ask, what power does this middle finger hold? Where does it come from? Before I'm done you will know the origin—or origins—of the middle finger curse." In substance and liveliness the speech proper lived up to its thrilling introduction. Of course the class applauded raucously, and I did too, though a bit less raucously than they. I assigned a grade of A+ to Wilson, which in over forty years of teaching college speech classes I've done fewer than ten times.

For all our theories of teaching and our knowledge of different learning styles, only concrete, specific guidance that grows from experience will be helpful in the long run. For example, certainly students fall into no more than a handful of categories. These are indicated by level of preparation, intellectual acumen, understanding of the enterprise of higher education and (especially) of liberal education, and willingness to learn *this* material (whatever it is). In short, level of maturity, intellectual ability, and predisposition. Those variations, however, should not cause teachers to be varied in their manner of teaching. In fact, the response to those variations should be uniformity: of standards, expectations, and treatment, sometimes sever. If in answer to a question a student begins "I feel" I interrupt: "I'm not interested in your feelings. Tell me what you think." When a student invites a quarrel by disputing advice or instructions, I tell them, "you're about to hear what you think you want to hear but, really, you are wrong. Here it is: do it your way." So I say to young colleagues (I've mentored many), stick to your own requirements and instructions. Teachers must use their well-earned magisterium as well as the pedagogic imperium that comes with it.

But that is in the classroom, and a category is not a person. During my career I have been privileged to receive certificates of recognition, plaques, and certain high honors: induction into the International Spanish Honor Society, recognition for my "outstanding contributions to the York College Male Initiative Program and the Surrounding Community," and the Distinguished Faculty Award of the York College Alumni Association. These are matter to me yet together matter less than that one student who finally gets it, and says so. The reason for this asymmetry is simple: every single student has a story. What you see in class is the tip of complex humanity, people learning as much about the process and about themselves as learners as they are the material. Only conversation can reveal that person, and—although the performance in a given class can be graded—only that whole person can be *educed*: that is, *led forth*. Then personal flaws of immaturity, uncertainty or insecurity matter very much less than at first sight. Much more important still: the institution, with all its constraints, intrusions and pedagogic silliness seem to disappear.

THREE

PRESENCE
Building a Performance

[He] recognized, intuitively, that the presence of other people, even the humblest and fewest, constitutes an audience, and towards an audience one has certain duties. They are always giving a performance in the role for which they have cast themselves . . . tacitly inviting others to collaborate . . . it is the recognition of a duty that is binding on everyone. . . . The Creator . . . has equipped them with a certain identity, and they are all the time . . . out to get, and to give, as much fun as possible. . .

— John Wain, on his tutor C. S. Lewis

THERE ARE people who, though lacking a mass audience, are the very people we want at our dinner table. They seem to run their own talk shows. How do they do it? To one degree or another a number of elements interanimate each other, almost like magic, in their minds, imaginations, then in their talk, and finally in us. The results of this mix may be idiosyncratic, but its elements are knowable, and it is their mix that often makes for conversations that are at least enjoyable, often memorable.

The old lady, Miss Edna, age seventy-eight, more bent over than usual, shuffled very slowly to the front of the classroom; apparently her arthritis was acting up. She was a superb student and already popular with her young classmates, so there would be much patience with her. But as she moved between the chairs, she looked over her shoulder at her classmates and smacked her lips: once or twice she wiped a bit of drool from those lips with the back of her hand. She was leering. When she arrived at her spot she paused and, stooped, looked over the entire room, still leering. Then, as she turned her head steadily from right to left and back again, she spoke these words: "I love sex!"

The class was stunned at first, but soon it irrupted in howls of laughter. Then it became silent when she continued. "You heard me. I said 'love.' Not 'loved.' Well, I'm on my fourth husband." Pause. "I buried the first three." The house fell apart. "That's right," she continued, "old Edna has had lots and lots of sex. But, do you want to know something?" Silence. "All those times I had sex? Sex never had me. No sir!" Dead silence. "Do you know why? I'll tell you why. Because I've kept sex in its proper place." Then one student spoke, whether as a plant or not I do not know: "where's that, Miss Edna?" Others chimed their agreement. "Okay. Okay," said Miss Edna. "I'll tell you." Then, slowly and most emphatically, pausing after the major beats, she said, *the only place for sex is in marriage!*" The class of young people clapped and cheered and then listened to Miss Edna give a wonderfully persuasive speech on both the virtues and practical advantages of chastity. I've never had a student, before or since, who brought more presence to her performances. No American public official that I know of has outdone Miss Edna.

This extraordinary woman, like C. S. Lewis, had *sprezzatura*, a combination of verve, self-assurance, and command. As a result she was able to . . . connect. What did she know, whether consciously or intuitively?

An answer, I suspect, begins with conviction, *belief* in oneself, in the affirmational function of conversation (the *re-creational* benefits of the engagement), and in the willingness of your partners to play along. You might also believe in what you are saying; more important, though, is your belief *that* what you are saying (even if hypothetical or experimental or even just playful) is useful.

Belief is not such a simple concept as its definition, "intellectual assent," leads us to think. Is it knowledge? Or *certain* knowledge? Or is it faith beyond knowledge? Or is it the acceptance of only probabilities—perhaps even mere possibilities? Is it something to be acted upon? Are there degrees of belief? How do we acquire our beliefs? Do we test them? If we believe *in* rather than merely *that*, does the belief work on us from the inside, like faith or personal trust? Does such a "belief in" not require what we commonly call *proof*? Or does it require a different sort of proof than when we believe that something—something outside of us—is true?

And yet, amid our uncertainty lies this certainty which we all hold: no one believes anything which he holds to be downright false: if it's not real, we don't believe, either *in* or *that*. Saul on his way to Tarsus is struck from his donkey and has a vision: that reality is so unquestionably actual that his life changes even unto the point of martyrdom.

Prior to that experience, he did not seem to be either stupid or nuts. Socrates, who would be a war hero, goes into the battle of Potidaea and famously experiences twenty-four hours of trance-like rapture (described in Plato's *Symposium*). Thereafter he will represent the concept of *soul* in terms unlike any heard before, and it will become his life's mission to lead people to the belief that this soul must be made good, that it will survive, and that it will be judged. He also does this unto martyrdom.

Looming large within and around any discussion of belief—around any beliefs, really—are two concepts that pervade the discussion almost invisibly. These are *controversy* and *persuasion*. Each requires a good rinse to separate its essential features from its typical ones. Essentially controversy is marked by disagreement that lends itself to the possibility of dispute. (We don't dispute all disagreements; sometimes we agree to disagree or we just walk away, physically or mentally.) It does not require passion, let alone anger or cataclysmic divisiveness. Thus the phrase "mildly controversial" is apt, since the concept does allow for degrees of intensity.

As for the resolution of controversy, we know of the limited number of ways to attempt it: 1/ violence, 2/ coercion (*e.g.* "your money or your life," "if you *really* loved me you would ..."; and by the way, propaganda is a form of coercion, since one way or another it rules out alternatives), 3/ chance (we can flip a coin, for example), and 4/ persuasion. The first two, especially if we lose, leaves us frustrated: we're basically kicking the can down the road (a glaring example being the Treaty of Versailles that ended World War I, but left the Germans so deeply frustrated that they were vulnerable even to the rants of a cartoon madman). We might reconcile ourselves to a chance outcome, but we'll know that we diminished ourselves by abdicating the seat of free will; we've checked our brains at the door and have fled into the hands of randomness.

Only persuasion allows for *reasonableness*, the full engagement of our humanity in thought, word, and affect. It is the *willing assent to change of some kind* (not necessarily conversion). It does this "by sweetness," which is what persuasion means. Strictly speaking, it talks no one into anything; rather, it allows someone to talk himself into everything. In short, all persuasion is, somehow and to some degree, *self*-persuasion, than which there is no more effective means of gaining assent. Its means is proof (from a Latin root meaning to test; it's cognate with our 'probe'). It is not that which "establishes truth." Such a meaning is the case in mathematics and in the laboratory, and maybe in theology, but not in the work-a-day world we occupy. Here it means "to establish belief." Of course we hope that what we believe is also true, but by the time we were five years old we knew better; whether it was "belief in" that true friend who turned out to be the very person spreading those nasty rumors, or because "mommy says" turned out to be a disciplinary ploy—we know that belief and truth are often different.

"By sweetness" works in three ways. First it relies upon authority, called "ethical proof" (from the Greek word *ethos*, meaning character). The question "who says" continues to come readily to mind no matter our age or stage of life. And if the answer is a source we regard as knowledgeable, trustworthy (*e.g.* truthful), and of good will (*i.e.* looking out for others) then we trust it. The second way proof works is by establishing the grounds for emotion. When blatant, *pathe* (not so much 'emotion' as the conditions from which an emotion arises) can backfire—it is and is often seen to be—manipulative, and the effects are notoriously short-lived. Correctly used, emotional proof first addresses the imagination. That way, self-persuasion has concrete raw material—images—to work upon. The rule is simple: Aristotle long ago told us "to set it before the eyes," because he knew that where the imagination goes, the rest is sure to follow. Two more features of these two types of proof matter: 1/ precisely because we intuit our own vulnerability to them they are suspect and therefore 2/they must work very quickly.

Neither is true of *logical* proof. The gathering, authentication, and deployment of evidence is hard work; reasoning with it, especially if the process is complex and must be sustained, is taxing. The payoff, though, is that it is outside of us; it does not depend upon trust coming from some vibe or on a subjective response at the mercy of often impulsive emotional twitches. It can be assessed objectively, by others as well as by ourselves. So because it is hard and outside and subject to examination, we trust it. No skillful speaker—no matter his emphasis on *ethos* or *pathos*—ever omits it from his message, even if its inclusion is perfunctory, because its mere appearance carries authority and *gravitas*.

So Miss Edna won our trust: she showed extraordinary good will— by way of familiarity with us and by her humor—and (shall we say) her claim to expertise. We also inferred that she had no reason to lie. In short, intuiting the requirements for establishing reciprocal re-creative conversation, she engaged us, as though she and we were gears meshing and spinning in sync.

Here is what, somehow, she knew.

1/ *All meaning derives from connectedness; in fact, all meaning is connectedness.* Once something, anything, is connected to us, no matter how, it is meaningful. And just here we need clarification. The word *meaningful*, bless its heart, is just too warm and fuzzy for its own good. What I mean is this: has anyone reading these words ever used *meaningful* to refer to something bad, twisted, unhappy, lamentable or sorry? "Are you in a meaningful relationship?" never means, "does your partner routinely cheat on you?" My point is straightforward: a connection may be trivial, temporary, shallow or bad. It doesn't matter. If there was a connection, whatever was connected was meaningful. And what sort of connection might that be? Any kind: intellectual, physical, emotional, spiritual or any combination of these. And we may even be unconscious of it, as when (because we're rushing, for example) we let a door swing into the person behind us, who then concludes that we are rude. That's right: the connection may be entirely misbegotten.

2/ *Human beings are meaning machines.* We cannot *not* make connections. we solve crossword puzzles, play find-a-word, record our favorite soap operas to find out what happens next (*i.e.* how the future is connected to the present or to the past), hold to superstitions that connect broken mirrors to misfortune. Along with our long lost cousin we gaze at a low, plump, rotund cloud and chuckle together: "Aunt Mable, right?" We don't say, "oh what a lovely cumulous collection of water vapor." In short, our internal switch-board, which *compels us to make meaning*, compels us to see connections which, cumulatively, establish patterns. These patterns explain the past, help us to manage the present, and form the basis for our predictions of the future.

3/ *Our greatest source of connectedness is other human beings.* Some decades ago there lived and flourished one of the toughest chieftains of one of the toughest gangs in U.S. history. He was both brutal and sadistic: he was known to have mutilated, then killed, his enemies *in front of their families.* He was caught, tried, convicted and sent to prison, from which he continued to direct his horrors. Unfortunately for him, the judge in his case found that out and re-sentenced the man to almost absolute solitary confinement—perpetually. There was no physical abuse or deprivation of any kind—except that of human company. After some months the tough guy wrote the judge begging him to relent: solitary was driving the poor guy crazy. The judge did relent, allowing the prisoner a couple of hours a month of human contact.

4/ *As meaning machines we are the most contagious agents on the planet.* Try this. Board an empty subway car at one end. When a second person enters, sits, and does not notice you, you (and here you must use your good judgment) turn your head to that person and stare at him blankly. You will see that soon enough that poor, clueless guinea pig will feel your stare and look back at you. Have you been taught, as I had been, that when in a social gathering "a bad mood is bad manners"?

Decades ago in a seminar was one of the strongest students I've ever had. I'll call him Bobby. He had a quick, incisive and well-stocked mind. Alas, he was also extremely shy, with long hair dangling in front of his always-down-turned faced; and he seemed perpetually morose. You can imagine my surprise when one day he came to me for advice: he wanted to be a stand-up comic! I told him that, as he was still young, he should give it a try for a fixed period: if he failed he could go on to graduate school. He then asked, Would I hear his routine? With very great trepidation (which somehow I managed to mask) I not only assented but gathered a group of friendly students for the event. It was . . . awful. Some time later he told me that he would be auditioning at a Manhattan comedy club. Would I attend? Once again I assented and, with the same group of students, went to the club. But I had instructed our small group to sprinkle ourselves about the room and, given that we knew the routine, be sure to laugh at the punch lines. At first we were alone in our laughter; but soon more and more people were laughing with us. Bobby was a hit—and has stayed one. He has since made his living doing stand-up (and voice-over work). If you see the film *Neverland*, about James M. Barrie writing *Peter Pan* and having it staged, you will notice that Barrie, in giving free tickets to local orphans and sprinkling them about the house, uses the very same . . .er, trick. Shills have been around for a very long time!

People with presence—people like C. S. Lewis and Miss Edna— seem to live by these premises. They know that when among others the here and now matters much more than the there and then; they are present in time and in place, to others and to themselves (that is, they are self-possessed, not self-conscious). Wherever they are, they are at home: they belong. They know a secret and they embrace it, as some of us do not. And what they know is this: whether we are aware of it or not, particularly care or not, and whether we like it or not, *when interacting with others we are performers*. We cannot choose *not* to perform, only to perform badly.

So then, the next question is, What are our performance instruments? That answer begins with an explanation first of what it is we do with what we have, and that is D.O.C.: Direct Oral Communication, by which I mean nothing other than people speaking with each other "same time, same place, face-to-face," the prototype of all human communication.

Now, assuming normal good health, every participant in a conversation has use of three "sections" of his orchestra, of his self: *verbal, vocalic,* and *kinesic.*

Verbal. Our first step is to clarify this universally misused word: "verbal" does not mean "oral." If you speak an agreement with a friend you have an oral agreement; if you write it down you have a—written agreement. Both, however, are verbal agreements. And why is that? Because "verbal" means one simple thing and one only: words. Words, no matter their medium of expression, form or format. No matter anything. If it's words, it's verbal; if it's not words—like the punctuation on this and on every page you've ever read, like every facial expression and gesture—it's non-verbal. If, as a whisper, I ask, as a question, "shut the door?" and then shout, as a command, "shut the door!" I have uttered two verbally identical sentences: same words, same order. The great difference in meaning between the two does not lie in the words.

Vocalic. From a Latin root meaning "to call," and giving us, for example, the word "vocation," a "calling," vocalic communication derives from the expressiveness of our voice, what we ordinarily refer to as "tone of voice" or "vocal intonation" (but not the word "tone" by itself, which has a larger field of reference that includes, but is not limited to, vocal expressiveness). Very early—some say while we are still in the womb—we begin to learn the features of vocalic communication. There are four of them. One is largely beyond our control, but three of them we learn to control and to mix-and-match. These three are pitch, volume, and speed. The fourth element is timbre, pronounced *tambre,* and is the vocal signature that we recognize when, for example, we hear a voice over the phone.

Kinesic. If the verbal is what we say, and the vocalic is how we sound when we say it, then the kinesic is how we look—that is, what we do, how we act—as we say it (from the Greek *kinesis,* movement). This feature, often referred to by the tiresome phrase "body language," has five elements. In reverse order of their importance (that is, their impact on other participants who are listening and watching) they are:

5/ *Dress, grooming and posture.* We are what we look like, both under exceptional circumstances (like that first date or the job interview) and routinely (as in the workplace or at leisure). 4/ *Large bodily movement.* These are movements, like pacing or strolling, that take us from one spot to another. Of course, as with all features and their elements, this element can easily be overdone. If we do use it, then we absolutely must employ what comes next. 3/ *Gesture.* These are any movements—any—that do not require us to move from one spot to another. They include arm and hand movements, of course, but also a turn of the head, a twist of the torso, and even a peek of the eyes. Whereas we can do without large bodily movement, we cannot do without gestures all together. 2/ *Facial expression.* The face is the most telling indication of affect: emotion, attitude, engagement. The absence of facial expression is entirely unnatural; among humans we see it only in the dead. Thus, to freeze our faces when we converse is an indication of either fear, boredom, disengagement, hostility, doubt, or uncertainty—nothing good. It is an attempt to hide in plain sight. But we are very astute at reading expressions. After all, even horses can do it, as the carnival animal Clever Hans has shown. His trainers presented him as a horse who could solve mathematical problems. In fact the horse was responding to subtle facial cues from the trainers, and he was never wrong!

1/ *Eye contact.* This element is not only the most important but the most difficult to deploy: we must provide an "eyeshake" but we must not stare. Do we really want the windows to our soul to be unshaded? Are we surprised when others are troubled when we peer into their windows? Complicating the matter is culture, because different cultures prescribe different regulations. And by the way, all mammals value eye-contact.

Perhaps you've heard actors refer to their "instrument." I have a different take. We do not have an instrument; rather, we have an entire orchestra that I've referred to earlier, with these sections called verbal, vocalic and kinesic. The natural tendency of those sections is to play, and they do—unless we drop the conduor's baton, or throw the "off" switch. It may be useful to think of conversation as like a song, with both words (the verbal section) and music (the vocalic and kinesic sections). Together they provide our overall *tone*, that set of attitudes towards ourselves, our subject, and towards those with whom we converse: a prevailing mood, or vibe. So we must ask: what kind of music will I make? We must remember: the opposite of monotony is variety, purposeful and directed. Especially we must remember: The only perfectly still human being is a dead one.

And yet . . . And yet, no matter our attentiveness, effort and skills, there are laws that we disregard at our peril. These are not statutes. Those we might violate and still go unpunished. Instead these laws, if violated, will strike, like the law of gravity: if you step out of that fifth floor window you are not going up—as simple as that. These are The Five Laws of Direct Oral Communication. 1/ *We get what we give.* How could it be otherwise, given how infectious we are? As is often the case, we here stumble upon the moral dimension of conversation, for where there are other people, there moral concerns must be. In other words, performance is intimately tied to our debt to all the other participants. 2/ *There is always a loss of meaning when human beings communicate.* Not occasionally, or frequently but—always. Given the delicacy of our attentiveness, of our understanding, and of our patience; given the rigor of our perceptual screening processes—how could this not be? In other words, somehow communication is always failing, and therefore, somehow, we must bring humility to the act, along with tender, ever-loving care, especially patience.

3/ *Intent never equals impact.* Actually a corollary of the second law, this warns us to be patient with, and prepared for, misunderstanding. Communication is behavior, and almost always behavior is motivated; that is, at some level of our awareness we intend our actions to achieve some end, or impact. As with the second law, this one is absolute: that second word is not "usually" or "sometimes" or anything other than *never*. A dramatic example is when an utterance intended as a compliment ("my goodness, Annie, you have lost that weight, haven't you? You look great!") is taken as an insult ("what?! Are you saying I looked . . . ugly . . . before I lost the weight? I'm supposed to be thrilled now that you approve?")

The last two laws are identical except for one word. 4/ *Without form there is no fixed or reliable meaning.* By form I mean nothing more than a discernible pattern. It may not be immediately apparent but it works on us, as music works on dancers. Now, notice carefully the wording of the law: "no *fixed* or *reliable* meaning." Of course, since we are meaning machines, there will be meaning. There may be no form, but will it be what the speaker intends? 5/ And finally, *Without context there is no fixed or reliable meaning.* There is no mystery here. Context functions as a sort of frame—sort of, because unlike a picture frame, communication contexts interact with what happens within, as though the frame overflowed into the picture. Context fills in the gaps, tells us the *kind* of thing we're engaging, provides direction, and *colors how we see what we see.* Moreover, context is *everything*, in time and space, that surrounds the conversation.

Good speakers try to control all aspects of context but, of course, cannot. The reason for this is "noise." Noise, in communication, is anything that disrupts or tends to disrupt communication. It could be the lights going out when you're reading, or a belly rumbling with hunger, or the distractions of a quarrel you've had and know you'll be getting back to. Anything. And it is everywhere and always: *there is no such thing as noiseless communication.* Contexts are breeding grounds for noise.

To coordinate the premises, instruments and laws, the following guidelines are always helpful: 1/ When speaking with others, think "conversation." 2/ A conversationalist is always a performer. 3/ Make the music that goes with your words (as with a song). 4/ Remember, the process is not about you; rather it's about your "guests" who, after all, are in your "house." 5/ In public communication, there are only individual listeners; there is no such thing as an "audience." 6/ Animate and pervade your conversation with your character: *sign your work.*

It begins with a state of mind. One philosopher described presence as turning space into place: you belong, where you stand is now *your* address. That's useful. But the best conception of presence comes from the actress Glenn Close. She said "it's a movement of the air," and she's right.

That's what makes a *performance*, and each one of us is capable of giving. We cannot *not* perform—whether we know it or not, care or not—or like it or not. The real key is self-awareness, being the conductor who gets all the musicians—verbal, vocalic and kinesic; *ethos, pathos* and *logos*—on the same page. When speaking—whether publically, socially, in a small group or privately: it's all conversation—think of yourself as the host of a small party, the listeners as your guests. It's your house, your address, and you would have them be welcome; then, since you get what you give, they will welcome you. Right here is one of the great secrets of effective conversation and its rhetoric.

The diagram below summarizes the relationship of its parts to the whole of a performance in the present tense. Our objective is at the apex of this Performance Pyramid. At the very bottom are four elements that we must bring with, the four "con-" elements. Together these form our base: they give rise to a robust orchestra of verbal, vocalic and kinesic communication, all variously—not discordantly. We do not want mixed messages, nor monotony, directed at our listeners. Since we get what we give, we must believe, feel and communicate enthusiasm for this particular event: there was life before that was more important, and surely there is more important life after. But during this event nothing matters more that speaking with these people about this subject. Moreover, if I am in tune with my subject—if I myself am responding to my own subject as it invites or even compels me to respond, and if I remember that this engagement is a conversation—then I will achieve those features of spontaneity and immediacy that are at the heart of vitality. My listener will forgive any number of mistakes (well, not any number) but will not forgive an imitation of a corpse. A perfectly still human being is a dead human being.

Presence

VITALITY
Spontaneity and Immediacy
Responsiveness/Emphasis/Expressiveness

VARIETY
DIRECTNESS
"Enthusiasm for the Event"

VOCALIC: Pitch, Volume, Rate, Timbre
KINESIC: Eyes, Face, Gestures, Movement, Appearance

CON: -TROL -VICTION -CENTRATION -FIDENCE

Some years ago the roundest student I've ever had in a course rose to the front of the class to speak. She was no more than five feet tall, but she was also a good three feet front-to-back and side-to-side. She approached her spot with an exaggerated waddle, all the while slowly rubbing her considerable belly with both hands—as she smacked her lips. We could not take our eyes off of her. When she finally arrived, she paused, looked us all over, eye-to-eye, and said, "as you can see, I've had my share of sweet potato pie. In fact, I've had my share, your share"—here and in what followed she pointed around the room—"his share and her share, too." And then she laughed, and we laughed right along with her. "Well," she continued, "the truth is, we black folk know a little something about sweet potato pie. Especially"—this after a brief pause, as she looked, first down, then again right at us—"we know the meaning of sweet potato pie to the warmth and comfort and security of a close family and the enduring love it assures us. Why? Because besides building bellies, for many of us sweet potato pie builds memories. And I will tell you how." Her speech then explained the association between sensory recall and emotional responsiveness; and it was a speech as wonderful as its opening.

Its conclusion, not so by-the-way, did not disappoint, and you should know it, for its charm, its wit, and its lessons. Some weeks before she spoke she came to my office for a chat. Soon enough she mentioned my Italian-American heritage and asked if I liked good food. I assured her I did. And dessert too, she wondered. Is that also a favorite?" Then came my shame: I had to confess that I'd never in my life tasted sweet potato pie. "*What?!*" she screamed. "That is a sorry, sorry fact, professor. Maybe someday I'll do something about that." Soon thereafter she left. As she was giving her speech I must say that I did not recall that conversation, but she certainly did. Near the end, she told the class, "you know, there is one sorry person in this room whom I know has never had sweet potato pie. Professor," she said, looking at me, "would you like a piece of pie?" I said, sure; she handed me the piece on a paper plate with a fork, and I ate one of the most delicious foods of my entire life. "I don't have to ask how you liked that, do I professor?" she said. "No," I answered, "you surely do not." Well then," she almost drawled, "do you think you'll remember this event?" "I certainly will, and please thank your granny for me won't you?"

She had signed her work

FOUR

MEANING
Seeing, Knowing, and Thinking

IN 1922 WALTER LIPPMANN (who in *Public Opinion* was the first to teach us about stereotypes) complained that, in a "complicated civilization," we mistakenly assume "that somehow mysteriously there exists in the hearts of men a knowledge of the world beyond their reach." He goes on to argue that "representative government . . . cannot be worked successfully . . . unless there is an independent, expert organization for making the unseen facts intelligible to those who have to make decisions." I have no idea what organization he could have meant: federal agencies? universities? think tanks? He certainly did not mean the press. About that estate (and remember that he was essentially a journalist) he tells us that the main concern is to get our attention: "It is a problem of provoking *feeling* [my emph.] in the reader, of inducing him to feel [again] a sense of personal identification with the stories he is reading."

Well, why not? The press, according to Lippmann, plays into a basic human need, according to Robin Dunbar in his *Grooming, Gossip and the Evolution of Language*: ". . . language [in fact, *human communication*] is someone actively trying to influence the mind of another individual. The human mind seems to have been built in such a way that it assumes other individuals are trying to communicate with it." And at the end of the day—*feelings* or not, *identification* or not—we should be of good cheer, for according to Jeremy Campbell (in his *Grammatical Man*) all will be well: "information theory shows that there are good reasons why the forces of anti-chance are as universal as the forces of chance. . . . Sense and order, the theory says, can prevail against nonsense and chaos." In this world. Really.

My own scepticism derives from those annoying "unexamined assumptions" that we constantly make; we all know they can get us into trouble, as in "oh, I just assumed . . ." They are committed enemies of cogent communication. Here are two simple instances (actually two riddles) illustrating how the affliction works. Remember: our difficulty is not with any old assumptions, which we must make, but with assumptions we don't examine, largely because *we don't even know we're making them.* They make bigots of us all.

1/ *The Row Boat.* Two fathers and two sons go out on a local lake in a row boat to fish. Each catches one fish, neither more nor less. They come back to shore and lay out the catch. Now, no one has lost, or eaten, or thrown back or in any way gotten rid of his fish, and yet the two fathers and two sons count three fish. Well, 2+2 has equaled 4 for a long time, and you learned that a long time ago. So how do we get three fish instead of four? Easy. If you are puzzled it's because you're assuming that two fathers and two sons are four people; you can probably see them out there on that boat. But if you work backwards you'll see your mistake. If each caught a fish, and no fish were lost, then there must be three people. So the problem becomes, How can two fathers and two sons be three people? By the end of that sentence I'm sure you realized—if you were puzzled in the first place—that a grandfather, his son, and that son's son are two fathers and two sons: three people.

2/ *The Car Crash.* A father is driving along at very high speed, his small (biological) son next to him. They crash horribly. The father is killed immediately, but the son, still alive, is rushed to the nearest emergency room. There the doctor on duty—can you visualize the scene?—rushes to the boy, stops in horror, and wails, "I can't operate on that boy. He's my son!" Here I say that I was not fooled by the row boat riddle but that this one caught me, precisely because I *did* visualize the scene. And what I saw was a male doctor, which contradicts the fact of the riddle. What I did not see was a female doctor, the boy being her son: chaos, not clarity.

Every word comes with assumptions, right? Consider. A honeybee never gets confused. The scouts fly for miles, locate pollen, fly back to the hive (never getting lost), do a hemispherical dance (never mis-stepping) as other bees watch, then often die. The bees who were watching then fly to the exact point at which they will find the pollen—because the dying bee's dance told them exactly where to find it. Neither the dancer nor the watcher ever mistakes the movement. No dancer bee ever decides to "do his own thing." Why? Because *bees have no concepts, only senses and a pre-programmed navigational apparatus.* Unlike us they cannot philosophize about pollen, and they make no assumptions.

Those poor bees are "incompletely individuated," to use the language of Susanne K. Langer in her *Philosophical Sketches*, whereas we function by way of "imagination" (her word again), which enables us to envision connections. In other words, we use this "specialized function, imagination [vision, wonder]. . . . The result is that we live in a web of ideas, a fabric of our own making" that arises from "figments of all sorts that serve as *symbols for ideas.*" In other words, we are *Homo very sapiens.* So not only can much go wrong in conception, but much more in transmission and reception. Then again, it is concepts that make the world—known, unknown, past, future, imagined—both possible *and portable,* which it isn't for any animal we know of (with the possible exception of elephants: see the fascinating *When Elephants Weep,* by Jeffrey Moussaieff Masson). The price for this wonder is the possibility of confusion, often owing to unexamined assumption.

Here is an example of handling concepts. What do we mean by charity? Our mental survey uncovers the obvious, as it often does. Charity is either stuff or an organization that collects, then distributes, stuff to the needy. A layer down comes associations with generosity of spirit, as in "now, don't be uncharitable," that is, mean-spirited or unkind. Step two, however, gets us much deeper than that. Perhaps the most famous passage dealing with charity—beware the translation—is from St. Paul's first letter to the Corinthians, 13:3-8, where we are told that if we do not have "charity, we gain nothing . . . ," that "charity is patient, charity is kind . . . it does not seek it's own interests. . . . [It] rejoices with the truth . . . believes all things, hopes all things, endures all things. Charity never fails." Next, the *New Catholic Encyclopedia* refers us to St. Jerome, who translated the Bible from Greek into Latin. In his original he found the Greek *agape,* which only meekly translates as our word "love," meekly because Greek has a number of other words for love but we have none for this special kind of love: God's love for his creation, his self-sacrificing love, which never fails and is undeserved. For some reason unfathomable to us, we are *cara,* dear or precious beyond measure, to Him, and *cara,* according to an etymological search, is the Latin root of *caritas,* which is St. Jerome's word for *agape* and which becomes our *charity.*

How, then, does *love,* the usual contemporary translation of *agape,* enter the picture? Well, that is simple: we have corrupted *charity* to mean . . . stuff. Our lovely four-letter English word has it's own etymology, of course, originating in the German *lubig.* But do you really want to use a word for *agape* that is commonly applied to actors, clothing, and sweet potato pie? Precisely here is where examples can help. Consider a man walking along a forest path. At the bottom of the slope that descends from the path is a deep lake.

Example 1: The man sees a very young girl playing at the bank of the lake. He worries. If she falls in surely she will drown. He knows the child and loves both her and her family, who live in his village. She falls in. He cannot swim. As he watches the child first struggle, then gurgle, then sink beneath the surface, his anguish grows so much that he weeps and trembles and wrings his hands and cries out. But he does nothing to save her. Clearly, his feelings are strong and sympathetic. Is this *charity*? Or is it, rather, compassion, from the Latin *com* = "along with" and *passio* = "suffering"? Certainly he feels her pain; that is, he is compassionate. But just as certainly feelings are insufficient—they are not *giving*.

Example 2: Here we have exactly the same scenario but with a very different man. This one is old and angry. He doesn't like children; he particularly does not like that little girl, there by the lake, or her parents. Like his counterpart, this man cannot swim, but when the little girl falls in, he immediately whips of his shoes and jacket, dashes down to the lake, dives in, and, with his last ounce of energy, lifts her above the surface so that she can grasp a low-hanging branch, thus saving herself. He, however, drowns.

By comparing the two scenarios in light of our previous work, we see that charity is indeed giving, but not the giving of *stuff*. Instead, it's giving of the *self*, and, as with *agape*, it is extended to those who are dear though not necessarily deserving; that is, dear because they are in need and we can help. It is not a feeling (though *typically* sympathetic feelings are present) no matter how strong, but an act of will. We also see that when we begin to give of ourselves we may not stop until the other's need is satisfied, even perhaps at the cost of our very lives. We don't give charity, or *to* charity, but *from* it. We expect nothing in return, not even a warm feeling of self-satisfaction, because charity is sacrifice not stuff. It is not about the lover but the beloved.

Can you recall the story of Helen Keller, who very near birth became both blind and deaf? The wonderful movie about her and her teacher, Annie Sullivan, is *The Miracle Worker*. The climactic scene occurs at the well. Annie has been struggling, often physically, to teach language to Helen, who has been little more than an ill-tempered, pampered pet. But teach how? The pre-adolescent girl can neither hear the sounds of speech nor see the mouths that make them: she has nothing to imitate. But Annie knows that Helen, as a human being, has her human benediction: her *logos*. The switch-board is there and it will make connections, if only it can be turned on. Annie has been signing into the palm of Helen's hand and has been putting Helen's hands to mouth and throat, her own and Helen's.

Finally, at the well, Helen frantically pumps water to drink. Annie seizes the opportunity to sign w-a-t-e-r into Helen's hand. And the coin drops. For the first time in her life Helen connects these movements, first to that very liquid which in this instant happens to be running over her hands and arms, then to the concept of that liquid. She knows that things combine into concepts that we can carry with us—and that they have names.

Helen, of course, would grow up to be an effective writer and lecturer. Other children, feral children who have been deprived and abused, have not been as blessed as Helen. We know of some who, after their rescue and much care and instruction, die young or become feral once again. We are more blessed, so blessed that we take for granted the gift of *logos*. Do you remember struggling to learn how to speak? If you've learned a second language late, and in school, you have some idea of the struggle. Now imagine having to do that at age twelve, like Helen—without being able to see or hear how it's done! Really, we must not take this ability for granted. And we must be vigilant in preventing its abuse, by ourselves or by others.

So: much more than "personal identification" is required to satisfy what Mr. Dunbar identifies as our need to communicate and, yes, Mr. Campbell, much *can* go wrong.

2.

We hope we know what we're talking about, of course. And to obtain that knowledge, curiosity surely helps. But to satisfy curiosity we must work. First we must overcome what Francis Bacon, in his *Novum Organum*, called Idols of the Mind, ways of thinking beyond which it never occurs to us to move. He discusses four: 1/ *Idols of the Tribe*. Owing to our inclination to perceive our preconceived notions about things, this is our tendency to perceive more order and regularity in systems than is actually the case (as when we talk of political parties or movements as though they are homogeneous). 2/ *Idols of the Cave*. Personal flaws in reasoning due to likes and dislikes; that is, bigotries (*e.g.* political bigotries) of all kinds. 3/ *Idols of the Marketplace*. Confusions in the use of language (such as 'poverty,' 'gay', 'race', 'liberal', 'conservative' and the like). 4/ *Idols of the Theatre*. The following of dogma without question (as when a confused colleague couldn't answer a question on public affairs until she found out "what the liberal position would be").

We cannot know, argue, opine or conclude accurately until we can see what is actually there to be seen. We must struggle—it's rarely easy—past the idols and pay attention (to what actually is there to be seen). Nathaniel Southgate Shaler, the Harvard paleontologist and geologist of the late nineteenth- and early twentieth-century (and a man troubling for many of his racial theories—withal his mind had its many idols), was taught the difficulty of actually seeing what's there to be seen—the hard, slow, patient work of it—by the great Louis Agassiz, the godfather of American paleontology. This edited selection is from "How Agassiz Taught Professor Shaler" in *The Autobiography of Nathaniel Southgate Shaler* (1907: education was different then, don't you think?)

I had my first contact with the man who was to have the most influence on my life of any of the teachers to whom I am indebted. . . . Agassiz's laboratory . . . occupied one room about thirty feet long and fifteen feet wide. . . . In this place, already packed, I had assigned to me a small pine table with a rusty tin pan upon it. . . . When I sat me down before my tin pan, Agassiz brought me a small fish, placing it before me with the rather stern requirement that I should study it, but should on no account talk to any one concerning it, nor read anything relating to fishes, until I had his permission so to do. To my inquiry, 'What shall I do?' he said in effect: 'Find out what you can without damaging the specimen; when I think that you have done the work I will question you.' In the course of an hour I thought I had compassed that fish; it was rather an unsavory object, giving forth the stench of old alcohol, then loathsome to me. . . . It appeared to me to be a case for a summary report, which I was anxious to make and get on to the next stage of the business. But Agassiz, though always within call, concerned himself no further with me that day, nor the next, nor for a week. . . . So I set my wits to work upon the thing, and in the course of a hundred hours or so thought I had done much—a hundred times as much as seemed possible at the start. . . . Finally, I felt full of the subject, and probably expressed it in my bearing. . . . At length, on the seventh day, came the question, 'Well?' and my disgorge of learning to him as he sat on the edge of my table puffing his cigar. At the end of the hour's telling, he swung off and away, saying: 'That is not right.' . . . I went at the task anew, discarded my first notes, and in another week of ten hours a day labor I had results which astonished myself and satisfied him. Still there was no trace of praise in words or manner. He signified that it would do by placing before me about a half a peck of bones, telling me to see what I could make of them, with no further directions to guide me. . . . Two months or more went to this task with no other help than an occasional looking over my grouping with the stereotyped remark: 'That is not right.' Finally, the task was done, and I was again set upon alcoholic specimens – this time a remarkable lot of specimens representing, perhaps, twenty species. . . . I shall never forget the sense of power in dealing with things which I felt in beginning the more extended work on a groups of animals. I had learned the art of comparing objects.

Sustained looking, seeing as much as there is, from every angle, driving the eye into ever-greater detail no matter the size or number of those details, and doing so from every height—close, so as to see the texture of the bark on the tree, farther away, to see the variations in the bark, farthest, to see the forest—is hard *and therefore* rewarding work. It is the great antidote to mental idols of all kinds.

Shaler's lesson, though, is not the only lesson. For the rest of it we must turn briefly to C. S. Lewis and his short essay "Meditation in a Toolshed." Lewis places himself in the dark corner of a closed shed. The door does not have a tight fit, so a beam of sunlight enters through a crack near the top of the jamb. He notices certain features of the beam and of his surroundings: the interior remains dark and barely visible, the beam itself is sharply defined, with dust motes sharply defined as well as they float about inside the beam; and he can discern the dimensions of the beam very clearly. Then the world changes. He steps into the beam, turning his eyes upwards toward the crack through which the beam enters. Now, instead of looking at the beam he is looking along the beam.

The first obvious difference brought by this new perspective is that there is no longer a beam, only a bath of light; and the shed has just about disappeared; and Lewis can now see through the crack to the leaves on the tree outside the door and even to the source of the light, the sun beyond the tree. The two experiences are entirely different. Lewis' point, in its simplicity, is elegant and momentous. If we stand only outside an experience (*e.g.* religious faith), we can study it and, know nothing of the interior experience and denying its validity, we can (if we care to do so) easily debunk reports from the inside. But that would be only half the story—Shaler's half.

Is this sounding too easy? Perhaps so, since it ignores the process of Selective Perception that makes seeing and knowing so difficult. We cannot give our attention to everything, so we give it to that small portion of the world that promises some return. For example, as a lover of movies, I see these but not those movies simply because I don't have the temporal or psychic space to see more (let alone all) of them. Most of movie reality has thus been excluded as dots that I might connect. But at least I do see this movie. Or do I? In fact, most of us look at about one-third of the screen, and it is the third which, if not the very center, is the one third the director wants us to pay attention to. So having practiced selective exposure, we go on to practice selective attention, and the world of dots to connect is further diminished. Then comes faulty recall: of that part of the screen that we did pay attention to, how much do we remember—either when we leave the theater or, worse, days, week and months later? *Selective recall* further shrinks the number of dots that we can connect. Selective exposure, selective attention, and selective recall make for an ever smaller world of meaning—unless we work very hard indeed to counteract the process of selective perception.

Very many factors account for selectivity; prominent among these is expectation. From time-to-time I've done the following class experiment, never lasting more than two minutes. If there is a student whom I've known prior to his entrance into the particular class and whom I trust, I enlist him as an accomplice. My instructions are for him to be truculent for the first week or two, while I am patient and tolerant with him in return. Soon enough he arrives late to class, again, and I uncharacteristically interrupt myself and the class to call him on it at once. He answers angrily and rudely, but not threateningly or profanely. He certainly does not shout. I, on the other hand, become personally abusive, and loudly so. I use profanity. I even go so far as to threaten him with some academic punishment as I gesture menacingly. I say we must go to Security. He abruptly leaves, saying "no way" as he does so. I turn to the class and tell them that they were witnesses and ask them write what they've seen and heard.

Over the decades perhaps a hundred students have complied: the preponderance get it wrong. Fewer than twenty have reported me as the one using profanity, being personally abusive, and gesturing menacingly; most have reported the student behaving in that way—the opposite of what actually has happened. Teachers, and particularly this one who had been so gentle so far, do not behave that way! In the minds of my students, their classmate was defined as the thug, and *the power to define is the power to rule.*

3.

Another barrier to open attentiveness, idol-free thinking, and assuming varied perspectives is described by Eric Hoffer in his classic *The True Believer* (1951). Although Hoffer is most interested in mass movements, he does delineate two features of the true-believing mind: 1/ frustration, which "can generate most of the characteristics of the true believer"; and 2/ "that an effective technique of conversion consists basically in the inculcation and fixation of proclivities and responses indigenous to the frustrated mind." He goes on to add this: "For though ours is a godless age, it is the very opposite of irreligious. The true believer is everywhere on the march, and both by converting and antagonizing he is shaping the world. . . ." Or, as Freud has somewhere said, "everyone will have a religion; it's only a matter of which." Hoffer is non-judgmental, allowing that much "true belief" is necessary for goodness and justice to prevail; on the other hand we know that some true belief is, in the big picture, trivial, for example rabid allegiance to sports teams. And if you read his sorely neglected book it is difficult not to confess that you are, or have been, somehow, a true believer yourself.

Here is an example of many intellectual errors militating against fixed, open attentiveness, idol-free thinking, and multi-perspective knowing—all at once. Nearly five decades ago my bride-to-be, my mother-in-law-to-be(!) and I traveled from Lima high into the Andes, finally to see the old Inca capital of Cuzco and the ruins of Machu Picchu. (Both far exceeded expectations and continue to do so.) In order to see the sights around Cuzco we hired a car with a driver-guide named Alejandro, a man fluent in both Spanish (as the three of us are) and Qechua (which none of us is).

At one point we pulled over so I could climb the grassy, protuberant mound of one of the peaks. Once on the rounded height it seemed to me that I was at the top of the world, such was the view, until I turned and saw the mountain peak looming behind me. I'd never felt such over-whelming—and comforting—solitude: the experience was the very essence of the concept numinous. And I would have knelt and prayed there and then if, coming over the mound from the other direction, a little boy leading a herd of llama had not appeared, as if out of the clouds (at that height one looks both up and down to see clouds, unless one is inside a cloud). I tried to strike up a conversation.

Fortuitously, Alejandro appeared and was able to translate. The boy (he could not have been ten years old) was utterly poised, unaffected and cheerful—and seemingly impoverished. Yes, he said, he lives nearby, no more than a half-day walk from where we stood; no, he had never heard of Lima—was it bigger than Pisac (the market village nearby)? Would he go so far as to leave Peru? Was that possible? Wasn't Peru the world? Then I made a grievous mistake: I offered the boy a few *soles* (maybe two dollars worth). He was utterly puzzled; Alejandro was utterly nonplussed. With exquisite courtesy the man told me that this simply wasn't done here: the *altiplano* was *not* Lima, *serranos* are neither beggars—there is no Qechua word for the act—nor hustlers. The boy, who did not understand our Spanish, asked what he was to do with the money. I answered that, maybe, his parents would find it useful. He allowed that not only did he think they wouldn't need it—what would they use it for?—but that they would be angry if he were to accept it.

I was chastened, of course: a geographical Other World had within it a cultural Other World as well. I've never learned more than a few words in Qechua, but I am unsurprised at the true tale of a man who mistook the word for "terrorist" to mean a certain species of bird.

4.

Culture makes life-as-we-live-it, and conversation makes culture; inauthentic conversation makes inauthentic culture. Therefore if an inauthentic cultural claim molds your identity, then your identity is not, so to speak, worth the oxygen it took to speak the words. Here Thomas Sowell (in *Intellectuals and Society*) teaches us something pertinent, in this case about a particularly influential group of communicators. The "public intellectual"—for which read any civil authority who holds sway over a group—creates

> . . . a general set of assumptions, beliefs and imperatives—a vision—that serves as a general framework for the way particular issues and events that come along are perceived. . . . What John Maynard Keynes called 'the gradual encroachment of ideas' can change the way we see the world as it exists and change how we think the world ought to be.

—but only if those assumptions are examined. Or, and on a more personal level, the lesson is one taught by Malcolm X in one of his very last speeches: "look for yourself, think for yourself, then make up your own mind."

FIVE

ARGUMENTS
Making Them and Having Them

Rarely do we find men who engage in hard, solid thinking. There is an almost universal quest for easy answers and half-baked solutions. Nothing pains some people more than having to think.
—Martin Luther King, Jr.

Dialectic and Logic generally mean the very same thing . . . the same doctrine of reasoning well about anything. . .
—Peter Ramus, *Dialectic* (1572)

ABOUT TWENTY-FIVE years ago I was invited to participate in a debate on abortion. I cannot recall who extended the invitation, but it would be under the auspices of an the Arts and Works Ensemble Theater Company, then performing at a venue in Greenwich Village. The program was enticing to me. Five or six (I cannot remember) very short plays would be performed, each dramatically rendering a side in the debate. After the performances the debaters would take the stage. Seated at stage-left were the pro-choice people, Bill Baird (a leading abortionist who was also a spokesmen for his cause on many a TV program) along with a number of women from either the National Organization of Women or Planned Parenthood. They were behind a table stacked with much printed matter. At stage-right were the pro-life people: I alone seated on a chair, an empty one to my left, with no table or printed matter.

I had been promised a partner, a famous convert to my side who, as a nurse, had assisted at many an abortion until the repulsion overcame her and morality took hold. Whereas I was unknown (except very locally as a capable debater), she was very well known and feared by the pro-choice people. As I watched the plays preceding the debate I said a few prayers, some petitioning that my partner would appear. She did, but after the debate proper had begun. By then I had made a handful of telling points that had the opposition very much on the defensive. I know the points were telling because I was not only applauded at the time of making the points but thanked later by many in the audience. That is worth knowing because of who made up that audience: young, hip, New York liberals who were looking for some kind of excitement in Greenwich Village, than which there was, and isn't, a more pro-choice territory on this side of time.

The opposition spoke first, and they made their big mistake right at the beginning. Mr. Baird committed the fallacy of the Strawman, that is, he attributed to me a position I did not hold. He should have known better, since he did not know me from a bug. What he did was attribute to me attacks upon himself: he was craven, he was immoral, he was cruel, he was self-aggrandizing, he was callous, he was greedy. All wrong, he protested, pointing out that he has been harassed for his beliefs and has spent much of him own money in defending them and putting them into practice. (At the time he was among the leading abortion-providers in the country.)

Then it was my turn, and I could not believe how easy he had made it for me. He had not only attacked a strawman (attributing to me a position I had neither made nor implied) but committed an *ad hominem* (a personal attack, in this case tricky, since his attack consisted of attributing nastiness to me against him). Sitting upright and alone (with an empty chair to my left: the nurse had not yet arrived), I pointed out that Mr. Baird could not be right, for the simple reason that I had never met him, had never uttered a word about him, and that—contrary to what he claimed I thought of him—I assumed he was an honorable man who believed what he proclaimed and a brave one, too, for his was willingness to sacrifice on behalf of his beliefs. My objections, in short, were not to Mr. Baird but to his beliefs: "Simply put," I said, I believe he, like many principled people, is wrong. I am here to explore that disagreement," I added, "not to defame anyone or, for that matter, to be defamed." There came the first round of applause.

Baird having been first to defend his position (his wasted opportunity), it was now my turn to defend my position (after which Baird would be afforded an opportunity, as I had been, to respond). I promised to be brief and I was. I claimed to be the real liberal, for was it not Liberalism that historically stood up for the invisible, the voiceless and the defenseless? As for choice, the accumulation of which defines personal identity: "think," I said, "of all the choices *not* made because of abortion. I speak in defense of those choices, perhaps billions. So," I concluded, "who is the real pro-choice advocate here?"

In his response Baird fell back. "A woman's right" became his mantra, "a right to do with her body as she pleases, especially with a non-human entity." Now, I'll wager that any reader could write my answer. First, she certainly does not have such a right; none of us does. In New York State, for example, you may not have a healthy limb amputated; nor can you abuse "non-human entities" known as animals. "Moreover," I asked, "how can you be so sure the life in that mother is non-human? [We can now, of course, with advances in embryology and the science of DNA.] Has a human mother ever given birth, say, to a lamb, a tree or a stone? Has a human mother ever given birth to anything *other than* a human being?" There came the second round of applause. (To be honest, I believe the audience was enjoying the gamesmanship more than the substance of my arguments.)

There were a few more exchanges involving the definition of person: Baird said the embryo was not one, I countered with a request for a definition of "person," he answered by example: we on stage were persons, I then with a question: were you as much a person twenty years ago as you are now? "Well then," I concluded, "neither is that unborn child as much of a person that she will be once she begins making all those choices we here all favor." There came the third round of applause.

At that point the nurse showed up and Baird and his vestals really became over-wrought. She knew the science, it showed, and Baird was done for. After she arrived I never said another word; thank God I didn't have to. As I was leaving some twenty people stopped me to say they would re-think their pro-choice position now: their orthodoxy had been unsettled which, short of outright conversion (a very great rarity) counts as a victory.

Trying to revive use of the old word "quarrel" (now fallen into disuse and what Baird was trying for), I juxtapose it to "argument," which we ordinarily use when we mean "quarrel." But, then, what do we mean by "argument"? The simple answer is, "evidence plus reasoning leading to a conclusion," which is a beginning, but only that. To "have an argument" is to have a clash of ideas (my objective in the debate), not a clash of personalities—the essence of a quarrel. The obvious implication is that arguments are marked by logic rather than by passion or vanity.

These days my subject is called "critical thinking," a trendy designation if ever there was one. But the very same subject has been known as "decision-making" theory, "argumentation" theory, and—going very far back—"dialectic." Of course, bells and whistles have been added, but the matter *per se*, the discipline at its core, remains as central to human thinking as it has always been. It's important to remember that, whether with or without academic or philosophical systems, this subject—this system—is the way the mind works when it's trying to make a point rationally. Even when working badly it is what the mind is *trying* to do well.

Here is an overview of critical thinking. It is thinking that is 1/ reasonable, 2/ conducive to judgment that relies upon objective criteria, 3/ sensitive to context, and 4/ self-corrective. It depends greatly on premises that are identified and examines (unexamined assumptions are lethal), terms that are candidly and fairly defined, evidence that is substantial and reliable, and logic that can be examined transparently. Our first great teacher of the . . . I will call it an "art" . . . is Plato who, in his dialogues teaches the need for definition, the division of ideas into their constituent parts, the civility of exchange (in his case by way of questions-and-answers), and the refusal to over-claim (with respect to what we know or what can be known and with respect to our own knowledge).

Plato's pupil Aristotle later comes along with his *organon*, a group of at least eight works (depending on what we choose to include) that together, and with considerable thoroughness, map the touchstones and requirements of reliable thinking, especially when such thinking seeks to arrive at a rational conclusion. The most important among these eight are the *Prior Analytics*, which introduces us to the syllogism, and the *Posterior Analytics*, which treats of knowledge, or, more particularly, how arguments may demonstrate the truth of what we think we know. Apart from the *organon* is the *Rhetoric*, which (among other things) describes the avenues of thinking ("topics") along which we may profitably argue. (Some three hundred years later Cicero would amplify upon this with his own books, *Topica* and *de Inventione*, which means how to find ideas and arguments.) Thereafter all is amplification, more or less, up to the present day. One emphasis since has been on methods of refutation, and one elaboration has been the practice of formal debate, as in the Lincoln-Douglas debates and in academic debating, where teams are formed for tournament competition.

We begin with a claim, some statement—a complete sentence, but not a question—that stakes a claim to our belief. These statements can be of fact (something did, does, or shall exist), value (something is worth this or that or nothing), or policy (here is what we ought to do). A *proposition* is either true, false, or more probably one than the other. In any controversy—mutually exclusive alternatives competing for selection—the proposition clarifies the alternatives by separating them distinctively; a proposition does not bridge, it divides (*e.g.* capital punishment should be abolished). Now, these propositions yield closed-ended *questions*—points of *stasis*, or "strife,": issues that constitute the proposition: Is capital punishment immoral? Is imprisonment sufficient punishment to fit all crimes? Does imprisonment deter other commission of crimes? That sort of thing. These questions are directly related to the proposition; they are dispositive.

Answers are called *contentions*. The different sides on the debate answer the questions differently, of course, and those answers—the contentions—become *primary reasons* for one side or the other. They must be argued before a decision-maker can choose the more reasonable alternative. Finding the issues, the real issues as opposed to phony ones, can be a chore. Much fraudulence is perpetrated, time wasted, and ill-will accumulated because of the purveying of phony issues. ("Is Mitt Romney super rich?" has nothing to do with "Vote for Mitt Romney," especially since he is no more rich than were FDR or JFK.) In other words, not every little annoyance or emotional tic deserves our attention.

Now for argument *per se*. The arguments are small reasons in support of our big reasons, secondary reasons in support of the primary ones. For example, a big reason for a claim, or proposition, that capital punishment be abolished is that it is immoral; my reasons for that reason would be my arguments. To make arguments we must match something in the world ("evidence") to something in our minds (a "warrant," some conception which ought to be as clear and as systematic as we can make it, excluding, for example, unexamined assumptions, platitudes, clichés, and slogans); then we infer a claim, even if (depending on the degree of the match) only a partial one.

Thus the parts of an argument are Evidence, Backing (for the Evidence: "Who says, how, and why?"), Claim (perhaps "qualified"), Warrant (which joins the evidence to the claim), Backing (a source for the Warrant), and Reservations (possible exceptions, the number and force of which determine the degree of qualification). A quick device for checking an argument is to link these parts by (in order) the common words "therefore," "since," "after all" (to link Backings) and "unless." This all sounds very complicated but in fact is what we do all the time. Now we're merely breaking down our normal process into its parts and giving those parts names. Here is a closer look. But before we take that look, this reminder: *reasons are not motives.* Reasons are objective and connect directly to our main claim; motives are personal preferences, tastes or drives from within.

The tour proper begins with the diagram below.

An Argument:
According to Stephen Toulmin

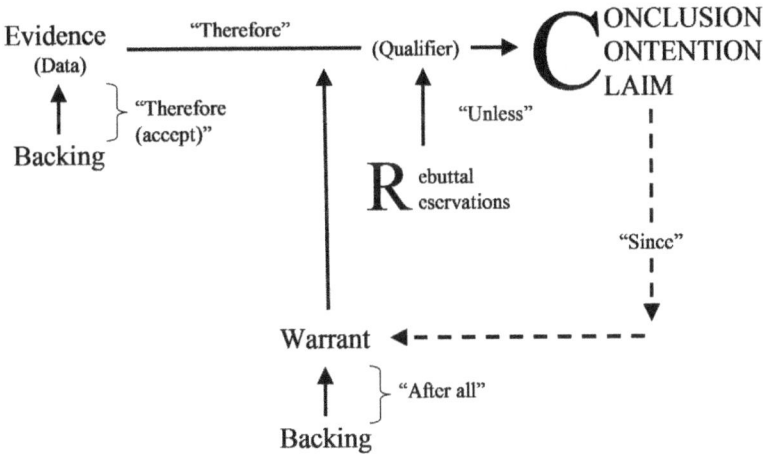

That is a schematic rendition—a map of our minds when we argue, whether we know it or not—adapted from the model formulated by the philosopher Stephen Toulmin (1922-2009) in his *The Uses of Argument* (1964) and in common (though not universal) use for nearly five decades. (Even the barbershop needs a method.)

Our understanding of this model begins with Aristotle's discovery the workings of the human mind when it reasons: the *syllogism*. Here is Aristotle's classic example: All men are mortal; Socrates is a man; therefore Socrates is _____. That's right. The first statement is the Major Premise, a general statement understood to be generally, if not universally, held as true. That will be our Warrant. It exists in people's minds, as do all beliefs. (Here we must recall that concepts also exist only in people's minds. So we are reminded to ask, What do we mean by "mortal"?) The second statement is the Minor Premise, a specific statement about something in the world, in this case good old Socrates. That is our Evidence.

Now just here we notice the very heart of all argument: *there is a match*; or, as logicians say, the middle term, "men," is "distributed," appearing in both the Warrant and in the Evidence, first as the subject then as the object. There is the match. And so we may conclude that Socrates shares the characteristics of all men: he is mortal. Now, the problem with the syllogism is the number and complexity of their types; that is why Toulmin devised his model. He notes that we don't all know those syllogisms and that we do not usually begin our arguments with a statement of general principle. So he put Evidence—that stuff in the world expressed by the Minor Premise—first, because that is how we usually begin our arguments. He connects that to the Conclusion, because that is what we do. And he buried the Major Premise—the Warrant, that which allows us to bridge the Evidence-Conclusion gap, because that is what we usually do: bury it when we bother with it at all.

Here's another example. Harry was born in Bermuda, therefore Harry is a British subject, since Bermuda is British territory; "after all" (see the diagram), Parliamentary law xyz long ago Anglified the island. Now for the sake of this exercise you can take the evidence, warrant, and backing as true. In that light, can you come up with any reservations, any "unless-es"? Here we must do what we do intuitively, examine the evidence by asking questions: Was Harry born in Bermuda when it was already British territory? Was he born of foreign parents who claimed their citizenship for him? Has he changed his own citizenship? Was he born in a foreign mission on the island of Bermuda that would have allowed for foreign citizenship? Is Harry alive? Is he *human*? (We are allowed no unexamined assumptions.)

Of course we may not know the answers to these questions, but if Harry matters enough, these questions guide further research so that we might have more evidence. But note: if even one reservation persists, we may no longer say "Harry is." We would then qualify our conclusion. We would have to scale down our certainty to something like, "Harry almost certainly is" or, if we have a few reservations, "Harry probably is" or, if we have many reservations, "Harry possibly is" or. . . . Clearly we are dealing with probability, not with the certainty of math equations or laboratory experiments or theological dogma.

That is why refutation is possible: probability always invites questions. For example, it is the wholesale acceptance of likelihood and the consequent absence of refutation that leads the jealous Othello to kill his wife. In his *The Improbability of Othello*, Joel B. Altman, while examining the history of rhetorical influence in the Renaissance and its roots, explains that no one in the play applies the variety of *enthymemes*—lines of reasoning and argument with *repressed* warrants—that we use to examine claims. Examining opposites, or definitions, or the relationship of parts to their whole, or the proportion of results to presumed causes, or prior mistakes, attributed motives, the reliability of authority, and so many others—Aristotle numbered twenty-eight altogether and his list is incomplete. These help us to see and to entertain alternatives, which Othello never does.

Refutation is itself an art, consisting of both it own method and a number of techniques. The method is fairly simple: identify the target (fairly: no distortion allowed), take a shot (here is where techniques enters the picture), examine the accuracy of the shot, and display its effectiveness to all and sundry. This four-step process is easily remembered if one imagines an archer shooting at a circular target with a red bulls-eye in the middle. Techniques vary, but one devastating tool can be the knowledge and application the fallacy inventory. Here is an abbreviated version (there are actually dozens) the knowledge of which can help disarm any careless, deceptive or lying adversary. If one thinks of the Toulmin model and its parts as limbs with joints to be tested, then fallacies are like diseases in the body: diagnose them, kill them, and display the dead tissue for the audience to behold.

FALLACY
Any error, abuse, or neglect of reasoning

Fallacies are at the heart of *demagogy*, rhetoric that distorts a subject and deceives an audience, usually by way of an abundance of hyper-emotional language. It is a variety of the more general *diseased speech*, tha t way of addressing each other, privately *or* publicly, which de-humanizes both the speaker and the audience. The following dozen fallacies are the most common and deceptive.

1. *Begging the Question*: Assuming part of the proposition (that which must be proved) to be true at the start, without first having offered any proof: as when asking a man accused of beating his wife, "when did you stop beating her?" as though the act itself had already been proven.

2. *Post hoc, ergo propter hoc* ("after this, therefore because of this"): Inferring that something which usually follows something else is necessarily caused by it, *e.g.* assuming lightening causes thunder because it comes first.

3. *Composition*: Assuming that something true of a single part of a whole is therefore true of the whole: that policeman is racist, so the police must be at war with black people.

4. *Division*: Assuming that something true of a whole is therefore true of one or more its parts. "You're from America? What a rich country! You must be rich."

5. *Hasty Generalization*: Drawing a conclusion on the basis of too small, or too unrepresentative, a sample of the larger group, as in "unbe-

lievable that Nixon won. Everyone I know voted for McGovern," when spoken by a resident of the People's Republic of the Upper West Side in Manhattan. (I know: a cheap shot.)

6. *Faulty Analogy*: The literal comparison of unlike things, or a failure to keep the basis of comparison (*e.g.* for statistical comparisons) constant, as when we compare "apples to oranges," let alone to chairs.

7. *Red Herring*: The introduction of a dramatic and irrelevant issue in order to distract from the actual argument. "What?! Mitt Romney drove with his dog on the roof of his car???"

8. *Smokescreen*: Excessive attention to context and detail in order to avoid the heart of the matter at hand, as when you cannot get a straight answer to a yes-no question but instead hear about, say, grandchildren.

9. *Ad Populum* ("argument to the crowd [or mob]"): An appeal to prejudice or an excessive appeal to emotion in place of rational argument, designed merely to arouse an excited response. A common—and base— form of demagogy, as with almost anything Al Sharpton says.

10. *Equivocation*: Shifting the meaning of an expression during an argument to suit a momentary convenience. (If you really want to annoy an adversary, simply ask, "by the way, exactly what do you mean by _____?"

11. *Ad Hominem* ("argument against the man"): Any attempt to distract from the subject to a speaker; the most offensive of many forms is name-calling, as with almost anything said on the Left about Dick Cheney.

12. *Strawman*: Attributing to an opponent something he did not say, or clearly did not mean, usually to make a spectacle of "refuting" it. (See the beginning of this chapter.)

I suggest that the reader do some homework and add to the list, listen for them, cringe, then correct.

For at the end of the day, as at its beginning and middle, we find ourselves in disagreement with others: from living room debates, to casual and spontaneous conversation, on to formal debate and especially public controversy. Short of an ugly quarrel we ought to know how to handle ourselves, even if only to see through the nonsense around us. I've been on a number of stages, but, really, Will is right: "all the world is a stage," and as players upon it we have a job to do: to think clearly, to dispel confusion in others, and to resist—even to combat—diseased speech when we are either tempted to it or encounter it in others.

SIX

"THE TONGUE IS ALSO A FIRE"
Ethics, Manners and Madness on the Left

"Wait, hold on here. Is this a barbershop? If we can't talk straight
in a barbershop, then where can we talk straight? We can't talk
straight nowhere else. You know, this ain't nothin' but healthy con-
versation, that's all. . . . nobody is exempt in the barbershop."
                 – Eddie the Barber, *Barbershop*

First, the disease.

O N JUNE 23, 1987, the late Senator Edward Kennedy said the
following about Robert Bork, a nominee to the United States
Supreme Court:

> Robert Bork's America is a land in which women would be
> forced into back-alley abortions, blacks would sit at segregated
> lunch counters, rogue police could break down citizens' doors
> in midnight raids, schoolchildren could not be taught about
> evolution, writers and artists would be censored at the whim
> of government.

The *ad hominem* burst like a giant pustule, and yet no one asked
him, as Joseph Welch famously asked of Sen. Joe McCarthy, "have you
no decency, sir?"

    I am not here arguing that Kennedy is the one who pulled the cork
out of the bottle of rhetorical toxins, which have been circulating in the

Republic since its founding. His rant was merely a particularly venomous instance of invective, which no amount of "compartmentalizing" as "politics as usual" can excuse. Rather I do claim that, in public places both high and low, *diseased speech* has never been more rampant, and never has the Left owned it more than it does now. It is where Neo-McCarthyism—in both toxicity and falsehood—has pitched its tent. Now, I do not claim the Right is a non-practitioner of eristic—from Eris, the goddess of strife—or of fraudulent speech but that it does not come close—in frequency, malice, prominence of the practitioner, or indulgence—to the Left. (When anti-Semitism rattled its forked tongue within the precincts of *National Review* it was its editor, William Buckley, who decapitated that snake. Now on the Left we do not have snake hunters but snake handlers, and just who is handling whom remains an open question.)

There she was, a lovely little girl, picking daisies, until a nuclear bomb blew her to bits. That was LBJ's contribution some fifty years ago against Barry Goldwater, part of a "vast Right Wing conspiracy" *avant la lettre.* (*La lettre* proper came with the First Lady's attribution of the plight of her philandering and rapist husband—Juanita Broderick was his victim—to a "vast Right Wing conspiracy." By the way, in her mendacity does not Hillary remind you, as she does me, of Lillian Hellman, though not as pretty?)

More than thirty years ago Janet Cook cooked up "Jimmy's World," a report for the *Washington Post* on a life of inner city misery. It was all fabricated. Jayson Blair perpetrated similar falsehoods for the *New York Times.* Recently a horrific campus gang rape by Duke athletes was reported, with the Left jumping through hoops to condemn it fastest and most furiously: it, too, was pure fiction, as was a second rape "reported" in *Rolling Stone* (for which enormity no one has been fired). Decades ago, Rigoberta Menchu won a Nobel Prize for her harrowing and inspiring Third World autobiography, which turned out to be largely an invention.

An anchorman for MSNBC suggested a fecal diet for Sarah Pailin; Whoopi Goldberg grabbed her crotch and punned on "bush" during a presidential election cycle; a former Secretary of State actually suggested that a sitting president already had Osama bin Laden captive but was waiting for the politically opportune time to release the news. (Madeline Albright would later claim she was joking, but her charge is on video—no one believed that.) Where to stop?

Peter Arnett of CNN cuts a deal with Sadam Hussein: in exchange for favorable reporting Arnett gets a privileged position from which to view the Allied attack on Iraq as well as unique access to high-ranking Iraqi officials. (He was fired.) The Democrat Senate Majority leader ridicules a sitting Republican president as dumb, repeatedly excoriates (by name) citizen-donors to the opposition party, and lies (along with his president) about policy consequences. When he is caught in a lie about a presidential nominee his answer is, "he lost, didn't he?" "Hands up, don't shoot," which was all lie, becomes an anthem of the Newest Left. (Not-so-by-the-way, I have failed to find any such enormities on Fox News Channel)

So: Where to stop? With the savaging of Dick Cheney, or of President Bush? Or of Sarah Palin, who for a while was held indirectly responsible for the shooting of Congresswoman Gabrielle Giffords—until, of course, the news of her shooter's Leftist leanings came out? And—of course—no apologies. There never are. But there remain the plagiarists: Martin Luther King, Junior, Joe Biden . . . but by comparison with their siblings they seem almost innocent in their fraudulence.

I believe any reader not only gets the point but could add to the list amply: the instances of diseased speech proliferate, and as they do such depredations—like cheap currency—matter less and less. Here is an example of what I mean. Two White House guests of President Obama pose in front of the portrait of Ronald Reagan and give him the middle-finger salute; they photograph themselves; they post the picture online, and they go on to say, "that's right, f**k Reagan." Nary a peep from the press. (Of course Al Sharpton is a one-man neo-McCarthyite bobblehead doll, with nary a peep from the press.) Now, just do the Reversal Test: here come members of the Tea Party movement, and here is a portrait of, say, FDR, and here are you, honestly answering this question: Can you in the most hallucinatory pipe dream imagine the same gesture being made? And, if you can, could we not write the *New York Times* editorial the next day? This license extends even to its own (sort of): see Juan Williams' *Muzzled*, the trials of a center-left black man persecuted by PBS, abuse still less than that suffered by Sharyl Attkisson, a prize-winning journalist who names the names of CBS bosses who stifled reliable reports damaging to Obama. (Obviously for the Left black lists work in one direction only.)

At work, apparently, is belief in some greater Cause (as the incomparable Charles McCarry dissects it in his *Shelly's Heart*). It matters more than both truth and American interests. When not too long ago Edward Koch, a quintessential public servant, a Democrat (among my all-time favorites), a patriot, and a Jew, died, a number of New York Jews mourned qualifiedly, because "he had betrayed the [C]ause."

The Cause comes first, and so the use of means damnably disproportionate to the ends sought is not only permissible but obligatory for those whose troth is pledged to it, such is the self-righteousness of the crypto-religious True Believer. Of course, in this carnival of fraudulence the *New York Times* plays its role. It has yet to return a Pulitzer Prize given to Walter Duranty, one of its reporters, who lied about the Stalin regime, and it prints—on the front page—an entirely false story about the adultery of a presidential candidate from the party it disfavors. But rather than cherry-pick from that amply-stocked basket, I'll take the higher road.

How the *Times* is trending has been shown by its own advertising. One TV ad depicted a couple trading sections of the Sunday edition—*e.g.* the Arts, the Book review—but not the Main (that is, the news) Section; in other words, the paper confesses to being a feature rag rather than a newspaper. The second ad sold the paper because, in the words of a voice-over, "it makes me feel like I'm in the know." Bad grammar aside, note the claim is not "puts me in the know" but rather to feel that way. It reminds me of an old TV ad for the Barbizon School for Modeling, which taught its pupils to be models "or just look like one," as though models did more than "look like." It's what happens when you check your brain at the door on behalf of the Cause.

I've heard one political operative speak for many in both political parties: if your guy is behind and the election is close, anything goes, as long as it's legal—ethics and morality be damned. This view, extended well beyond the electoral season, is, I think, why some time ago *New York Times* columnist Matt Miller asked "Is Persuasion Dead?" He was not complaining that persuasion does not work; in fact he cited an instance when (lamentably in his opinion) it had worked on him. Instead he regretted its abandonment in favor of the snipe and that demonizing smear that dominate public discourse. These noxious irruptions have become not only commonplace but wanton, like trolling, "the act [as Julie Zhuo has put it in another *New York Times* article] of posting inflammatory, derogatory, or provocative messages in public forums."

Second, a cure.

My purpose here is more diagnostic than prescriptive. Still, I offer these suggestions for conversation down the road. Consider the Nobel Laureate in Physics William Shockley, co-inventor of the transistor—probably a genius. In the sixties he went about claiming, quite calmly and benignly, just like your gramps, that black people are genetically inferior to white people with respect to intelligence and should be subjected to selective eugenic procedures (a program long-held by such figures of the Left as G.B. Shaw, H.G. Wells, and Margaret Sanger). He had a mountain of evidence, almost all of it based on the results of IQ tests. He got quite a play, this genius and Nobel Laureate in Physics. You noticed, I'm sure, that the word is 'physics', not 'genetics' or 'psycho-metrics'. In short, he had no expertise in the field he was now plowing.

Alas, despite his tranquil, respectful, and slightly avuncular manner, he was so odious to most audiences that, most of the time, he wasn't allowed to speak when he was invited to do so. And then the great public communicator Tony Brown had him on his PBS *Black Journal* to debate the psychiatrist Frances Cress Welsing (an extremist of a different stripe). Brown's mediation was key: Welsing stuck to the topic—Shockley's theory—and avoided her own broader program, while Shockley was allowed, temperately and thoroughly, to expound. The winner was open, rational debate (as well as Tony Brown), and Truth, as Shockley's views were exposed as pre-baked, half-baked, and finally utterly unbaked.

Protagoras was the great fifth century B.C. sophist and the subject of one of Plato's greatest dialogues. He set exercises for his students emphasizing eristic oratory, de-emphasized righteousness, and often encouraged a design that would make the weaker case seem the stronger. Debate (Do you remember *Firing Line?*) is one antidote to all the Protagorases of the world.

There are others. I've touched upon one old one, an instrument of ethical diagnosis whereby the propriety of means is determined by (among other elements) its proportion-ality to the moral worth of the end sought (but that requires a fixed notion of moral worth—objective, not subjective). Another is the application of a fallacy inventory. One can easily learn the informal fallacies (*e.g. ad hominem*, red-herring, smokescreen, composition and division, and perhaps ten others): recognizing them becomes easy, the practice becomes compulsive; the destruction of the falsehood is immediate. Yet another is more demanding: the Toulmin analysis of argument, from the philosopher Stephen Toulmin's *The Uses of Argument*. It requires some command of a very natural, logical paradigm and the application to a truth-claim of a sequence of words—therefore, since, unless, after all—in the light of that schemata. As with the use of the fallacy inventory, this too becomes second nature once the practitioner pays some dues. What matters most, however, is that *the enormities be called out in the first place* and tallies kept. And let us remember: the devil cannot stand to be mocked.

A Roadblock

We populate terrain heavily marked by a great psycho-ideological divide, a chasm so deep and jagged that it may as well be theological.

Such divides happen in private and social discourse, to be sure, and even though cures, palliatives and appeals apply to all levels of diseased speech, my subject here is limited to public discourse. In that light, a question: What stops us from crossing the chasm?

I am no more equipped to address the 'psycho' element of the divide than anyone else on either side of it, and we are all less well-equipped than Eric Hoffer, whose *The True Believer* remains as discerning today as it was some sixty years ago when first published. The ideological element, however, offers all of us an opportunity for real *debate*. My claim—no reader should be surprised, I think—is that the divide is preponderantly the work of the Left, or at least the far (or radical, now dominant) Left. It is they and their sympathizers who, though finding their *modus operandi* distasteful, nevertheless go along: "they are bastards but they are our bastards"; that sort of thing.[1]

So it is the Left who must, as young people have been saying for some time now, get over themselves, their "illiberal liberal"[2] selves. But that cannot be easy: with that *Weltanschauung* on their backs there's may be too heavy lifting, and it's locked up so tight that hardly anyone ever gets out. Still, it is locked on the inside, so just maybe . . .

Previously I've attacked the fraudulence of the Left. Now for their pretense to tyranny; that is, what they would keep out of the public arena, and how. These days race comes first; a close second is sex (including the fiat that we refer to it as gender); then, of course, religion in the public square, especially Christianity, *especially* Evangelical Christianity and Catholicism (but not Islam—here we must make nice); then the cause *du jour*, climate change; Israel, too, is always a fallback target; and finally conservatives, conservatism and the Fox News Channel. (Repugnantly, Barack Obama has blazed the trail on all and each.) On these, the Left jumps *jihad* when they see an opening, with *fatwa*'s scattered . . . liberally: you had better treat these nerve endings *just right*, or else. . . . My file bursts with examples; in fact, so promiscuously does the Left abuse the public square with its demonizing impositions that I was not looking forward to this discussion: just too much stuff.[3] Then along came Kirsten Powers' new

---

1 All patterns of thought and feeling have, like many garments, a fringe, often a lunatic fringe—except the Left, apparently. For example, how in the world can they abide Noam Chomsky, who has defended both Pol Pot and Bin Laden? Where is the dissociation, the housekeeping?

2 A designation borrowed from Kirsten Powers, on whose book *The Silencing* more presently.

3 Including professional stuff relating to my participation in this or that academic controversy. Surely Henry Kissinger is right: the most vicious politics was not practiced in

book—and I am spared.

Her *The Silencing: How the Left is Killing Free Speech* (Regnery 2015) is the first of three books that demand notice. But here only notice: all three should be required reading, discussed, debated, and generally purveyed, because each is authoritative, responsible, highly readable and *dispositive* in its own right; together they provide a rounded, rich, accurate and compelling portrait of the Left. In fact together they have it surrounded.

Powers' advantage is that she speaks of liberals ("illiberals") as an insider. Of course her view of conservatives was stereotypical, because, she tells us, she didn't know any - bigotry like any other. For example, she confesses to having believed that a woman nominee to the Supreme Court was not a woman—because she was both conservative and an Evangelical Christian. Such settled views lead, not to disagreement but to discrimination and then to intolerance, which "is not a passive matter of opinion. It's an aggressive, illiberal impulse to silence people. . . . an existential threat to those who hold orthodox religious beliefs." She continues, "I've followed this trend closely as a columnists with growing concern. It's become clear that the attempts . . . to silence dissent from the liberal worldview aren't isolated outbursts. They are part of a bigger story."

In telling that bigger story, Powers first anatomizes, then documents, and finally pulverizes the silencing syndrome which seems devoted to nothing less than living up—that is, down—to Herbert Marcuse's admonition that "suppression of . . . regressive [politics] is a prerequisite for the strengthening of progressive ones."[4] The result, she shows, is the deadening of what Tocqueville designated the "habits of the heart" of freedom-loving Americans. In short, Powers takes no prisoners: testimony (from both perpetrators and victims, and, not-so-by-the-way, from all points on the political spectrum), statistics, and documented accounts, all told temperately, are devastating, both singly and collectively. So reading the book becomes like watching an old Polaroid photo gradually developing: Is that . . . ? Can it be . . . ? Yes, it really is—that repugnant, that menacing. Moreover, she runs the table of high crimes and misdemeanors (by the way, if you are an illiberal feminist you really don't want to be in her sights). But if you merely sample the wreckage by dipping here and there, you will miss the Big Story. Finally you think: this Kirsten Powers is one massively-muscled

---

the Nixon White House but in the halls of Harvard, which stands in for every university in, well, at least in the United States. My one literary controversy was as bad.

4 A recent example: New York Governor Andrew Cuomo not long ago said that people who hold pro-life views have "no place" in New York. Regard that in light of my discussion of Jonah Goldberg's *Liberal Fascism*, below. Of course, no one raised an eyebrow.

journalistic *mensch*.

The real Terror—Robespierre would be exalting in the Seventh Circle of Hell—lies deeper than the polemical tyranny practiced by neo-McCarthyite polemicists. In *Left Illusions: An Intellectual Odyssey* David Horowitz (Spence, 2003)—a "red diaper baby" who speaks as a former insider and therefore as a direct witness to the horror—tells all.[5] In fact, in collecting work from prior decades, Horowitz gives us at least four books: a history of Communist activity going back to the fifties (usually first hand), an eye-witness account of New Left enormities, a chronicle and refutation of attacks upon him, essentially for letting all those cats out of all those bags, and a philosophical-historical seminar (he is as good a scholar as he is a witness and a debater).

In this case, unlike with *The Silencing*, one may cherry-pick profitably; you will not miss the big story: yes, there were American Communists at home working against us, the New Left inherited their mantle, "useful idiots" who cover and front for them abound, and, yes, though they have self-indulgent, utopian illusions, it is we who are deluded if we do not call them out. Doing that—with compelling detail and with formidable and varied authority, is precisely Horowitz's service to us.

The Progressive pampering of the murderous Black Panthers; the hypocrisies of Tom Hayden and the other Port Huron New Leftists; the calculated anti-Americanism of the Viet Nam War resistance; the screeching denials (and psychological denial) over Alger Hiss and the Rosenbergs; the working of the Communist Party *per se*; the vitriolic, self-righteous, often-mendacious response to anyone who breaks ranks: these are Horowitz's subjects. Along with cunning. Horowitz reports that when red diaper baby Carl Bernstein was writing his autobiography, his father urged him not to tell the whole truth: "you're going to prove McCarthy right, because all he was saying was that the system was loaded with Communists. And he was right." Since then we have had a number of post-Fall-of-Communism morphologies. Horowitz writes:

> . . . the collapse of communism has disintegrated the marxist idea and fragmented the culture of the international left. The result is a proliferation of post-marxian theories and identity politics that no longer base themselves on the universalist cat-

---

5 His autobiography, *Radical Son*, is a compelling tale of life as a maturing red diaper baby who, awakened gradually by the immoralities, enormities, and hypocrisies that he witnesses and is party to, eventually comes to his senses. See also his *The Black Book of the American Left: The Collected Conservative Writings of David Horowitz*.

egory of economic class but on the particularist identities of gender, ethnicity, and race. . . . the class struggle has been replaced by . . . the universalist idea [of] quasi-fascist doctrines of racial solidarity, group rights, and antiliberal political agendas.

"The line separating good and evil," as the heroic dissident Solzhenitsyn reminded us at Harvard, "passes not through states, nor between classes, nor between political parties, but right through every human heart—and through all human hearts"—but some more than others, as Jonah Golberg dispositively shows in his *Liberal Fascism: The Secret History of the American Left, from Mussolini to the Politics of Change* (Doubleday 2007), our third nail.

A working journalist, Goldberg proves himself to be a high-caliber scholar as well, in this case writing as a social and intellectual historian. Powers' book should be read *seriatim*, Golberg's must be (no mere cherry-picking here, except for his endnotes, which nearly make for a second book: start on those and you will finish them before you get to the book *per se*). Goldberg has a story to tell, from which his argument emerges inexorably. The early twentieth-century American progressives and British Left (for example in their support for eugenics), the Frankfurt School of cultural criticism (which would eventually diagnosis anyone to the Right as mentally ill), Mussolini (praised for a decade by the Left and himself a man of the Left), Hitler (one of whose goals was to eliminate the line dividing rich from poor and who thought marriage a "thing against nature"), a smorgasbord of Communist dictatorships, and now the constellation of victimologists (from platforms of gender, race, or class), most academics, and a majority of editorial boards—these were either outright totalitarians or crypto-totalitarians. In the event, their collective progeny is liberalism: if not "totalitarian," then

"holistic" if you prefer—in that liberalism today sees no realm of human life that is beyond political significance, from what you eat to what you smoke to what you say. Sex is political. Food is political. Sports, entertainment, your inner motives and outer appearance, all have political salience for liberal fascists.

Finally the inherency to the contemporary American Left of smug self-righteousness, disingenuousness, intolerance, unexamined assumptions, and lazy, self-indulgent (though fervent) sentimentalism is unpacked to its ugly root—a root that illiberal liberals, like twisted progeny who don't so much blame but deny their ruinous parents, would refuse to recognize—except in others.

A *Weltanschauung*—that amoeba-like, self-contained, self-defined state of mind—is a hard reality to pierce, because from the inside every attack upon it from the outside must be paranoid, or evil, and certainly ignorant. Adherents ask (usually of each other), "Is not our way of thinking that which Nature herself has ordained? After all, could it otherwise feel, and feel so sincerely, so *good*? You see, the heart wants what the heart wants, and our hearts are liberal, and its feelings cannot be wrong."

A tough safe to crack.

Finally, an appeal.

So I am not sanguine about our ability, or even our willingness to try, to overcome such a roadblock. Nevertheless . . .

In her 1999 lecture to the National Communication Association,[6] Kathleen Hall Jamieson (at the time Director of the Annenberg Public Policy Center of the University of Pennsylvania) reported that people who are subjected to verbal aggression often suffer "a loss of self-esteem, a sense of loss of control, feelings of powerlessness, high blood pressure, increased heart rates, increased aggression [and] self reports of anger and dissatisfaction. . . ." Her point—and mine—is that the aggressor should care about such effects—and have in mind Ben Franklin's own experience (as quoted by Jameison):

> When another asserted something that I thought an error I deny'd myself the pleasure of contradicting him abruptly, and of showing immediately some absurdity in his proposition; and in answering I began by observing that in certain cases of circumstances his opinion would be right, bit in the present case there appear'd . . .to me some difference. I soon found the advantage of this change in my manner; the conversations I engag'd in went on more pleasantly. The modest way in which I propos'd my opinions procur'd them a readier reception and less contradiction; I had less mortification when I was found to be in the wrong and I more easily pre-vail'd with others to give up their mistakes and join with me when I happened to be in the right.[7]

---

6 "Incivility and Its Discontents," The Carroll C. Arnold Distinguished Lecture (Allyn and Bacon).

7 On the other hand, Senator Daniel Patrick Moynihan, a superb public servant on the

That reminds me of something I read from nearly forty years ago. In May of 1978 my long-time colleague Samuel Hux published "Confession of a Conservative Socialist" in *Moment.*

There Sam (a Social Democrat) would wind up wondering why conservatives seemed to be investing more in capital than in "the cultivation of mind and sensibility, in the family, in the community of man . . . a love of what's good from the past." When he visited my seminar on political discourse I argued that he was wrong about conservatives generally. Then he reminded me of his reason for visiting the seminar in the first place by referring to the beginning of the article: "I find it easier to talk to, to enjoy the company of, people of cautious conservative reflexes; I find myself edgy, distrustful, around people whose immediate, habitual response to this or that is a liberal, progressive one," a response I share when surrounded by conservatives who share the tic that Sam has described. I noted that neither of us seemed typical of his ilk, that neither had used a "devil term" to designate the other, with "liberal," "conservative," and "socialist" used strictly as descriptions, not as judgments (let alone slurs). At the ground level of interaction such a stance held in common would be a wonderful stride against diseased (public) speech.

What follows is my own favorite way of defining ethical behavior, especially the ethics of communication, favorite because it has boundaries, and even barbershops need those. And because it is powerful. If enough people knew it, and abided by it, much hash would be settled. It is a view, not from ground level but from a thousand feet up; it has served me well during the nearly forty years I taught Ethics and the Freedom of Speech.

In July,1924, "Law and Manners" by John Fletcher, Lord Moulton, parliamentarian and judge, appeared in the *Atlantic Monthly.* He provides a second way, and he gets right down to business:

> . . . follow me in examining the three great domains of Human Action. First comes the domain of Positive Law, where our actions are prescribed by laws binding upon us which must be obeyed. Next comes the domain of Free Choice, which includes all those actions as to which we . . . enjoy complete freedom. But between these two there is a third . . . important domain in which there rules neither Positive Law nor Absolute Freedom. In that domain there is no law which inexorably determines our course of action, and yet we feel that we are not

---

Left, once called his colleague James Buckley a "Nazi"—and then publicly apologized. *Comme il faut.*

free to choose as we would.

He continues, "the degree of this sense of a lack of complete freedom in this domain varies in every case. It grades from a consciousness of a Duty nearly as strong as Positive Law, to a feeling that the matter is all but a question of personal choice."

Then Moulton gives us a phrase for the ages. This Middle Domain, he wrote, "is the domain of Obedience to the Unenforceable . . . the obedience . . . of a man to that which he cannot be forced to obey. He is the enforcer of the law upon himself." He then expands on the idea:

> [The] country which lies between Law and Free Choice I always think of as the domain of Manners. To me, Manners in this broad sense signifies the doing that which you should do although you are not obliged to do it. I do not wish to call it Duty, for that is too narrow to describe it, nor would I call it Morals for the same reason. It might include both, but it extends beyond them. . . . the real greatness of a nation, its true civilization, is measured by the extent of this land.

In other words, "between 'can do' and 'may do' ought to exists the whole realm which recognizes the sway of duty, fairness, sympathy, taste, and all the other things that make life beautiful and society possible . . . in some form or other . . . strong in the hearts of all except the most depraved." Mouton's conclusion deserves quotation-in-full:

> It must be evident to you that Manners must include all things which a man should impose upon himself, from duty to good taste. I have borne in mind the great motto of William of Wykeham—"Manners makyth Man." It is in this sense—loyalty to the rule of Obedience to the Unenforceable, throughout the whole realm of personal action—that we should use the word 'Manners' if we would truly say that 'Manners makyth Man.'

Of course the question is, How do we bring people into the Middle Domain intellectually?

Simple mutual respect (more of which would prevent the proliferation of speech codes, most of them silly—though, alas, not all of them) often suffices: occupancy of the Middle Domain becomes natural. Consider this, on the wall of a gym I used to frequent. The owner clearly occupies the Middle Domain and asks others to do the same:

> To our valued members: Use of the "F" word & the "N" word. We, at Powerhouse, have always encouraged our members to support each other during their workouts—by this we mean that we have never had a problem with members yelling and shouting to motivate each other, on which many other facilities do have these restriction. We have noticed recently, however, that this practice has begun to include derogatory words such as "F" word and "N" word (you all know what we mean). Many members find it insulting. This is not acceptable and we would appreciate it if you would respect your fellow members by refraining from the use of this language.

Whether in the barbershop, the gym, or in the public square certain lines should not crossed.

That is, either we obey the unenforceable—yes, that's right, some self-censorship—or we continue to navigate the diatribe, calumny, demagoguery, contumely, vituperation, and sheer rhetorical treachery now commonly midwived by those for whom eristic is what flames were for Torquemada.[8] In that light note the epiphany (and its date) of Imam Anwar Al-Awlaki who, in a *New York Times* article headlined "Influential American Muslims Temper Their Tone" (the date: October 19, 2001), is reported to have said "now we realize that talk can be taken seriously." Indeed.

In his *Speaking Into the Air*, John Durham Peters suggests how we might fill the Domain once we decide to occupy it. "'Communication'," he writes, "is . . . from the Latin *communicare*, meaning to impart, share or to make common." . . . The key root is *mun*- (not *uni*-) related to . . . 'munificent', 'community', 'meaning'. . . . *munus* has to do with gifts or duties offered publicly": freely, yet obediently. Or we can try this, from Stephen L. Carter, quoting the legal scholar Michael Perry, in his superb

---

8 This *Jihadist* approach, epitomized by LGBT fanaticism, must have roots deep in a person's psyche: as Freud said somewhere, everybody needs a religion, its merely a matter of which one a person chooses. Culturally, however, I believe the roots of this *Jihad* go back fifty years to Tom Hayden's Port Huron statement and, of course, to Alinsky's *Rules for Radicals*. Together they called forth and gave license to the New Left, which exercised that license at the 1968 Democrat National Convention in Chicago and has never looked back. Since then the movement, its current, muted, avatar being the president himself, has hijacked most of the Party, at least for now.

Civility: "conversation that admits the possibility of error is the only kind of conversation that love for others allows."

And yet the Middle Domain is elusive, certainly for elements of the Left, *who simply do not care*. Near the end of his "August 1968" W. H. Auden shows us what that Ogre looks like. It "cannot master speech," he writes, and "stalks with hands on hips/ While drivel gushes from his lips." The stalking undead walk among us now more than ever. Thus the admonitory importance of St. James' Letter in the New Testament. "Consider," he tells us, "how small a fire can set a huge forest ablaze. *The tongue is also a fire.*"

SEVEN

HIS OWN SELF-ORGANIZING SELF
President Obama's Rhetoric

TO PARAPHRASE the old polymath and critic Buffon, a man's rhetoric is the man himself, and since the skilled production of rhetoric is regarded as among President's Obama's singular strengths, a look at some of it should prove useful.

He opines that the world is not messier now than under his predecessors but just seems messier because of the amplifying effect of social media; he regrets grinning it up on the links right after his press conference on the first horrific beheading because "I should have anticipated the optics," not the indecency of his behavior; the Islamist rampage at Fort Hood was "workplace violence," not a jihadist terrorist attack. Rarely downright inarticulate, his gaffes ("I don't speak Austrian," "I campaigned in all fifty-seven states," "the Marine corpse") bespeak a broad lack of cultivation. But more troubling—and clearly so—are his non-gaffes.

He has referred to the troops "who are fighting for *me*"; when the BP oil disaster happened and he was criticized for doing nothing his response was, "do they expect me to plug it myself"; to the Queen of England he presented a collection of his own speeches; he will, on foreign soil, criticize his country and dismiss its policies because "I wasn't even born yet," as though all meaningful history began with his entrance. These, along with his "present" votes earlier in his legislative career and much finger-pointing, are of-a-piece: he is a (pathological?) narcissist who *will* avoid accountability.[1]

---

1 For a rich discussion of Obama's narcissistic character and behavior, see Jonathan

83

So he ranges between the merely puerile and a crypto-Fifth Column menace. Yet he is now what he has always been: a Community Organizer—a cooler version of Al Sharpton (a frequent White House visitor)—for whom the opposition is to be coerced and demeaned, not reasoned with, and by whom "the people" are to be kept in a constant state of disaffection. Because the Organizer serves the higher good of social justice, downright lies as well as racialist, classist, self-righteous, and belligerent rhetoric are justified.

That is why he favors what ancient Greek rhetoricians called *epideictic* oratory, the practice of "praise and blame"; and that is why he must regale safe hallelujah choruses or stick to insulated venues. Just so does he passionately rail against Republicans as though they, not jihadists or Putin, were imminent threats, and unprecedentedly lambastes the Supreme Court in a State of the Union address. In fact he has little facility with deliberative (policy) speechmaking or forensic (factual) case-making, the other two types of oratory identified by the Ancients. (*E.g.* about his change in our Cuba policy he would simply assert, over and again, "it's the right thing to do," not an argument, let alone a case.) Moreover, this Organizer, not bothering with actual persuasion ("by sweetness," etymologically), simply seems to have a chip on his shoulder: he'll show us.

Like most people I found his 2004 Democratic convention keynote address thrilling, for its message of one America and for his joyful conviction in its delivery. Was I fooled? Soon enough he seemed to be guided by a thought from Winston Churchill's "The Scaffolding of Rhetoric." Written in 1897, it reflects the presumption of a very young person. Of greatest relevance to President Obama is this passage: "To convince them he must himself believe. His opinions may change as their impressions fade, but *every orator means what he says at the moment he says it.*" (Was it movie mogul Sam Goldwyn who said "sincerity is everything, if you can fake that you've got it made"?)

This ability not only works but explains his many falsehoods. Has any president ever walked back, re-interpreted, or denied having said more of his *own* rhetoric? Or does he believe he has the power to evoke or to banish reality simply by affirming a falsehood or leaving a truth unspoken? The clownish rhetorical smokescreen surrounding the depredations of Benghazi; the "success" of our anti-terrorists policy in Yemen; "nothing" being wrong with abuses of the IRS, including its "lost" emails; the "red

V. Last, "American Narcissus, the vanity of Barack Obama," in *The Weekly Standard* of November 22, 2010. For Left-leaning disillusionment see David Bromwich, "What Went Wrong," *Harper's Magazine*, June 2015.

line" for Assad drawn in the shifting sands of Syria; the "junior varsity" that was ISIL (and the "setbacks" in opposing it), the "random" murders at the Jewish deli in Paris . . . Cherry-picking, sure, but his presidency provides a bowlful. And like the reverend Sharpton, the president has yet to admit, let alone to apologize for, his abiding fraudulence.

So he "pivots" to the not-yet-quite-bungled precincts—climate change, the minimum wage—because they remain much safer than the instigations of the Chinese routinely harassing our aircraft as they build an ever-bigger and more assertive navy, or the violations of a nuclear treaty by the Russians. Eventually, though, the magic is overcome by a cascade of scandal, crisis and incompetence. Now, for example, our leading non-Muslim Islamophiliac must wage a sort-of-war against non-Muslim non-terrorists—just "folks." That, or fall back on his three defaults: near-clownish condescension (as when presuming to lesson us all at a prayer breakfast), insulting Republicans, or, best of all, bashing Netanyahu.

He is The One, said the tingle running up Chris Matthews' leg. And such is their befuddlement that President Obama's smug True Believers (a version of Lenin's "useful idiots," though actually more fundamentalist) continue to exult in their New Normal: a disintegrating Constitutional contract, dysfunctional federal machinery, a divided and diminished sense of national identity, and bumbling American influence abroad. All this, while living "The Life of Julia," depicted in a Democrat TV ad about a young woman coddled by the federal government from cradle to grave. This constituency certainly has their perfect piper, a Narcissist-in-Chief who (by his own proclamation knowing more than this, that, and the other thing than the very people he put in charge of those things) can organize his own rabbit hole of denial, smugness, not-a-little *schadenfreude*, and improvisational—not to say random—policy-making the goal of which seems to be the spectrum-wide depletion of America. No emperor has ever been more undressed.

Alas, it so happens that the neighborhood is not populated by subjects but by citizens who have inflicted an insulting electoral rebuke, who, "clinging to their guns and bibles," must be unworthy of Barack Obama's stewardship. Thus is the jejune post-adolescent compelled to pontificate on the one hand and rule with tantrum-by-decree on the other. After all, it's so much easier than actually governing. You don't really have to persuade at all.

EIGHT

LBJ DECLINES
Being Critical

HOW DOES A rhetorical critic go about discussing an actual piece of oratory? A three-step process—description of the situation, analysis of the rhetorical tactics of the speech as a response to that situation, and finally a judgment—is conventional and useful. But within those steps a critic must be adroit: attentive to novelty, nuance, and to the twists of the speaker's purposes and idiosyncrasies. What follows is an attempt to understand in rhetorical terms a single speech which, though very surprising and of great importance, has been largely neglected. Indeed, nearly fifty years after-the-fact, it is virtually forgotten.

1.

On April 1, 1968, the American people were variously shocked, elated, and unbelieving when, the night before, at 9:00 P.M., on March 31, 1968, President Lyndon B. Johnson began to end both a war and a career. Political leaders scurried about, attempting to interpret and to seize upon new and fleeting opportunities. Diplomats the world over, stunned but happy, tore up the old script and began plotting anew. As with most rhetorical events, this particular one—its occurrence, nature, and effects—were determined by a combination of circumstances: issues, expectations, and other men's words and behavior. But why could the exigency (some "imperfection marked by urgency") be remedied only by a *non-oratorical* yet highly *rhetorical* gesture: political suicide?

To answer that, we must begin with the President's greatest rhetorical problem: a near-total lack of credibility. Certainly people were upset about the economy. Between 1964 and 1965, $80 billion had been added to the federal budget; the international price of the dollar was in peril; and a 10% surcharge on personal and corporate income had been imposed. And certainly in his 1966 State of the Union message, the President had promised specific proposals to avert strikes. *But he did not deliver.* Moreover, people were also greatly distressed over poverty and tense race relations: by 1967, race-riots wracked more than 90 cities. Though most people were unfamiliar with the history of our involvement in Viet Nam, they were somehow aware that they had been deceived. In 1963, they had been told that all but 1000 advisors would be withdrawn by 1965. The calendar of involvement was just the opposite. June 10, 1965: 54000; November 4, 1965: 154000; June 12, 1966: 285000; December 8, 1966: 362000; March 31, 1968: 525000. (The joke was that, if you voted for Goldwater in 1964, we would send half a million troops to Viet Nam. Sure enough: you voted for Goldwater—who lost by a 3-to-2 margin—and that's exactly what happened.)

On May 15, 1965, the first national teach-in on Viet Nam was held. In 1966 and early in 1968, Senator J. W. Fulbright held full-scale, nationally-televised hearings on Viet Nam,[1] with no semblance of partiality. By the time President Johnson was to give his speech, only 26% of the American people favored his Viet Nam policy, and his personal popularity had dropped to 36%.[2]

Mr. Johnson had had his problems with the press since 1963 (not helped by the contrast in style between him and his elegant, popular, assassinated predecessor), and they would persist in spite of a landslide electoral victory of his own. He once told them, for example, that they and their First Amendment should be investigated. He severely criticized *Fortune* magazine for estimating Viet Nam costs at over $21 billion; one month later he announced exactly that figure. Repeatedly, he misled the American people not only about troop build-ups but casualty figures and bombing targets as well. In short Mr. Johnson was viewed by many as a self-serving manipulator and liar.

This impression was reinforced by events from the President's past.[3] The 1948 primary vote from Texas elected Senator Johnson by only 87 votes; suddenly, box 13 was discovered, which contained the names of 203

---

1 Raskin and Fall, edd., *Viet Nam Reader* (New York, 1967), p. 477.

2 Gallup poll, in *The New York Times*, April 1, 1968, p. 27.

3 Two books on the subject came out in rapid succession, before the President spoke. Rowland Evans and Robert Novak, *Lyndon B. Johnson: The Exercise of Power*, New York, 1966; and Robert Sherrill, *The Accidental President*, New York, 1967, a bestseller billed as "the election year blockbuster on LBJ."

people—all listed *in alphabetical order* and all voting for Johnson. When an investigation was undertaken, the building containing box 13 burned down. In 1957, Senator Johnson (as Majority Leader) intimidated half the Senate so that he might make drought-relief grain available to R.M. Kleberg, Johnson's original patron and owner of the largest ranch in the world. The senator was seen as a man who relished acquiring and wielding political power and who did so, some said, wantonly. The result of these perceptions, in a context of growing discontent, and as an anti-war movement was reaching its peak, was that the public soon had a new phrase, "credibility gap." Moreover, the political environment within the Democratic Party itself—and Johnson was more a creature of politics than any elected official of his day—was dynamic and moving against the president.

Thus the speaker's purpose in the speech was to make a credible as well as a significant policy statement about the war in Viet Nam. Thus, if any political, military, or diplomatic act were to be effective, it would have to be accompanied by a gesture indicating sincerity, that is, some evidence that it was neither false, nor manipulative, nor (above all) self serving.

2.

The speech is 4300 words long and took Mr. Johnson 42 minutes to deliver. Some 60 million Americans heard it live over all of the major radio and television networks. The major themes were peace, national achievement, and unity, especially the latter. He would place that gesture within the context of what he considered a dispositive speech announcing and, by way of a historical rationale, defending new policies. The President's proposition—his blockbuster announcement—is simple: For the sake of unity, "I shall not seek, and will not accept, the nomination of my party for another term as your president."

Four rigorously necessary and sufficient divisions support this startling proposition. With their sub-divisions, they are:

I. The American people are currently disunited.
II. Unity is an urgent necessity.
 A. Only a united America can keep and enlarge its commitment.
 B. The elements of that commitment must be upheld.
 C. At stake is the security of Southeast Asia, the United States, and the rest of the world.
III. Because I am so distrusted, my withdrawal will expedite unity.
 A. Partisanship will be laid aside.
 B. My proposals will be more credible.

IV. No other alternative would be as expedient.

A. My time and effort may be devoted to more pressing matters than domestic politics.

B. The Congress and the people will be able to serve the national interest.

The President stated his proposals (military, economic, and diplomatic) in great detail, referring to his previous addresses in Manila, Johns Hopkins, and San Antonio to buttress the claim of consistency. It is fitting that these policy statements consume the most words. This is essentially a policy speech (the president's declination ostensibly being but one of those). But an analysis of the organization of the argument reveals that the theme of unity—the call for which is an exhortative appeal, not a policy prescription—is strategically situated and thus emphasized over all other themes.

To consider the speech according to a classical structure would be fruitless. There was a brief *exordium* of only 192 words; the slight *narration* was used to declare and support subsidiary policies (as well as the bombing-halt, a main policy initiative); *confirmation* was interspersed throughout the speech; refutation was present but scattered; and the *peroration* was only 46 words long.

Yet there exists an otherwise very studied structure. Four distinct parts barely intrude upon each other. The first 3/8 of the speech dealt almost exclusively with Viet Nam; the next 1/8 with the economy; the penultimate 1/4 with general Asian policy. The final 1/4 (but especially the final 1/8) contained emotional appeals, leading to the theme of disunity and the speaker's personal involvement with, and solution for, that disunity: his personal withdrawal from politics. Clearly, this tight organization does much tactical heavy-lifting, not least in preparing the way for surprise and pleasure.

Along the way, Mr. Johnson employed three different plans of adaptation. While discussing the new policies (military strategy, taxation, the re-equipping of South Viet Nam), the President *argued and appealed* alternately. For example, he demonstrated that the Tet offensive failed (the government did not collapse, a general uprising did not occur, the enemy took heavy casualties) and then appealed for negotiations to prevent the further loss of life. But this method of argument-appeal was used sparingly and only in the first third of the speech, as though the speaker wanted it to serve as context (*narration*) as well (in part) as proof (*confirmation*). Evident throughout the speech, though not in strict order, was the *motivated sequence* (the ordered steps of attention, satisfaction, visualization, need, action).

Expecting to hear about Viet Nam, the audience's attention was captured when that expectation was satisfied:

> Tonight I want to speak to you of peace in Viet Nam and South-east Asia. No other question so preoccupies our people. No other dream so absorbs the 250 million people who live in that part of the world.[4]

Though hinted at early in the speech, the need for unity was not explicitly stated until the dramatic *last eighth* of the text (some 300 words after a vision of what peace could mean to Asia):

> And in these times, as in times before it, it is true that a house divided against itself by the spirit of faction, of party, of region, of religion, of race, is a house that cannot stand. There is division in the American house right now. There is divisiveness among us all tonight. And holding the trust that is mine, as President of all the people, I cannot disregard the peril to the progress of the American people. . . .

The action step—Mr. Johnson's declination *per se*—was to follow and conclude the speech: rising, or *climactic order*, at its best.

But by the time that step arrived, a third pattern (actually a combination of two) had done its work. The answer to our disunity was implicit throughout; "you," we can imagine the audience inferring, "are the causes of our disunity," yet no one could have suspected the action. How could they have? Until this last one-eighth, the speech had been somewhat typical (though more momentous than usual): a stagnant congress and rampant partisanship sounded too familiarly self-serving. So that when the President stated the action he was taking he at once confirmed the audience's growing inference, concluded the motivated sequence, and (to psychologically punctuate the effect) entirely reversed the movement of the speech to that point:

> With American sons in the field far away, with America's future under challenge right here at home, with our hopes and

---

4 Quotation are from a tape-recording of the speech. The text of *The New York Times* (April 1, 1968) is accurate; *Vital Speeches* contains many errors.

the world's hopes for peace in the balance every day, I do not believe that I should devote an hour or a day of my time to any personal partisan causes or to any duties other than the awesome duties of this office—the Presidency of your country. Accordingly, *I shall not seek, and I will not accept, the nomination of my party for another term as your President.*

In short, Mr. Johnson ended his speech as a good story-teller ends his narrative, with logical and psychological inevitability.

Indeed, the organization of the speech compensates for Mr. Johnson's characteristic difficulties with style. Though his sentences were straightforward, sometimes long but never incomprehensible, he used figures of speech in abundance, often distractingly so. *Homoeoprophoron* (beginning successive clauses with like sounds) and *isocolon* (phrases of similar length) were especially common, for example:

> Our purpose . . . is to bring about a reduction in the level of violence that now exists. It is to save the lives of brave men— and to save the lives of innocent children. It is to permit the contending forces to move closer to a political settlement.

Both *asyndeton* (the lack of connectives) and *continuatio* (the frequent insertion of conjunctions, especially 'and') appeared often; and one phrase, "just must," was used several times: "we just must not now," "we just must preserve," "we just must not allow." The most striking figure, however, appeared no fewer than four times, all in the final 3/8 of the speech: the *personification* of America as a mother, with American soldiers as her sons.

The presence of so many figures of speech, and the nature of those figures, were no doubt intended to help provide a certain tone: gravitas, sincerity, tragedy, good-will, a sort of old-fashioned eloquence. In fact, they probably served to reinforce Mr. Johnson's unfavorable image; the audience saw the same devices, even in the same language, that they had seen for five years. Of course, such skepticism ultimately would serve to make the reversal (the *self-denying* act of withdrawal) more effective than it ordinarily would have been.

Mr. Johnson's deployment of proofs is artful, with one item used many times or with a single item functioning in many ways at once. Early in the speech, for example, when discussing his policies, the President employs logical proof: 30 previous peace efforts, a real income gain of 30%

in seven years, (Viet Nams'). President Thieu's affirmation to assume an even greater burden (with statistics from the South Vietnamese military to support the affirmation), the failures of the Viet Cong's Tet Offensive, successes in Indonesia. In fact, only in the final 3/8 of the speech did the speaker rely upon emotional proof. He spoke feelingly of poverty, nobly of peace and prosperity and security, and inspiringly of pride and patriotism:

> United we have kept that commitment. And united we have enlarged that commitment. And through all time to come I think America will be a stronger nation, a more just society, a land of greater opportunity and fulfillment because of what we have all done together in these years of unparalleled achievement.

No particular attempt was made—except, of course, for the final reversal—at personal proof, but both logical and emotional proof served to demonstrate the speaker's intelligence, virtue, and good-will. His command of statistics, for example, showed that he was well-informed; emotional appeals about poverty and war demonstrated concern, just as his appeals to patriotism showed that he was a patriot. He referred, though infrequently, to prayer and to God; the House Divided (cannot stand) quotation served, of course, to bring to mind *The Bible* and Abraham Lincoln. And by paraphrasing President Kennedy's inaugural address, the speaker firmly placed himself within a potent and enduring context:

> Yet I believe that now, no less that when the decade began, this generation is willing to pay any price, bear and burden, meet any hardship, support any friend, oppose any foe, to assure the survival, and the success, of liberty.

The images of tragedy, sacrifice, and sincerity was reinforced by the president's delivery. He was seated and seemed to be reading from a manuscript, the pages of which he turned only five times. He spoke slowly and deliberately, and his face was drawn and gaunt, even grim. He was obviously fatigued. Had the years taken their toll? (Mr. Johnson was never an effective public orator, in contrast to what many in the Senate had said of his personal persuasiveness). For the most part, Mr. Johnson's facial expressions were appropriate to the text, though ill-timed smiles (a trait of Mr. Johnson's, and not helpful) were occasionally distracting. Generally, though, his appeals and delivery were in harmony, providing a tonal unity not lacking in force.

3.

The immediate and intermediate effects of the speech were varied, though substantially favorable. Nelson Rockefeller (R.) and Hubert Humphrey (D. and the eventual Democrat nominee who would lose to Richard Nixon) declared their candidacy for the rejected office; Hanoi agreed to peace talks, and the war was viewed (mistakenly) as being in its "final stages;" the American people did become more unified, especially on the war issue, even to the point of camaraderie; and, most astonishing of all, the President's own stock rose significantly. Without question, the speech achieved its objectives.

Because it was part of an enduring and overwhelming controversy, the long-range effects of the speech would be difficult to calculate. Intervening variables (*e.g.*, succeeding pronouncements by Mr. Johnson, his successor's policy of Vietnamization, the Pentagon Papers imbroglio), the eventual betrayal of our Vietnamese ally in violation of a pledge, and the "sleeper effect" (a sharp incline of approval, followed by a slow restoration of pre-speech opinion) cloud any ultimate conclusions.

But its short-range success should not surprise us. Lyndon Johnson himself became more popular, as indicated by a Gallup poll one week after the speech. (Indeed, in newspapers as far away as Peru, the President was hailed as a hero). The most useful explanation for this seems to be Congruity Theory. It assumes, first, that judgmental frames tend towards maximum simplicity and, second, that when change in evaluation or attitude occurs it does so in the direction of increased congruity with the prevailing frames of reference. We seem to need consistency. The paradigm involves three attitudes: listener to speaker, listener to object, and speaker to subject. According to Marie Jahoda, "incongruity is said to exist when the attitudes towards the source and the object are similar and the assertion is negative, or when they are dissimilar and the assertion is positive."[5] When the attitudes toward the person and his assertion are congruent, there is no change; but when those attitudes differ, attitudes change towards both the speaker and the subject in favor of congruity.

Congruity Theory predicts that with an originally negative attitude toward a source which makes a positive statement about a subject which itself is viewed favorably then the resulting attitude change toward the source will be double in a positive direction (whereas the attitude towards the subject will remain unchanged). With Lyndon Johnson as the source,

---

5 Marie Jahoda and Neil Warren, edd., *Attitudes* (Baltimore: 1966), p. 267.

making a positive statement about a favorably viewed object, withdrawal and his own departure, the attitudes toward the speaker had to rise, becoming either positive or less negative. Thus, we can account for the one, very surprising, effect unexplained by the text itself: the great spike in the president's approval rating.

At the end of the first edition of the ground-breaking *Speech Criticism* (now viewed as dated and so largely neglected, though never actually debunked) Lester Thonsenn and A. Craig Baird write:

> Great orators will unquestionably arise to meet the recurring crises in man's quest for ... freedom ... The inviolable logic of discourse is to secure ... liberty ... The spoken word is eternal ... Some few men there will always be, when the future of the state is in doubt, who will come forward to express the aspirations of the people. ... .[6]

As an orator Lyndon Johnson was second rate at best, but when the fate of our blood, treasure, and prestige were at stake, his decision-making, patriotism, and astute sense of rhetorical need rose to the occasion. He expressed and executed the aspirations of the people. The speech was a part of a momentous controversy, and, though flawed, was successful. Such a combination of its elements—timely, generous, momentous, cogent and convincing—is rare enough. Discourse which achieves that mix should be valued; certainly it should be remembered.

6 (New York, 1948), p. 472.

NINE

Sinners in the Hands of a Great Tradition
An Idiosyncratic Survey of Eloquence in America

To be genuine the qualities of force and beauty, in their higher signifi-cance, must come for the most part unsought, rising naturally out of the character [of the speaker] and the demands of the subject-matter.
— John F. Genung, *The Practical Elements of Rhetoric*, 1886

The main attribute of eloquence is gratuitousness: its place in the world is to be without place or function. . . . . Like beauty, it claims only the privilege of being a grace note in the culture that permits it.
— Denis Donoghue, *On Eloquence*, 2010

DO WE KNOW what eloquence is or whence it arises? On the one hand we have Genung, whose thinking is rhetorical through-and-through: it arises from the interanimation of situation, subject and speaker. On the other hand we have Donoghue, whose conception might be termed ornamental and, as such, utterly non-utilitarian. So subjective is our discernment of eloquence—we usually know it when we hear it, when it stops our breath, jangles our nerves, or elevates our spirit—that argument for or against a conception of it, let alone for its presence, is futile.

Focusing on a central theme, however, by gathering a set of congruent case studies within a thriving and compelling tradition might be

revealing. The American rhetorical heritage is such a tradition; in my opinion the most compelling of all rhetorical traditions precisely because its
central (but not sole) theme—freedom—is also central to our humanity.
No subject better merits or invites eloquence than freedom, and we are the
avatars of that eloquence.

Of course, this tradition has been both celebrated and adopted, from
the movement for South American independence to Tiananman Square.
But I propose a bit of a twist. I suggest that the eloquence of American
expression on the theme of freedom, especially as interanimated with that
of salvation, is so pervasive that it stretches, not merely beyond time and
space, but beyond the well-known, monumental figures like Jefferson and
Lincoln. In other words, it is deep. Here, then, is my idiosyncratic collection of (mostly) less-studied figures from our eloquent tradition, all too
few and too briefly presented, along with my judgments. (I am mindful
that they may not be yours).

1.

Peitho was the goddess of persuasion, of seduction, and of charming
speech, and a close companion of Aphrodite. She was usually depicted as
a woman with her hand lifted in the act. In her magisterial *Ratification*
Pauline Maier depicts the drama of the closely fought debates over the
ratification of the U.S. Constitution in the various states (incredibly, a tale
previously untold). Apparently, Peitho both ruled and was kicked about,
not least by a central figure in the controversy, Patrick Henry, who in his
day was known for much more than "give me liberty or give me death."
His opposition to the Constitution was almost febrile. He was generally
regarded as the greatest orator alive and struck real fear into the hearts of
supporters of the Constitution. Jefferson, who despised him, said of Henry
that he was "the best humored man that ever lived" and had "a consummate knowledge of the human heart . . . [which] enabled him to attain
a degree of popularity with the people at large never perhaps equaled."
Simply put, this man, who was (this is Jefferson speaking again, to Henry's
own grandson) "avaritious & rotten hearted" was also "the greatest orator
who ever lived." Henry certainly did not seem a friend of Aphrodite.

Virtually uneducated, he was a school dropout, and the greatest legal
scholar in Virginia (George Wythe) voted against his licensing to the profession. In that light, he would trouble our old friend Cicero, for it was the
great Roman rhetorician who told us (in *De inventione*) that wisdom without eloquence is of little benefit and eloquence without wisdom a great
danger. That seemed to be Henry to perfection, if we allow that eloquence

is the ability to rivet, then move, and finally to win over a listener by the spoken word—truth, right, and wrong be damned.

Cicero's standard, however, is so much higher than that. In *De Oratore* he tells us:

> In my opinion, indeed, no man can be an orator possessed of every praiseworthy accomplishment, unless he has attained the knowledge of every thing important, and of all liberal arts, for his language must be ornate and copious from knowledge, since, unless there be beneath the surface matter understood and felt by the speaker, oratory becomes an empty and almost puerile flow of words.

He does relent, even if only slightly, on the "everything important" standard, but at the end allows that the practice of rhetoric is "an immense and infinite undertaking."

2.

That is the standard that marked American eloquence well before the stirring of a Republic, and it was not political. For example our sermonic eloquence is as dysentropic as any and goes back to our beginning. Take Samuel Danforth's Election Day sermon of 1670, "A Brief Recognition of New England's Errand into the Wilderness": "To what purpose came we into this place . . . ?" And the tradition is exceedingly rich. Following are speakers who did—and who still ought to—stand out.

One who does, though he does not quite fit here but whom I include here for the sheer fun of it, is Jonathan Edwards (1703-1758), he of our most frightening sermon. He preached "Sinners in the Hands of an Angry God" on July 8, 1741, in Enfield, Connecticut where, although a religious Awakening was already in progress, he managed to raise his congregants' zeal to a frenzy. His text, the biblical verse upon which a sermon is based, is from Deuteronomy (xxxii, 35): "their foot shall slide in due time." He begins, "in this verse is threatened the vengeance of God on the wicked unbelieving Israelites. . . ."—an unpromising beginning: colorless, conventional, even trite. But it proves to be portentous, for never has vengeance been made more instant, concrete, unremitting, nor more absolute than that wrought by the Almighty as depicted in this sermon.

Edwards, however, will not be rushed. Before we see how we will be destroyed, we are told that only the "sovereign" pleasure of God restrains his "arbitrary" will. And lest you believe that your goodness has anything to do with his restraint, be assured that you not only deserve to be "cast into hell" but may already be "under a sentence of condemnation" to hell. For God is as angry with you as "with many of those miserable creatures that he is now tormenting in hell."

> 'Tis ascribed to nothing else, that you did not go to hell the last night, that you was suffered to awake again in this world after you closed your eyes to sleep; and there is not other reason to be given why you have not dropped into hell since you arose in the morning, but that God's hand has held you up. There is no other reason to be given why you han't gone to hell since you have sat here in the house of God, provoking his pure eyes by your sinful wicked manner of attending his solemn worship. Yea, there is nothing else that is to be given as a reason why you don't this very moment drop down into hell.

In its simplicity, directness, immediacy and cumulative rhythm, that passage is eloquent; something about your response is involuntary, inevitable.

Then there is the how we shall suffer. "'Tis a great furnace of wrath, a wide and bottomless pit . . . ." Well, we've heard that before. But we haven't heard this: "the creation groans with you; the creature is made subject to the bondage of your corruption, not willingly; the sun don't willingly shine upon you to give you light to serve sin and Satan . . . the air don't willingly serve you for breath . . . ." This, after having heard that "your healthy constitution, and your own care and prudence, and best contrivance, and all your righteousness, would have no more influence to uphold you and keep you back than a spider's web would have to stop a falling rock." (Noteworthy is the fact that, at age thirteen, Edwards had spent very many long hours studying spiders before writing his treatise on them.) In a cinematic age, and as Aristotle instructs, movie-making masters have "set it before [our] eyes" so often that we take horror for granted. That, however, was not the case when Edwards spoke. He, not the moving image, made people see:

> The bow of God's wrath is bent, and the arrow made ready on the string, and justice bends the arrow at your heart, and strains the bow, and it is nothing but the mere pleasure of God, and that of an angry God, without any promise or obligation at all, that keeps the arrow one moment from being made drunk

with your blood.

Eloquence need not be soft and sweet, but it must compel us to apprehend its thought, to be able to snatch it. It is by accretion of thought—bow to string, string to arrow, arrow to heart—in perfect order, in the company of convulsive imagery—the bow is God's wrath, its arrow, as though alive, would be made *drunk with your blood*—that constitutes the eloquence of this passage, as well as of most of the sermon.

Almost incredibly, Edwards will end with a call to hope: Christ the Saviour waits at the open door of the mansion of salvation; but he won't wait much longer. You must rush to Him. Rush, because the anger is pitiless, unremitting and worse:

> . . . and though he will know that you can't bear the weight of omnipotence treading upon you, yet he won't regard that, but he will crush you under his feet without mercy; he'll crush out your blood, and make it fly, and it shall be sprinkled on his garments, so as to stain all his raiment. He will not only hate you, but he will have you in the utmost contempt; no place shall be thought fit for you but under his feet, to be trodden down as the mire of the streets.

"He will not only hate you . . . ." Aristotle warns that hatred is a dangerous emotion to arouse: it is marked by a desire for the destruction of the hated and, when directed by overwhelming force, leads to . . . hopelessness. Not-so-by-the-way, and notwithstanding his un-Aristotelian use of hatred, Edwards would almost certainly have known his Aristotle, for his deployment of Anger, Fear and Hope are directly out of the *Rhetoric* (Book II, sections 2, 4-5, and 9).

Edwards had been invited to Enfield precisely to duplicate the Awakening already going on in neighboring Suffield. Edwards, whose voice was weak and who lacked the dramatic delivery that his colleague George Whitefield could achieve, decided to add some vivid imagery to the conventional realism of sermons on Hell and he practiced assiduously so that he knew his text by heart. During his delivery, he seemed to look fixedly at the bell rope in the back of the church.

Now, recall our cinematic age. I was at the first commercial screening of *The Exorcist*, having waited in a long line on a frigid morning in 1973. There, at two or three moments in the film, I witnessed people, not only screaming but running from the theatre in fear as they screamed. We are told that something like that very thing happened during Edwards' sermon, notwithstanding the dryness of his delivery. Many of his congregants fled. The terror this calm and goodly pastor stirred—one fellow minister records that "the shrieks and cries were piercing and amazing"—was so tumultuous that most in the congregation *did not hear Edwards' call for hope* with which he ended: "Therefore let every one that is out of CHRIST [sic], now awake and fly from the Wrath to come. The Wrath of almighty God is now undoubtedly hanging over a great Part of this Congregation: Let every one fly out of Sodom: *Haste and escape for your Lives, look not behind you, escape to the Mountain, least you be consumed.*" Close call: to close to be eloquent?

3.

Fifty years later the subject had changed; or a second had been introduced, and the subject was as frightening as Edwards'. James Dana (1735-1812) was a Congregationalist minister who, in 1791, delivered "The African Slave Trade: a Discourse" in New Haven before the Connecticut society for the Promotion of Freedom. The sermon is marked by two features, a great breadth of historical learning and supreme cogency. Dana takes his time (rather like Lincoln in his Cooper Union Address, where he establishes the record of the Founders respecting slavery), going so far as to include two pages of numerical tables documenting the size of the slave trade, state-by-state and beyond, from 1702 to 1778: "We suppose, then, that eight millions of slaves have been shipped in Africa for the West-India islands and the United States." His logic is systematic, proceeding issue-by-issue, his language undramatic: "With what reason or truth is it urged, that the conditions of the Africans is meliorated by their slavery?" The effect is cumulatively horrific; indeed, his passionate conclusion invoking the New Jerusalem and the Gospel of Jesus Christ, is almost anti-climactic. If electronic media had existed in 1790, slavery would have ended seventy years sooner—in part because of this speech.

Then in March of 1807 the United States Congress, following England, voted to abolish the Transatlantic Slave Trade; the prohibition became effective on January 1, 1808. On that very day, in St. Thomas' (an African Episcopal church) in Philadelphia, the Abolitionist Reverend Absalom Jones (1746-1818) preached his Thanksgiving sermon. His leitmotif, enduring to the present day in Black churches, was a comparison of African Americans to Ancient Israelites during the Egyptian captivity and their deliverance therefrom (Exodus, 3:7-8). Here eloquence arises from two sources, the parade of horrors and a reversal: an expression of gratitude. All the slave might have is "a scanty allowance of roots"; the master has withheld religious instruction and access to the means of obtaining it; and God has seen all the means of torture: whip, screws, pincers, and "the red hot iron." Moreover, God has even seen masters and mistresses, "educated in the fashionable life [who] exceed even their overseers in cruelty."

But now, he enjoins his congregation, "let us give thanks" and let it not "be confined to this day." In fact, he calls for January 1 to be "a perpetual day of remembrance of the deliverance," for black people must never forget "that an African slave, ready to perish, was our father or our grandfather." He begins his peroration with, "let us be grateful to our benefactors," whom he hopes will be rewarded. He ends with a Christian prayer: "hasten that glorious time, when the knowledge of the Gospel of Jesus Christ, shall cover the earth, as the waters cover the sea"; and he ends: "now, O Lord, we desire, with angels and archangels, and all the company of Heaven, evermore to praise thee saying, Holy, Holy Holy, Lord God Almighty: the whole earth is full of thy glory. Amen."

4.

The intertwining of the Gospel with social justice is a commonplace of American rhetoric not confined to the Black Church. A second call for civil liberties came from elsewhere. Women have often carried the call, not least with respect to their own standing. Many stand out, but four are particularly interesting in their display of achievement and eloquence. (Note the diversity of appeals.)

Sarah Grimke (1792-1873) famously refuted the General Association of Congregational Ministers of Massachusetts Pastoral Letter on "the powers of women" with her own letter (1837). She thought the pastoral letter too compromising; and since she would not be patronized, she accused. Women, she said, have surrendered their dearest rights to men, who have "adorned the creature whom God gave him as a companion, with baubles and gewgaws, turned her attention to personal attractions, offered incense to her vanity, and made her the instrument of his selfish gratification, a plaything to please his eye and amuse his hours of leisure." Lucretia Mott (1793-1880), Quaker, abolitionist, godmother of the movement to gain political rights for women, delivered a sermon on November 4, 1849, entitled "Abuses and Uses of the Bible." "The Spirit of the Lord is upon them [the down-trodden]. . . . Whoever giveth them mouth and wisdom, tongue, and utterance to speak that which he commandeth, strength and perseverance is in accordance with right. . . ."

Julia A. J. Foote (1823-1900) might very well agree. She preached to her "dear sisters" that if they unite with the heavenly host, they "will not let what man may say or do, keep you from doing the will of the Lord" and living a holy and righteous life. In 1884 she became the first woman to be ordained a deacon in the African Methodist Episcopal Zion denomination. During the year of her death she became only the second woman to be ordained an AMEZ elder. Foote talked about herself because her subject explicitly was herself, and she treated that self almost as a specimen: I am an example, she seemed to be saying, but only one.

Thea Bowman (1937-1990) would applaud. Like Foote, Bowman would speak to her co-religionists, but not as a woman only. A Roman Catholic, she was invited in 1989 by the U.S. Catholic bishops to be the keynote speaker at their conference on black Catholics. She pulled no punches. "To be black and Catholic means to get in touch with the world church . . . ." She continues, "in Africa right now three hundred people become Christian every day, and 75 per cent of them are becoming Roman Catholics." She concludes by calling the church "a family" that will build "a holy city, a new Jerusalem, a city set apart where they'll know we are his because we love one another." Not merely their presence, but the accumulation of conviction among these women itself bears eloquent witness, both to the offense and to its solution.

5.

Malcolm X (1925-1965) was a rhetorical genius, I think, and capable of bursts of great eloquence delivered intensely, though rarely melodramatically. What intruded upon his eloquence, however, was his cleverness and the narrowness of his agenda: before his *haj* to Mecca and his conversion to orthodox Islam that resulted from it (after which his anti-white hostility disappeared and his appeal broadened), he did more to influence black separatism than any person in the country. Then his great integrity caused him to break with the Nation of Islam, and he accurately predicted his own murder at their hands.

His appeal lay in his uncompromising intellectual defiance, his ability to sustain a complex argument (often without a text) over great spans of speech, and in the boldness of his incisive re-definition of assumptions. For example, as a portrait of militant Black thinking in the sixties, and as an argument which would be daunting to any debate opponent, his 1964 "The Ballot or the Bullet" remains dispositive. It is sometimes too coy, sometimes self-subversive in its insults (he was still a furious racist when he delivered it) and it is some thirty per cent too long, but it remains a fountain of identity for a large minority of black Americans: "No, I'm not an American. I'm one of the twenty-two million black people who are the victims of Americanism." It is a great shame that he did not live longer than he did after his conversion; he might have had much to say to Dana, Jones, Foote, and Bowman. At the end of the day, his gifts, his authenticity, and his integrity place him among the greatest—perhaps the very greatest—speakers of the Sixties—and staunchly within our tradition of freedom-speech—even if he was mostly wrong.

On the other hand, there is Frederick Douglass (1817?-1895), a rhetorical giant even among Olympians like Clay, Calhoun and Webster. (I do not include Lincoln only because he is the Zeus of English-speaking oratory, with the Gettysburg Address being the greatest speech of all speeches in English.) A former slave whose literacy and oratory were self-taught (the former with the help, illegally rendered, of his owner's wife, the latter with a close and relentless study of *The Columbian Orator*, a popular anthology of rhetorical masterpieces), Douglass was already famous when, on July Fourth (a Sunday) in 1852 he delivered "What to the Slave is the Fourth of July?" in Rochester, New York. Douglass was under vicious *ad hominem* attack by his former Abolitionist colleagues, including William Lloyd Garrison. Douglass, though, would never sink into the gutter with them. That refusal, in addition to extraordinary platform gifts of voice, stature and gesture, help make this speech an American masterpiece, still standing on its own more than a century-and-a-half after its delivery as very much more than a mere historical artifact.

From the beginning Douglass makes clear his position (had Malcolm read Douglass? Probably): "The sunlight that brought life and healing to you, has brought stripes [scars from whippings] . . . to me. This Fourth of July is yours, not mine. You may rejoice, I must mourn. . . . Do you mean, citizens, to mock me, by asking me to speak today?" He then declares the near-futility of making a case that ought to need no making at all: "How should I look today in the presence of Americans, dividing and sub-diving a discourse, to show that men have a natural right to freedom, speaking of it relatively and positively, negatively and affirmatively? . . . There is not a man beneath the canopy of heaven that does not know that slavery is wrong for *him*." He goes on to use historical narration, description, analysis, definition, exposition, and especially argument, alternately and organically, to make his case.

His range of tools is staggering. He is unsparing but never insulting. His style is largely plain, until he needs more: "the flesh-mongers gather up their victims by dozens. . . . In the deep still darkness of midnight, I have been often aroused by the dead heavy footsteps, and the piteous cries of the chained gangs that passed our door." At the end, he looks prophetically to the future and is hopeful: "I do not despair of this country. . . . my spirit is also cheered by the obvious tendencies of the age." Space is comparatively annihilated. "Thoughts expressed on one side of the Atlantic are distinctly heard on the other."

6.

At its root (Latin, present participle *eloqui*) 'eloquence' means simply "to speak out." Textbooks tell us that qualities such as concreteness, variety (of rhythm and of figures of speech like metaphor), vividness (of imagery), appropriateness (of diction), and of course clarity make for sound style. The etymology implies none of these, and newer textbooks let us down as well, because they leave out *perspicuousness*: clear and intelligible expression *based upon acuteness of perception and of discernment*. In other words: pay attention, then say what you both see and what you discern (what lies behind what you see). Here is an example.

Lou Gehrig was among the greatest and most beloved gentleman-ballplayers who ever walked the earth. He certainly spoke heroically on Lou Gehrig Day, July 4, 1939. He knew he would soon be dead, from amyotrophic lateral sclerosis ("Lou Gehrig's Disease"). He knew that the seventy thousand people at Yankee Stadium knew it too, and they knew that he knew it. So, in nearly-flawless iambic rhythm (our natural English rhythm), does he dwell upon the disease ("a bad break" he calls it), or on its tragic consequence (a wasting away unto death), or even on the sadness he feels?

He does not. Rather, he *discerns*—in the midst of a loving multitude, with the greatest sports stadium in the world filled beyond capacity, at the center of the very place where he performed so splendidly for so long—he discerns his *good fortune*. "Today," he says, "I consider myself the luckiest man on the face of the earth." Do you find his line trivial or sentimental? Then you do not understand the rhetoric of baseball in America: this sport, as a metaphor speaking simply and directly, that is, eloquently, of our culture (as the great scholar Jacques Barzun has claimed). We all may have heard lines as eloquent as Lou Gehrig's, but in context none of us has heard any line more eloquent.

So: Genung, or Donoghue? Of course, a systematic attempt at an answer would include many examples beyond the oratorical. Bartoleme de las Casas, in the *Devastation of the Indies* and in live debate, successfully defended the humanity of Amerindians. "Ask not for whom the bells, toll/ They toll for thee," writes John Donne. "They also serve who only stand

and wait," writes John Milton. In his great American novel, *Winter's Tale,* a supreme poet (as in the Greek "maker") of *agape,* Mark Helprin writes:

> . . . he saw all before him all the many rich hours of every age and those to come, an infinitely light and deep universe . . . and then they were taken by a wind which arose suddenly and carried them up in full and triumphant faith. As they ascended, in mounting cascades, they saw that the great city about them was infinitely complex, holy, and alive. . . . the fine bays and rivers that surrounded the city had been moved to come alight, and for a hundred miles the bays and the rivers and the sea it-self were a pale shimmering gold. *They rose far enough to see that the swirling gold was real, and that it covered all the oceans, and rolled through all things with a promise of final benevolence that was certain to be kept. And then they were gently set down, in the heart of a new city that was all spring and sun.*

As Nietzsche has his Zarathustra ask, "are not words and [their] sounds given to things so that man can renew himself . . . ?"

Yet, not more than words, but also other. Juan Huarte, in his *Examen de ingenios para las ciencias* (1575), tells us the reason: "From a good imagination, spring all the Arts and Sciences, which consist in figure, correspondence, harmonie, and proportion." Van Gogh's "Starry Night," Artie Shaw's "Begin the Beguine," and E=MC2. And Taps. If it unsettles, or stands out, or re-arranges settled wisdom, or bears witness to truth: that's eloquence. Silence, too, may be eloquent. In other words, Genung is right, Donoghue wrong. Within the American tradition, though, and no matter race, ethnicity, sex, or religion, most threads of eloquence form our double helix of freedom and redemption.

A Postscript: During the Cold War, America led the Free World, and the Free World won. That is, freedom won. In that light, a brief look at the great rhetorical figures who arose late in that conflict might prove enlightening, for rhetoric—rhetoric inspired by the American ideal of freedom—mattered greatly. (And as Samuel Johnson has told us, people need to be reminded more often than instructed.)

Given their different styles and stations, comparisons between President Ronald Reagan, Aleksandr Solzhenitsyn (Soviet resister, novelist, and Nobel Prize-winner), and Pope John Paul II might prove useful. Together they sparked a rhetorical campaign contributing to the greatest irruption of freedom in human history. Here is what our three speakers intuited: That *the Soviet Union and the acceptance of it in certain precincts in the West as legitimate was entropic*; that is, ready to fall apart. They realized that most rhetoric is generated by orthodoxies: common, often unexamined, assumptions that we can think of as incorrigibles, because they are (or seem to be) products of nature itself: "givens." These produce what we might call a "hypothetical reality," a mini-worldview which, if closed and therefore unchallenged by newness, must become entropic (the tendency of any system to fall apart). Such a system may be "noisy," but there is no news. Furthermore, these three witness (for such is what they became) saw that rhetoric can be of three types: *confirmational,* rhetoric that assents to and reinforces the orthodoxies; *utilitarian,* that which applies those orthodoxies afresh; and the most transformative and therefore the most dangerous, *syntactical*—rhetoric which seeks to subvert the very structure of an orthodoxy.

We begin with Ronald Reagan, especially in the eighties as President of The United States. Before that his radio addresses especially reveal the consistency of his dysentropic—that is, the upsetting newness and freshness—of his thinking. His *In His Own Words* foreshadows his presidential emphasis on religious motifs, assertive optimism (a world apart from his predecessor's dreary imagery), and his triumphalist faith in individual enterprise and in Western values of freedom and democracy, which many "useful idiots" (to use Lenin's designation) on both sides of the Atlantic saw as morally equivalent to the values and practices of Soviet totalitarianism. Reagan's discourse was radically syntactic on both national and cultural levels, In spite of intense alarums raised by some verbalist elites, Reagan's electoral victory was pronounced, and the national landscape changed.

He (along with Prime Minister Margaret Thatcher, the Iron Lady of The United Kingdom) understood that the more deeply-rooted the orthodoxies being attacked, the more consistent, unambiguous, and hopeful that attack must be. Typical of this understanding are two of Reagan's most famous speeches. This first was "Remarks at the Annual Convention of the National Association of Evangelicals" on March 8, 1983, in which he called the Soviet Union an "evil empire." The second was "Remarks at the Brandenburg Gate" on June 12 1987, in which, to the screaming cheers of West Berliners, in front of the infamous Berlin Wall separating East Germany from West, he admonished his counterpart, "Mr. Gorbachev, tear down this wall." At the time, both were largely regarded by self-designated opinion-makers as absurdly irresponsible in their detachment from reality; now both have become catalytic artifacts of an entirely new reality they helped create. Thus Reagan has come to be considered a "transformative" president, in the words of President Obama, and his intellectual acuity (see Reagan's handwritten scripts for his *daily* radio program or his *Life in Letters*), as well as his eloquence[1] are—outside the precincts of the Hard Left—generally conceded.

The genuinely religious rhetoric most challenging to deeply rooted cultural incorrigibles was provided by Aleksandr Solzhenitsyn and Pope John Paul II, both contemporaries of Reagan. Solzhenitsyn most strikingly stunned the world with his Gulag Archipelago, the long, detailed account of the chain of Soviet political penitentiaries and the treatment of inmates there. The Soviet Union couldn't get rid of him fast enough, for older books would be brought back and others forthcoming. Moreover, Solzhenitsyn was unspeakably brave, an articulate, impassioned man who bore personal witness again and again to the depravities of a totalitarian state.

But he challenged the West generally, and the Left particularly, in his Harvard commencement address ("A World Split Apart," June 8, 1978). In this speech, he tells us that a chasm of evil runs through every human heart and that a materialist rot is despoiling our spiritual strength. His detailed, panscopic critique of Western values, but of America's in particular, was nothing new, yet, given the hostile response to it, the earth must have quaked; most noteworthy was the repulsion of those who recognized the basis of Solzhenitsyn's assault as essentially religious: notwithstanding his courteousness, he was patronized, scolded, dismissed, or ignored (though not actually refuted), apparently because he not only failed to respect the incorrigibles of the self-righteous but because he attacked secularist idols as well.

On the other hand, the pope, who substantially agreed with the Russian's critique, received little of the same reproach. Surely this muteness was directly related both to John Paul's station and to his personal character; but it is a function, too, of his method, which was prevailingly pastoral and philosophical. By traveling, however, he managed to transfuse his discourse with quite un-tranquil algorithms. For example, in Poland (where his reception was near-riotous), this Polish pope coupled liberty with solidarity in opposition to the Communist regime, clearly intimidating the dictator *de jour*. In Cuba the same thing happened: people could see Fidel Castro's legs actually wobbling. His appeal to youth was worldwide, and even his talks on sexuality encouraged people fearlessly to *ex-sistare*, to

---

1 See "Address to the Nation on the Challenger Disaster" or "Remarks at a Dinner Honoring Tip O'Neill," the Democrat Speaker of the House during Reagan's administration.

"stand out," from their State and Society into the non-conformity of moral conviction. Just so, perpetually fresh figures—with John Paul bearing witness—could show that politics and economics are not the engines of history.

These three men, with a spark provided by Polish labor leader Lech Walesa in front (he literally climbed the fence to lead his men to work) and the unrelenting will of Margaret Thatcher behind, collectivized their eloquence to destabilize the Communist bloc. "How many divisions does the pope have?" Josef Stalin once asked sneeringly. The answer: it doesn't take a division, merely unwavering witnesses who speak the truth, no matter the risks.

TEN

Rhetorical Peru
A Culture in Conversation

"Culture," an elusive concept, is a way of seeing, knowing, thinking, speaking and acting within a given community, whatever its designation (*e.g.* country, family, workplace). It so inheres to our lives that we often confuse our patterns of thought and practices within it as being ordained by nature itself. That is why culture often defines (that is, establishes boundaries, which is what "definition" means at its root) our very identities. But how do cultural variations in these patterns and practices affect rhetoric, that is, public expressions of that identity? Specifically, what are the parameters of public conversation when cultural conventions discourage vigorous argument, inviting only a confirmational rhetoric, one that re-affirms embedded assumptions? And what happens when there appears a syntactical rhetoric, one that seeks to uproot those assumptions?

I have been asking, and trying to answer, those questions for nearly fifty years, with Peru as both the subject of my self-styled fieldwork and my home-away-from home. I am married to a Peruvian, and there I have a wonderful extended family as well as friends and what ethnologists call "informants," and my wife and I have raised two children who (like their parents, reciprocally) are bi-lingual and virtually bi-cultural. This immersion, along with my palpable enjoyment of nearly all things Peruvian, has made for considerable cultural fluency, a certain ease and self-assurance that I've enjoyed when navigating the tricky currents of Peruvian conversation at all levels. Nevertheless, when in Peru I remain (in however authentically a friendly fashion) an alien.

I have learned that the useful question about Peru is not, What do we know? but How should we know it? Unlike English, Spanish (and many other languages) allows for two ways of knowing—*saber* and *conocer*—study from the outside and participatory, personal acquaintance from the inside. We in the United States are strong on the first, but our weakness on the second causes us to mediate our view of reality—usually without even knowing that we are doing so. How easy to assume, for example, that Peruvians "seek after continental models," as one American scholar has held. But they deny it. How much easier still to describe them as desirous of becoming "principal actors in the Latin American drama." But they do not care to be First Worldly-wise, and most Peruvian intellectuals avoid geopolitical prominence. They rely on rooted social institutions, which they do not see as weak at all. Gabriel García Márquez (a Colombian) said it best in his Nobel address: "The interpretation of reality through patterns not our own serves only to make us ever more unknown, ever less free, ever more solitary." Bolívar himself could not win over the Peruvians—despised them, in fact.

My purpose here is . . . well, I'm an old teacher, so my purpose is didactic. The country fascinates, invites, frustrates, compels. Over a span of thirty years I've published five articles on Peru: 1/ "The Habit of Peruvian Democracy" in *Worldview*, July 1985; 2/ "Prolonging Peru's Solitude?" in *National Review*, May 14, 1990; 3/ "'Chinochet'?" in *National Review*, September 14, 1992; 4/ "The Hero Storyteller" again in *National Review*, April 17, 1995; and 5/ "Letter from Peru: the Outgoing Tide" in *The New Criterion*, June 2011.

In 1990 the jury deciding the welfare of Peru was still out. The democracy restored by President Fernando Belaúnde Terry (1980) was threatened, not only by the ruinous presidency (1985-1990) of an arrogant and ideologically-driven president in his mid-thirties, but by two terrorist insurgencies: the urban MRTA and, especially, the Maoist Shining Path (on which more anon), who revered the butcher Pol Pot. Then came a national election (1990) that would forever change Peruvian society, nation, and culture—and thus its conversations, in fact its very manner of conversing. As a result Peru would (though later) flourish, under the leadership, no less, of a middle-aged and much-chastened Alan García, the very same man who almost brought the house down in the late eighties. Here I offer the fourth of these articles, "The Hero Storyteller," followed by two anecdotes.

2.
Lima, 1995.

There is no trust in the Americas, neither in individuals nor
in nations: The constitutions are books, the treaties scraps of
paper, the elections battles, liberty is anarchy, and life a torture.
                                    – Simón Bolívar, the Jamaica Letter, 1815

In 1995 Peru will elect a president, its *fourth* consecutive, legitimate
presidential election—astonishing for a country that has had only one
other such succession this century. Alberto Fujimori is running again (as
presidents could not until the new constitution was ratified by a majority
small enough to call Fujimori's popularity into question) and he will not
lose, not even to the universally-respected Javier Pérez de Cuéllar (the former Secretary General of the United Nations). And that virtual certainty
is accompanied by a second: there will be a campaign substantially unlike
any most Peruvians have ever known, for the rhetoric of liberal democracy,
free markets, private initiative, and personal freedom, as opposed to that of
ubiquitous statist intervention, *will be taken for granted by virtually everyone*, so radically have the deepest orthodoxies of the Peruvian nation and
culture been altered.

Until 1987, and notwithstanding the historic economic colloquia
of 1981, the most compelling feature of late twentieth-century Peru was
this: *no newness*, and so no hope. In fact, if we regard the entire culture as
a sort of human information system, we may say that it was saturated by
"noise," randomly distributed uncertainty and uniform disarray; that is, by
entropy. Is it any wonder that Mario Vargas Llosa, renowned novelist-brief-
ly-turned-politician, could feel "absurd and unreal" in his own country?
Was it at all likely that—in the face of four centuries of cultural inertia and
more than fifty years of aggressive and axiomatic political hostility—he
could have done something about it?

Yet, thanks in large part to Vargas Llosa and his heroic presidential
campaign of 1990, Peru (this "beggar sitting on a bench of gold," as the
Peruvian naturalist Raimondi described his country) has shown signs of
rising and, finally, of refuting Bolívar. Today Vargas Llosa's carping about
President Fujimori (amidst much necessary criticism of him) has earned
considerable ostracism, but tomorrow, when a whole pack of opportunists,
demagogues and technocrats are reduced to anomalous footnotes, he will
still be the hero who not only stood athwart Peruvian history and yelled
"Stop!" but went on to point out its proper direction and to propel it on

its historic way.

Until then, Peru hardly seemed worthy of exclusion from the Liberator's one-hundred-and-seventy-five-year-old judgment. A febrile, Khmer Rouge-like terrorist organization, *Sendero Luminoso* (Shining Path), was slowly numbing and eviscerating the country; hyper-inflation was de-valuing an absurd currency, just as an unraveling social contract was debasing standards of conduct, both public and private; the under-employed joined the unemployed, those who were merely hungry now starved, and the infrastructure deteriorated. Many of the people living in small towns or in the countryside away from the coast were *de facto* serfs, a neo-colonial population semi-indentured, not to multinational corporations or to old oligarchic interests, but to the barons of a great drug-trafficking empire and their ideologically maniacal counterparts. And all the while a helplessly mercantilist state presided, at once bloated and flaccid. Rampant and petty corruption (called *coima*) accompanied an obligatory shamming (*pillería*) in all aspects of bureaucratic life, and the state employed or otherwise ruled most of the Peruvian workforce. In some years more than a thousand executive decrees per month had been issued.

In the late sixties Peru had been, per capita, second on the continent in animal husbandry; in 1968 General Juan Velasco conducted a leftist military coup against President Fernando Belaúnde (who was spirited out of the presidential palace in his pajamas) and botched a land reform that broke up large estates. So began the decline in Peruvian husbandry: by 1990 (after the depredations of the García administration, 1985-90, and its shameless APRA—*Alianza Popular Revolucionaria Americana*—party) only Haiti had a lower per capita rate. President Belaúnde, vindicated by his re-election in 1980, told me that, indeed, decentralization (social as well as economic) was his policy; he would build roads and telecommunications facilities and encourage investment outside Lima. Syntactic rhetoric was changing the culture.

Under such bizarre circumstances, who better than a novelist—whose living is the invention of credible worlds—to summon forth a new vision after having lived through, assaulted, and finally discarded a ruinous one (Marxist-socialist "Castroism")? In person Vargas Llosa is charming, friendly, and supremely courteous—a cosmopolitan, multi-lingual figure (like one of his heroes, Jorge Luis Borges, the great Argentine writer and scholar), apparently at home with people of all kinds, who in turn have seemed at home with him. And as a national treasure he is unique: among the most indigenous writers his country has ever produced, he is also the most internationally renowned in its history.

So it was with exceptional authority that, in 1981, he spontaneously formed and led a large and varied group of demonstrators to the Soviet embassy to protest the imposition of martial law in Poland, and in July of 1987 raised an alarm in response to Alan García's plan to nationalize banks, insurance companies, and all other lending institutions (which would have effected a virtual state monopoly over all credit, especially damaging to newspapers, which rely upon it to buy newsprint). One month later, to the amazement of the continent, he led a rally of over one hundred thousand people in the Plaza San Martín—street-vendors and bus drivers, along with bankers, all protesting García's decision. That demonstration was the birth of *Libertad*, not a political party but a social movement, to that point the largest ever in Peru.

Thus by the late eighties Vargas Llosa was not only ideally suited to leadership but seemed to apprehend his role in its dynamic. In his novel *Hablador (The Storyteller*, the proofs of which he was correcting in 1987, as the plans for the Plaza demonstration were being laid), he tells the tale of Saúl Zuratas, a young and brilliant anthropology student who becomes so absorbed in the study of Amazon tribes that he abandons his scientific stance and enters as a native into the culture of the Machiguenga, a dwindling group who must walk (literally and figuratively) in order to survive as a people. For coherence—the basis of their very identity—they rely upon *un hablador*, a storyteller who recounts episodes, myths, biographies and visions. Zuratas—an outsider to his own society because of his Jewishness as well as to the Amazon tribe because of a birthmark that runs across half his face (they would have killed him at birth)—becomes the Machiguenga's *hablador*.

It is but a short allegorical reach to read Peru as the tribe and Vargas Llosa himself as the *hablador*. Twice within the first two pages the narrator tells us "I went in," anticipating the choice of his protagonist to enter the tribal culture. And from that inside, the *hablador* can recount Tasurinchi's (the shaman's) resolute optimism: "The sun hasn't fallen yet. . . . we must help it. We have suffered evil and death, but we keep on walking. . . . No. We are alive. We are moving." From the outside, however, the narrator tells us that "the Shapras [another tribe: Ecuador? Bolivia?] were more isolated . . . but one did not find among them any of those symptoms of depression or moral disintegration that the [linguists] had described in the Machiguengas"; that is, in the allegorical Peru. "For the Machiguengas," the narrator says, "history marches neither forward nor backward: it goes around and around in circles, repeats itself." It is intelligible from within; but, from without, random and uncertain—*profoundly entropic.*

Yet Vargas Llosa, unlike his *hablador*, had transcended the entropic reality, and would have his countrymen do the same. Manuel D'Ornellas, formerly editor of the daily *Expreso* (and now a critic of the expatriate Vargas Llosa, who has taken Spanish citizenship), has aptly noted that Peruvians "have been accustomed to the harsh and aggressive rhetoric of [their] military dictators, or to the cooing or capricious words of their civilian governors." So Vargas Llosa seemed new indeed when, for example, he endorsed the candidacy of Belaúnde (in 1980) by describing his support for "the progress of liberty, change without cataclysmic trauma, and respect for law, criticism, and the *plurality of information"*—by way of rhetoric. After all, "it is necessary to transform reality by means of words," he wrote in 1983, "even though these words are themselves a distortion of reality."

Moreover, he is refreshingly unambiguous with respect to the question of responsibility. Speaking of his countrymen during a lecture in Edinburgh, in 1986, he said, "one of our worst defects—our best fictions—is to believe that our miseries have been imposed upon us from abroad, that others have always had responsibility for our problems; for instance, the *conquistadores*. . . . We are the *conquistadores*. They gave us the habit of passing to the devil the responsibility for any evil we do." A bit earlier he had already noted that, with respect to the same colonial period, "almost five centuries later this is still an unfinished business. We have not yet, properly speaking, seen the light. We don't yet," he said in 1986, "constitute [a] real nation."

In a speech in San José, Costa Rica, representing *Libertad*, he said (October 22, 1988):

> Our peoples, weighed down by hunger, economic injustice, the lack of work, of schools, of hospitals—weighed down by all the misfortune and hopelessness that life is for them—have not lost their appetite for liberty.

As a presidential candidate in 1990 he attacked "elites," largely of the private sector and always in league with high-ranking bureaucrats and *"cacasenos"*—some party hacks and "shitheads." These diminish both economic and political liberty, and turn democracy into a formalistic sham. He championed Hernando de Soto's groundbreaking *El Otro Sendero* (*The Other Path*). "Vote," he has often said, "not for the rich, but for a system that could make you rich." He promised to end the "folkloric unreality" that reigns and to punish "the reprobates." His Peru would be one of "the possible and the impossible."

As late as the close of his first-round campaign, Vargas Llosa gave no indication of oratorical distemper. For example, on April 5, 1990, in his farewell to Arequipa, his home Department, he addressed tens of thousands of wildly cheering people from a balcony and, quite musically and with a lover's zeal, promised the throng a government "as pure, as clean, as transparent as the air of Arequipa," with ideas "as luminous as are the stars that shine in the heavens and in the eyes of Arequipan women." Perhaps because he (like most Peruvians) anticipated his second-round loss and was disgusted with the first-round results, his heart was not in the second round campaign, though that would be with the exceptions (according to his son Álvaro, the campaign press officer) of his last speech and (in my judgment) of the formal debates with Fujimori. He closed his campaign, on June, 1990, with an address to the nation in which he compared Peru to a book:

> An ancient, beautiful, never-ending book. It contains pages of great beauty telling us of a great civilization built by Peruvians in this very same 'roof of the world', pages written on the stones of Machu Picchu and Chavin, in the paintings of Nazca and Paracas, in the gold and silver of the Incas. There are pages of bravery, such as those describing Grau's ship and Bolognesi's sword.

He asked Peruvians to write a happy ending. When the next day he heard the results he said, "I feel sorry for Peru."

It seems he would instruct but not persuade, as though the two were mutually exclusive; and just so would he, recently, come to be seen (in the words of his former friend and renowned colleague De Soto) as the absentee "*hijo de puta*," repeated twice, on television, live—that is, a "son of a whore," substantially worse than a mere "son of a bitch."

Notwithstanding the utter novelty and daring of his campaign, Vargas Llosa's whiteness and his political alliances had made him nominally the establishment candidate, a status that would be exploited by the adroit Fujimori, who would assume the role of struggling opposition candidate. But in fact Vargas Llosa—like the facially disfigured and Jewish storyteller Zuratas—was (and remains to this day) the archetypal outsider. A fresh Peruvian identity, with a new political and economic culture, are unthinkable without the vision of Vargas Llosa.

Fujimori is still playing the tough cop (as he fends off the attacks of an even tougher cop, Mrs. Fujimori, and the coup may be his legacy, its enduringly bad fruit being his complicity with the genuinely wicked Vladimiro Montesinos, the latter's military cronies, and their evil doings. But as far dictators go, and notwithstanding continuing abuses both substantive and formal, Fujimori is small potatoes. Unlike both Vargas Llosa and Pérez de Cuéllar, Peruvians say, Fujimori is present, indeed, virtually ubiquitous. (Six weeks away from the election he was staying near the Peru-Ecuador border, inside a war zone.) He travels to public projects, walks among the poor, and visits the remotest, and hottest, spots in the republic. He is, in fact, the first Peruvian president in living memory to have visited Ecuador. Inflation, nearly 8,000% per year in 1990, should be around 9% in 1995; a GDP which shrunk by some 5% in 1990 grew by 12% (the fastest in the world) in 1994 and should appreciate (for the third consecutive year) by another 6% in 1995, when Fujimori has promised to turn his attention to the establishment of a social safety net (the linchpin of Pérez de Cuéllar's campaign). During those same five years per capita income has risen from nearly $1000 to over $1300 per year. Old public works painted over and dedicated as though brand new? Municipal (Lima) funds impounded when Mayor Belmont showed signs of gaining a sizable national following? A candidate excessively availing himself of incumbency (this a first, remember) by mixing political campaigning with official business? All nickels and dimes, when not mere abstractions, to the ordinary Peruvian. The *sol* is dependable, and both water and electricity run all the time. Forgotten is this: most of Fujimori's economic policies are taken from Vargas Llosa's platform.

Last November while in Lima I met with a number of district stalwarts of the Pérez de Cuéllar party, Union for Peru: housewives, pharmacists, physicians and dentists who are among the most earnest and self-sacrificing people I have ever known, mostly Catholic church people (led by the candidate's daughter-in-law, Luz) with a long history of religious devotion to hands-on charitable work among the poor. They have a grassroots strategy, high (and not entirely unrealistic) hopes for their legislative candidates (Fujimori's *Cambio 90* party may not win majorities in both houses), and no money. Not even Pérez de Cuéllar's promise to put the vastly popular Ketín Vidal (the low key, un-self-promoting Special Strike Force chief who actually captured Abimael Guzmán, the "maximum leader" of the Shining Path) in charge of all counter-terrorism has made an impression. Explosions and assassinations have virtually ceased, and people already feel safe. The other candidates, including two women (from the Popular Christian Party on the Right to APRA), stand no chance. Whereas I met no one who actually likes Fujimori, only a handful of those will vote against him.

Near the end of *The Storyteller* Zuratas says, "before, I wasn't what I am now. I became a storyteller after being what you are at this moment: listeners. . . . It happened without my willing it, little by little. Without even realizing it, I began to find my destiny. Slowly, calmly. It appeared bit by bit. Not with tobacco juice, or with *ayahuasco* (hallucinogenic) brews. Or with the help of the [demons]. I discovered it all by myself." The Peruvian poet Martín Adan chose to remove himself from social insanity by entering an insane asylum. He wrote, "*La cosa real, si la pretendes/ No es aprehenderla sino imaginarla*": "The real thing, if one aspires to it, is not to be apprehended but imagined"—all by oneself. But Vargas Llosa, having learned the same lesson about "*la cosa real*," would not tolerate some entropic refuge. During his speech in Costa Rica he said:

> . . . the option of freedom often manifests itself as an instinctive and blind hunger from the depths of the psyche rather than as a conscious and reasoned effort. It is a mysterious desire to reach a complete and supreme individuality, breaking away from the undifferentiated collectivity. It is the sovereignty of being. . . .

One of his characters, Santiago Zavala, famously asks in an early novel, *Conversation in the Cathedral* (1969, a remarkable attempt at a public conversation about the past, foreshadowing much of Vargas' later political and literary careers), "*cuando se jodió el Peru?*"—"When did Peru first f___ itself?" A number of answers could be given, but why not start with the early sixteenth century? Foreshadowing indigenous, literary Magic Realism is the fantastic eyewitness account of Spanish atrocities—"We are the *conquistadores*"—provided by Bartolome de Las Casas (the first priest ordained in the New World):

> In Peru. . . . massacres and robberies occurred without rhyme or reason. Entire settlements were destroyed, the population was reduced, and so many afflictions were imposed upon this country that we are certain no one would be able to list them, from now until the Day of Judgment.

If, on the other hand, the question were, "When did Peru first begin concretely to right itself?" I would say in 1981, when (with De Soto, the historian Hugh Thomas and others) Vargas Llosa sponsored that international economics colloquium, featuring Milton Friedman, bringing a seachange in Peruvian economic, political, and social discourse. What would work in Chile and (in modified form) is now working wonders in Peru was adumbrated there and then. (In a brief, private chat Friedman told me how a Peruvian safety net might work, a subject unfortunately omitted from the official program.) Earlier that year Prime and Finance Minister Manuel Ulloa stayed on his feet for over eight hours, debating and beating the opposition in an open, nationally-televised legislative session: unprecedented political theater. Elegant and poised throughout, this impressive man did not even break a sweat.

Recently Vargas Llosa, according to most Peruvians, is behaving foolishly at best, not only himself carping (often from abroad), but having Álvaro take out after Fujimori over the border war with Ecuador. (An article by Mario on this topic was recently killed by the prestigious *El Comercio*.) His fascinating *A Fish in the Water*, political reportage interspersed with memoir, exemplifies the problem. The book has been widely reviewed, so I will do no more than heartily recommend it with these caveats: He settles more than one score, occasionally falls prey to his particular literary failing of stylistic self-indulgence, and misses the point, implicitly *his own*: Fujimori's "self-coup" was necessary precisely because of the rot he describes; it worked; and it would have been quite beyond his own provenance.

Surely he remains serious in his belief that "a great liberal reform is possible under democratic rule, provided a clear majority votes for it, and to achieve it, it is necessary to be open and honest, explaining in detail what we want to do and the price we would exact for it. "Finally," Vargas Llosa has written, "I don't believe that I succeeded in putting across what I wanted to. Peruvians did not vote for ideas in the elections." Shortly after that passage, however, he quotes a passage from his last political speech, delivered after he lost, to his most loyal workers from *Libertad*:

> I know, I am certain, [and] Peru too will come to know and acknowledge. . . . [t]hat the seeds that we have sown together during these two and a half years will continue to germinate and finally produce those fruits that we desire for Peru: the fruits of modernity, justice, prosperity, peace and liberty.

After all, people who are inventing a culture must, after a period of proverbial "solitude," leave the asylum behind.

Fujimori won the election of 1990 with confirmational rhetoric that appealed to fundamental habits, including racism, but he did not change the culture. The great achievement of Vargas Llosa is that, after revealing the madhouse, he showed Peruvians that they could escape it. His great challenge was, and for some years thereafter would remain—to analyze without scolding, advise without obstructing (*Sendero* and APRA, after all, are virtually crushed and cleansed, respectively), define, remind, persuade, and prophesy. (And he might remember that Peruvians believe more in God and less in Karl Popper than he does.) This is not, of course, the business of electoral politics; it never really is. Rather it is the agenda of an *hablador*—new, fresh, effective and, notwithstanding his disdain for such a claim, victorious.

3.

Much has happened in Peru during the twenty years since that article first appeared. The Peruvian middle class has grown enormously; the poor (in part owing to the heroic—and I mean Heroic—efforts of Hernando de Soto: he was marked for death by *Sendero*) have gained title to their plots of homesteaded land and to their businesses; tourism helped vastly to elevate the quality of much of the infrastructure both in Lima and beyond; computers and cell-phones are ubiquitous; and elements of the bureaucracy-for-its-own-sake (with its attendant *coima*) have not only been tamed and trimmed but a lean administrative local machinery put effectively online. No longer, as was the case in 1981, would my wife and I have to spend a year to . . . marry . . . because Peru does not recognize as contractual Catholic wedding performed in New York. (Finally we did, after, as a "wedding gift," my brother-in-law did what I refused to do: pay off the mayor of a small suburb. The ceremony excited my nine-year-old son who, as witty then as now, had written on a blackboard, "hurray, I'm not a bastard anymore!")

I lament the absence of such journalistic giants as the Aprista Luis Alberto Sánchez (who, blind and an octogenarian, received me with the utmost courtesy and entertained my questions for over an hour), Manuel d'Ornellas, and the revered Alfonso Delboy. It was the Peruvian press, in the (Peruvian) spring of 1992, that held Fujimori's feet to the fire when his *autogolpe* struck—and at the same time did its due diligence, and more, with reporting and commentary on the trial of Abimael Guzmán. *El Comercio, Expreso, La República*, the magazine *Oiga*, together covering the political and socio-economic gamut, were strong *national* guarantors of real *information*. Their public conversations have built on the great strengths of a culture the roots of which trace back more than two millennia. I might have changed my mind with respect to an item or two, or three, in the essays above, but not with respect to the utter distinctiveness of a place as authentic as any on earth.

On October 7, 2010, Mario Vargas Llosa was awarded the Nobel Prize for literature for a body of fiction that renders a "cartography" of Peruvian (particularly) and of South American (generally) culture and that unremittingly defends liberal democracy. His conversations—including his *Conversation in the Cathedral*—actually do what the Nobel committee claims for them: victory indeed. But as far as I know neither the committee nor any report of the prize mentioned *El Hablador*, and neither is he mentioned as the *hablador* whose heroic stance and *syntactical* rhetoric helped restored Peru to itself.

4.

Two encounters are worthy of note, as much for their personal as their cultural significance. Even before arriving in Peru with my wife, Alexandra, and our two children to live 1981, I admired greatly the then-president Fernando Belaúnde Terry. An architect who had attended the University of Texas, admired FDR (whom he would call a key political and ideological model), had fought a duel, had been arrested by a dictator (finally swimming to safety after his escape from an island prison), he at last had won the presidency in 1962. Ousted by a *coup d'état* in 1968, he was re-elected in 1980, an enormous vindication. As it happened, a journalist friend of mine had managed to win for me an interview with him, scheduled for five minutes. It would last longer, nearly an hour, and would be marked throughout by pronounced good humor.

To appreciate an aspect of that humor the reader must know two items of Peruvian life at the time. The most dominating TV personality was the riotously funny Tulio Losa (if you're old enough, recall Buddy Hackett, but clean, and Red Skelton). One of his funniest bits was an imitation of Belaúnde obsessing over his pet-project (this is the second item), the construction of the Marginal Road running North-South and allowing for East-West links to the coast at various latitudes. It was a superb idea, and its eventual realization vastly improved Peruvian life; but Belaúnde's zeal was such that, whenever he discussed it, he would rush out a map on which to make a visual point. Of course, the darting to grasp that map, to wheel it up front, and to tap it almost everywhere with a pointer was Tulio's greatest gag, and it did not get tired.

A stocky, handsome man in his sixties, with a winning smile and a full head of gray hair combed back, he greeted me most graciously, invited me to sit, and instructed his aide to leave us alone (I had already been searched). He indicated a preference that I not record the session, though he permitted note-taking, and told me that I could proceed in either Spanish or English, as I wished. (It would be a mix.) I raised many topics, some caste as questions others as references, and an interview turned into a conversation. So we discussed Texas, FDR, Peruvian journalists and journalism, Peruvian café society, his impressive Prime Minister (Manuel Ulloa who, on his feet for nearly ten hours one day in the Senate, answered and outwitted and outdebated every question, taunt, argument and wee mousie of a congressman that came his way), his own past, and Peru's future.

Then, with the utmost deference, I asked if I might place a question of a sensitive nature. "Well of course, Professor Como. You may ask anything—though you know I may choose not to answer," and we both smiled. "It happens, Mr. President, that I am a great fan of Tulio Losa and—" I was interrupted by laughter, not a chuckle but a belly laugh. "I love that man," said the president. We have been friends for very many years. I'm delighted that you find him and our brand of Peruvian humor so amusing." He was speaking in English now. "Well," I said, "about El Marginal. It seems that his burlesque of your mapwork casts you in a ludicrous light and—" Another interruption, this time with side-splitting laughter. "That," he said, after catching his breath, "is the funniest thing I've ever seen him do. And do you realize," as he leaned back, "that by that burlesque Tulio has brought enormous attention to an idea of grave importance?" Then . . . then the *coup de grâce*. "Here," he said, "let me show you." And he sprang from the sofa, dashed (really) behind a wall, and rushed out The Map, pointer in hand! Thereupon he proceeded to explain, just as I had seen him explain so many times and had seen Losa mock so many times. Life imitating art imitating life.

It was too much for me. Like a second-grader who simply must laugh riotously but knows he may not, I felt all sorts of unidentified effluvia pressing forth from eyes, nose, and ears. But, when seeing my discomfort, the president stopped immediately and said, "well, professor, I see how very funny this must look." Pause. And then he joined me in great laughter. I left soon thereafter, more admiring than when I had entered, and given my initial admiration that was no easy achievement by this extraordinary man.

A very different one was with a Peruvian in the dining room of the Tourist Hotel in the southern city of Tacna; I was traveling alone. After dinner, while making some notes about my expenses, an old, very drunk gentlemen began to speak to me from the next table: to speak far too loudly. I greeted him politely (the exchange would proceed in Spanish) and turned back to my note-making. "Keeping track of expenses, my young friend?" he nearly shouted. I mumbled a "yes, yes" with a meek smile. "Oh, I don't have to," he said. "Would you like to know why?" At that point I noticed that the few other diners and all the staff had turned their backs on us. When I remained silent, the old man rose, approached me, and shouted, "go ahead, ask me why!" So I did. And he answered, while pounding his own chest, "because I am the king of cocaine in all of southern Peru!" I believe I really did hear a pin drop. He returned to his table, smiled at me once, and we both finished our meals and went our separate ways.

And there would be a coda. The next morning as I was checking out two large men in black suits approached me on either side at the front desk. Smiling they asked about the substance of the conversation, addressing me as "professor Como," which, to say the least, had a chilling effect. I told them that I wasn't sure as I had had much to much *pisco* (a lie, of course) and so was drunk. "Ah, good," said the chap to my right, with a smack on my back, "then you can return to Lima and continue your research." Hail fellow, well met. Once in my cab, the driver, who had witnessed the encounter, looking straight ahead, told me to say nothing, including to him, and to sit by myself at the airport, talking to no one. Someone would be watching. Not knowing anyone at the airport, I behaved normally, and upon returning to Lima it was business as usual which, so utterly innocent, must have been suspicious to all sorts of forces at work in a country fraught with tension.

President Belaúnde, though, was not tense, and his own good humor would relax the country for a spell and give license for ordinary Peruvians to undertake a "new normal." History would intervene, of course (it always does), and thugs continue to roam the land, but my friend—for such is what I felt him to be—became a touchstone that continues to serve the country as a model of equanimity, congeniality, and integrity.

ELEVEN

WHY SHAKESPEARE WENT TO SCHOOL
Rhetoric Renascent

NO ONE DOMINATES the great conversation that is Western civilization more than Shakespeare, and in English he is without peer. There is no explaining such genius, but if we take the work in small bits, and train just the right lens upon one of those, we might see what makes that genius live. In that light I will train my lens on one of the most famous speeches in English literature, Marc Antony's public oration over the butchered corpse of Julius Caesar. In doing so I will assume some familiarity with the play but not with the art behind its craft: I mean Rhetoric—my particular lens—without which there would be no Shakespeare as we know him; without which, in fact, there would be no Great Conversation.

Before our leading man enters, however, we must dress the stage with some history of rhetoric (a bit idiosyncratic) leading into the English Renaissance, a glance at how Shakespeare came to know and to master its moves, a primer on some mid-level strategy beyond those tactics emphasized in Shakespeare's day, and a survey of the spectrum of Antony's rhetorical displays in *The Tragedie of Julius Caesar*. That is part one. In part two I tighten the focus: the oration's the thing.[1]

---

1 *Love's Labour's Lost* is Shakespeare's *jeu d'esprit* on figures of rhetoric; see Sister Miriam Joseph's *Shakespeare's use of the Arts of Language.* For our play see Gary Wills, *Rome and Rhetoric: Shakespeare's Julius Caesar,* discussing Roman history, the textual history of *Julius Caesar,* the counterplay of the characters' psychology, and the effectiveness of many figures of speech. Brian Vickers, *Classical Rhetoric in English Poetry,* provides an analytical history of rhetoric (especially of the English Renaissance rheto-

1.

Whether called rhetoric or poetic, in the period of interest to us (as in many periods) the art of making verse or persuasive (or even expository) prose according to contemporaneous rhetorical theory was viewed skeptically, whether by moral or by artistic standards. Early on certain commanding figures of the age were of one mind on this. St. Augustine, a rhetorician by training and profession, was using rhetorical figures and tropes profusely, but he would also call rhetoric "the art of telling lies skilfully"; and as those "colors" of rhetoric began to dominate rhetorical theory, nearly reducing it to style only, Martianus Capella (in his *Marriage of Philology and Mercury*, 5th c.) personified the art as a pompous, decorated woman carrying weapons with which to wound her enemies. A bit later on a supreme *Grammaticus*, Rabanus Maurus (ninth century), would call it merely ornare ('decoration'). Its standing would never be lower. But there was dissent. St. Jerome (he of the Vulgate Bible, 5thc.) had already written that rhetoric is "a means of conveying hidden truth to the uninitiated"; and this early stage is punctuated by John of Salisbury who, in his *Metalogicon* (12th c.), would come to regard rhetoric as the "beautiful and fruitful union between reason and expression," with "eloquence" defined as "skill in uttering appropriately what the mind wishes to express."

Dante (1265-1321) agreed. We know him as a transitional figure, stepping from the Middle Ages into a Renaissance partly of his begetting. A student of rhetoric as well a practitioner, his view of the art in a way resembles Plato's: it is erotic, an exchange between lovers. In his *Convivio* (II.vii.52-56) he tells us so directly. The third concentric, crystalline sphere in his medieval cosmology was presided over by Venus. But it was also the sphere of rhetoric. Thus was love poetry regarded as the height of rhetorical expression. Petrarch (1304-74), a love poet who idolized Dante, was regarded as the master rhetorician—not least by Geoffrey Chaucer (1343-1400), who wrote of Petrarch that his "rhetoryke swete/ Enlumined al Itaille of poetrye."

At the time this all seemed . . . modern. (Petrarch had been the leading light of the movement known as the *dolce stil novo*—the "sweet new style.") Yet the greatest contemporary influence in the high Middle Ages and early Renaissance began his rule some thirteen centuries earlier than Dante: the great Roman lawyer, politician and philosopher Cicero (106-43 B.C.), referred to as the "*magister* [master, teacher] *eloquentiae*." Among his works the most consulted were *Orator, De oratore* and, especial-

---

ricians), an inventory of the deployment of figures in English poetry (and elsewhere), and a taxonomy of figures.

ly, the early *De inventione*. Between the eleventh and the fourteenth centuries that book has more than two dozen library references, an astonishing number in a world without printing. (Extant manuscript commentaries on Cicero's various rhetorics number in the hundreds.) He was unavoidable for students who studied the *Trivium*: the three Liberal Arts of Grammar, Rhetoric, and Logic. Early in his magisterial (and majestic) *European Literature and the Latin Middle Ages*, Ernst Robert Curtius summarizes the hegemony of rhetoric: "the reception of antique rhetoric was a determining factor of artistic self-expression in the West for long after the close of the Middle Ages."[2]

Transmitting this tradition was one particularly influential rhetorician whose work spread throughout the Continent and to England, Geoffroi of Vinsauf (*Poetria Nova*, c.1210). Of course Geoffroi makes no distinction between rhetoric and poetic and, yes, thinks himself modern. His book has nine parts, but two thousand hexameters (90% of the whole, all in verse) address figures of speech—of which he lists and exemplifies nearly seventy (even so, somewhat fewer than had been, and would be, the case with others). To appreciate Geoffroi's influence we need only note that dozens of manuscripts of the *Poetria Nova* are extant, an enormous number, especially given how many have probably been lost.

Virtually the whole of high medieval rhetorical doctrine could be found, completely exemplified, in Geoffroi's treatise, making it the most famous and influential work of the thirteenth century in its field (and which is why Chaucer would make him a laughing-stock here and there in his *Canterbury Tales*). By Shakespeare's day this tradition had been ripening for two centuries. Rhetoric textbooks abounded[3] and were pedagogical mainstays. In short, the wholeness of rhetorical theory, which is to say most of Cicero's and Geoffroi's rhetoric, had been purveyed, and young Will would come to know most of it.

How? We now know that Shakespeare, who never went to University, had a superb grammar school education typical of its day for families of a certain station (and Shakespeare's family was not without station). His schooldays were long (nearly dawn to nearly dusk), there were many

2 Pantheon Books, New York, 1953, p.78.

3 *E.g.* Cox, *The Art and Crafte of Rhetoryke*; Wilson, *The Arte of Rhetorique*; Fraunce, *The Arcadian Rhetorike*; Peacham, *The Garden of Eloquence*; and George Puttenham, *The Arte of English Poesie*. See also: James J. Murphy, *Rhetoric in the Middle Ages* as well as *Renaissance Eloquence*; Wilbur Samuel Howell, *Logic and Rhetoric in England, 1500-1700*, esp. 3.iii; and, still, Charles Sears Baldwin, *Medieval Rhetoric* and *Poetic and Renaissance Literary Theory and Practice*.

of them (six days a week, and virtually no summer vacation), and he went all the way through. And what he did there, day-after-day, year-after-year (though not hour-after-hour of course), was *study rhetoric*, both in Latin (he was drilled on Cicero[4]) and from those many English rhetoricians of his day. He must have completed thousands of drills (the *progymnasmata*) and mastered more than a hundred figures. At the end of the day rhetoric would have been hard-wired into his brain: he could not *not* have been a rhetorical master.[5]

This medieval-Renaissance tradition, however, was far from being about "*ornare*" only.[6] It was tuned also towards *effectiveness*: rhetoric as an instrumental, not a mimetic, art. At the beginning of his great work Aristotle defines "rhetoric" as "the faculty of observing in the particular case the available means of persuasion" (I.2). That means the verbal ("by words") *expression, transmission, or imposition of one's will upon another "by sweetness"* (the root of "persuasion") rather than by force or the threat of force. The practice of rhetoric may indeed be artful, but, before it becomes that, it is a faculty—a factory that makes or does like any other faculty but producing persuasion. The faculty comes with the species. We must rhetorize.

Six general items derive from this instrumental beginning and require special attention. 1. Three types of rhetoric exist: *forensic, deliberative*, and *epideictic*. These correspond to considerations of fact (what *is*, originally suitable to law courts), what to *do* about what is (often called policy, or "political," rhetoric because it urges a policy, or course of action), and *value* (what is the worth of what is, sometimes called ceremonial rhetoric, like a funeral oration). 2. Each of these types lends itself to different styles: the *plain*, the *intermediate*, and the *high* (the most florid, meaning much imagery and many attention-getting figures of speech and thought). 3. Each of these types also has its appropriate claims, or propositions, called respectively propositions of *fact, policy*, and *value*. Of course, in actual practice

---

4 The benchmark work on Shakespeare's schooling is T. W. Baldwin's *William Shakespeare's Small Latine and Lesse Greek)*, ch. XXXI-XXXVII. See also Jonathan Bate, *Soul of the Age: A Biography of the Mind of William Shakespeare*, 71-92. In his *Shakespeare and Classical Antiquity*, pp. 30-50 and *passim*, Colin Burrow disputes Baldwin's claims respecting the thoroughness of Shakespeare's grammar schooling, especially in rhetoric, but his argument seems a mere gesture.

5 Sister Miriam Joseph, *Shakespeare's Use of the Arts of Language, passim*.

6 Even as late as 1684, Samuel Butler could write in his *Hudibras*, "For all a rhetorician's rules/ Teach nothing but to name his tools." That is why the eighteenth- and nineteenth-century rhetorics, first from George Campbell and, later, from Richard Whately would be regarded as new: they went far beyond figures.

rhetoric is often less neat than this scheme suggests. That is certainly the case with Antony's funeral oration. 4. There are five parts, or canons, to rhetoric. The first is *Invention*, the discovery of ideas, material to amplify those ideas, and arguments and other devices to explain or support them. Second is *Disposition*, the arrangement of all the matter in its most understandable, interesting, and especially in its most persuasive form. Third is *Style*, the choice of signs and symbols (*i.e.* words, mostly) with which to express the matter. Fourth comes *Mastery*, or preparation for presentation; that is, practice, perhaps even memorization. The fifth step is *Presentation*.

Persuasion (*any* change in the listener) implies *proof.* Here the most important point is this one: proof is not that which necessarily establishes truth but that which establishes belief (that is, degrees of *probability*) or, in many cases, action. There are three types of proof: *logos* (logic appealing to the intellect), *ethos* (personal trust in the speaker) and *pathos* (the arousal and direction feelings, whether mild or strong). 6. Finally there is the *rhetorical situation.* This we have not met before. Authentic rhetoric arises in response to a need grounded in a combination of actual circumstances. That need is some exigency; for example, the ending of slavery. It is "an imperfection marked by urgency" and susceptible to correction by persuasion. This exigency occurs within an occasion, whether formal (like a wedding or the Fourth of July) or not (like a spontaneous rally, a domestic quarrel, or a death). The occasion includes *physical circumstances*, of course, but also its participants, especially the *audience* (which Aristotle sometimes refers to as the "judges"), the *speaker(s)* and his *purpose*, which may be honestly or dishonestly declared ("I come to bury Caesar not to praise him"), or entirely undeclared. Rhetorical situations do not last: if not acted upon the exigency triumphs.

That is an elevated view. At ground level are three particular parts of that larger landscape: *topoi, figures of speech,* and *enthymemes. Topoi* (or "places") are ways of thinking, or routes of inquiry (not exactly "topics" as we know them); definition is an example of a topic. *Figures of speech* are those combinations of language, images, and sounds that have so fascinated our ancient and medieval theorists (and our Will). Some tend towards mere *ornare* (*e.g.* alliteration), but the best known generally do not: metaphor, simile, personification, the rhetorical question. Moreover many others, such as *aporia, innuendo, aposiopesis,* and *paralepsis,* have their persuasive day as well (*i.e.* in the oration, anon).[7] They may gain their effects

---

7 Sister Mary Joseph and Gary Wills so ably describe and assess the figures in this oration that I am able to emphasize other tactics (though not to the complete neglect of some figures) and more encompassing strategies.

individually or cumulatively, often as patterns of language that are sometimes indiscernible to readers, viewers or listeners but somehow (as Vickers tells us Peacham has demonstrated) influential.[8]

For Aristotle, only examples and (especially) *enthymemes* can serve as proof. The latter are not merely shortened arguments, intellectual links connecting things in the world (evidence) to concepts in the mind (say, some conception of ambition), and thereby to particular conclusions. They can do that, but by nature they *imply*, drawing their premises from the audience's *own* underlying beliefs, whether true or false, bigoted or fair. Moreover, they can be drawn from all three types of proof and appeal to the whole person: will, emotion, intellect.[9]

2.

In fact Antony delivers three orations over the dead Caesar, not just the "friends, Romans, countrymen" one, which will be our subject. Moreover, a *fourth* funeral oration, over the corpse of his antagonist Brutus (V.5.68-75), nearly (but not quite) ends the play. That one is pitch-perfect in both fixing the essence of Brutus' character and enhancing Antony's; in victory he is his better self and vastly attractive as such. In a mere eight lines Antony assumes the right of proclamation and of judgment: it is his will. (The assumption, though, is mere presumption. An absurdly green Octavius has already contradicted the better general's tactical command, and at the very end his words are actions (V.5.76-81): Brutus will lie in state within the tent of greatest prestige, the young man's own. Caesar's will is secured.)

How different is this last oration from Antony's rhetorical opening (III.1.141-252), part deliberative, part epideictic—that first speech he delivers when, in the presence of the conspirators and knowing that his very life may hang in the balance, he first sees the remains of his mentor sliced to pieces, addresses the corpse (the figure known as apostrophe), then declares his friendship with the killers, soaking himself in Caesar's blood as he grasps arms with men he must already see as targets of his vengeance. Here is extraordinary self-possession. To be sure, the performance is not

---

8 Vickers: "No reader of [Peacham's *Garden of Eloquence*] could come away without seeing that the figures . . . have a great persuasive power." And Peacham is not alone. In his *On the Sublime Longinus* tells us, ". . . by some quality innate in them, the rhetorical figures reinforce the sublime, and in their turn derive a marvelous degree of support from it." Take that, Butler!

9 The very best online site for rhetoric that I know of is Gideon Burton's *Forest of Rhetoric* at <rhetoric.byu.edu>

impromptu; he had sent his servant ahead to feel out the mood and gain assurances. Yet it is remarkably disciplined. These two orations, the first and the last, are rather like bookends, the fake Antony and the good one holding in place the real Antony.

We begin to see *that* Antony in the second oration (III.1.254-275) over the corpse of Caesar; it is the fiercest *and follows almost immediately upon the first*. Antony, alone with the steeping, butchered body of his beloved friend and mentor, grieves over his loss, laments his own blood-soaked, self-saving duplicity of the first oration, and vows vengeance; again, this complex man is utterly himself. This speech is impromptu and Antony is quite overwrought, promising an absolute imposition of will (an agency central to any understanding of rhetoric and especially of this play); it strongly suggests the very great rhetorical ability he will marshal in the third, public, oration (III.2.75-263). Presently we will see an Antony who is much more than the athlete-soldier-playboy. Like Shakespeare, he has gone to school.[10] The result is an exertion of public rhetoric unexcelled in Shakespeare's work: Antony's astonishing rhetorical range at its apex.

Here, then, is a view of just how Antony managed his ascent, a rhetorical *explication de texte* in eight parts.[11] In a nutshell: he will make a sort of love to his listeners; not the sort that Dante had in mind, but certainly of a sort that Plato feared.

Exigency. The exigency Antony faces is intense and simple. After hearing Brutus, the populous now favors the conspirators and thus threatens both Antony's ambition and his life. Reducing the threat is insufficient; the will of the people must be reversed (actually uncommon in persuasion). All is at risk, *right now*. Somehow he must praise Caesar (and himself by association) *instead* of burying him *and* indict the conspirators, *but only by implication*. If Antony fails, the conspirators succeed: this speech, not the assassination, is the hinge upon which Western culture swings.

Situation. The restraints on Antony are appalling. The audience is a conventional, probably semi-literate, now-hostile (after Brutus's pedestrian prose speech), pliant mob. They will tolerate no bad-mouthing of the noble Brutus or any praise of Caesar who, so to speak, had it coming. The

---

10 According to Plutarch, in Greece, studying eloquence.

11 In his *The Death of Caesar* (2015), Barry Strauss convinces us that, in fact, Antony put on quite a show. Four of the five sources depict an Antony whose emotionalism went beyond even Will's depiction, with riots following. And yet the Bard seems to have gotten the patterns of persuasion—mollification, innuendo, veiled *ad hominem* and accusation, a re-definition of the act from patriotism to petulance, and the exaltation of Caesar—just right.

speech cannot be long (withal sustaining attention is no simple matter). And even were he permitted to praise Caesar or to criticize the conspirators to do so would be imprudent: the crowd might rip him to pieces. Moreover, the speech is occasioned by the bloody death of an admired national leader, one held in awe by many, so Antony is speaking at a funeral (permitting of no eulogy!) with violence in the air and Roman self-identity at stake. As is the case with angry mobs, the cause is taken personally, a temper of which Antony will make ironic and brilliant use. And, as is the case with angry mobs, thinking is not the fallback instrument of judgment; it will indeed flee "to brutish beasts." For all of Antony's insistence that his auditors are not "wood" or "stones," the irony is that he will chisel and carve upon them exactly as though they were. Finally, we must keep in our mind's eye the presence of Caesar's corpse, at first covered by his shredded toga and soaked in blood.

Enthymemes: *Implication* and *Definition*. *Implicatio* and *definitio*, along with *depictio*[12] (the English counterparts tell us what they are), together constitute the framework within which Antony deploys all other proofs; he has a high genius for rhetorical multi-tasking. His fundamental "*available means of persuasion*" are the larger *dispositions*, that is, the arrangement of proofs (as brief as the speech is, Antony never hastens an appeal), the *perceptions* and *emotions* of his listeners (along with that greatest prop in stage history), and *style* (word-choice, rhythms, tropes and figures-of-speech). For example, ponder the eventual impact of the *association* of verbal stimuli (to each other, to altered contexts, and to the conspirators) from this list of words: *friends, masters, honorable, noble; ambition, brute, brutish, Cassius, Casca, Brutus, traitors, mutiny; blocks, wood, stone; marred, wounds, sacred, blood, mouths, will, Caesar.* What do you see? What do you feel? Then: Whom to blame, to admire, to trust? And finally, What to do? As is the case with well-structured enthymemes, the listeners will fill in the blanks.

A Logic of Pathos. Antony's first, long oral paragraph is rather like an overture; the high drama will follow only after the most useful mood and expectations have been established. His first word, *friends*, is his first deception, as the next two, Romans and countrymen, are not. (He has reversed Brutus' order, where "lovers," that is, friends, follows 'Romans' and

---

12 There are many more fine sources for figures of speech and thought than those I've already cited; see especially Warren Taylor, *Tudor Figures of Rhetoric* (Whitewater, WI: The Language Press, 1972). The anonymous *Rhetorica ad herennium* (c. 90B.C.) is a wellspring, but my favorite is Willard R. Espy's take on Peacham, *The Garden of Eloquence: a Rhetorical Bestiary.*

'countrymen'.) They matter, of course, insofar as they establish a common *political* identity. *Friends*, however, is not political; it is *personal*. That first word marks Antony's first move in re-defining a political act—one remote to the mob, an abstraction relied upon by Brutus—into a concrete and personal one, an act quite understandable to every listener. This seed will bear fruit quickly, but not quite yet.

Antony's second line is his biggest lie: "I come to bury Caesar, not to praise him" is not only false, but exactly the opposite of what Antony must do. He will sustain Caesar's will precisely by praising Caesar—by implication, of course. But that, too, comes later. For now, the mob is reassured: Brutus will be neither maligned nor contradicted. Thus within two lines Antony has demonstrated restraint (establishing his personal proof), suggested an *alternative setting* for the assassination (personal rather than political), and insinuated a sphere of friendship that will include him, the crowd, and Caesar too—but not the conspirators.

His second move is brilliantly "invented" and executed. With his third and fourth lines—"The evil that men do lives after them,/ The good is oft interred with their bones"—Antony establishes an antithesis that invites thought. With an angry mob in front of him, and the dead body of all dead bodies behind, Antony first relies upon logic. To be sure, his is not the logic of a courtroom but of an address suited to an occasion (a funeral) respected by all; and given his restraints we know he can scarcely rebut, let alone accuse, Brutus and the others. So his case does not look like a case but rather like . . . *personal puzzlement*; the man is doing nothing more than trying to connect a few points: A, B, C, and D. The audience watches, and in watching is drawn to . . . participate.

The close friend of the deceased is sadly perplexed. In his perfectly legitimate grief, Antony is simply trying to find—meaning. But who wouldn't? After all, he is just like us. That is Point A. Point B will be a *cri de coeur* that would exact some meaning from this mystifying act. Exactly what meaning? Not the conspirators' motives, of course; Brutus has clarified that, and he must not be contradicted. Rather, Antony is wondering about the crowd, *his friends*. At the very end of the first oral paragraph, he turns away weeping: "My heart is in the coffin there with Caesar,/ And I must pause till it come back to me." But first he has *insinuated his frustration* and sadness by asking the crowd about the absence of theirs: "What cause withholds you then to mourn for him?/ O judgement thou hast fled to brutish beasts,/ And men have lost their reason!" Point C. Now, he seems to say, see me cry for a friend, a great man deserving tears, even if only those of a single mourner. How can we . . . *friends* . . . not be as one in our grief? Point D, and done.

A Logic of Ethos. At bottom, how does Antony make his connections? First we have an outright disjunction, a dilemma that argument must resolve: Caesar, he says, "was my friend, faithful and just to me"; yet "Brutus says, he was ambitious,/ And Brutus is an honorable man." That is, here am I, with my faithful and just friend; there is Brutus, claiming ambition drove my friend. Given Brutus' honor, this charge seems plausible. But what if the honorable man's conception of ambition is dubious? And if it is, would not then his honor also be dubious? So, Antony wonders: what must Brutus mean by "ambition"? After all, Caesar gave much of his ransom money to Rome; "when that the poor have cried, Caesar hath wept." "Was this ambition?" Do you all not believe it should be made of "sterner stuff"? Moreover, he turned down the crown three times—which you yourselves ("friends") did witness. Well then: there on the one hand is Brutus, whose honor compelled him to kill Caesar because of a (now-ambiguous) ambition; here on the other am I, Caesar's friend who, knowing better, must mourn for him. So while "men have lost their reason" and human judgment has gone to the dogs ("brutish beasts") I at least shall weep. I, who (just like you!) loves his friend, shall follow his heart "in the coffin there with Caesar."

Now, with the crowd no longer mumbling threats against Antony but wondering if he might not be right, he consolidates his gain. After referring to the crowd as his "masters" (the cynicism deepens), he resorts to the conditional tense, declaring that to stir them to "mutiny and rage" would wrong Brutus and Cassius—so he will not do so; instead he only insinuates those two violent states. There comes the *coup de grâce.* Antony draws a line: "I'd rather to choose/ to the wrong the dead, to wrong myself and you,/ Than I will wrong such honorable men"—the very same honorable men about whom he will presently wonder, "What private griefs they have, alas, I know not." Not political griefs, mind you, but *private*—that is, *personal*—ones.

Having thus *included* the crowd in the circle of friendship he adumbrated earlier, Antony has now *excluded* the conspirators from that circle: their act was not only not political but based upon "private" grievances. Do we suppose there is anyone in that audience who could not understand personal betrayal? Antony's argument against Caesar's ambition (*logos*—three pieces of evidence), his own personal standing as a man of the people along with Caesar (*ethos*), and the unease of intellectual doubt (without Caesar's ambition where lies the Brutus' honor?—more *logos*) are all in place: they need only be secured. There is no better way to achieve that than with a high tide of strong emotion. The time has come to recover Caesar: his body first, then his will.

Transition. ". . . Than I will wrong such honorable men./ But here's a parchment . . . " Perhaps Antony inhaled before that "but," though its abruptness suggests otherwise. And that abruptness suggests a question: if you are among the conspirators, and you are watching, do you intervene *right now*? For if you do not, then within fourteen words it will be too late: ". . . with the seal of Caesar;/ I found it in his closet; 'tis his will." You may not know it, of course, but right *here* the game is up. And all because you didn't act between the words "parchment" and "will." But how could you have? Antony's pace, his abruptness, made intervention virtually impossible. Now an epideictic speech (value, of Caesar) will become a forensic one (fact, why Caesar was butchered), and then—but only by implication—a deliberative one (policy, *i.e.* "mutiny" as the action to be taken).

After the hook of curiosity (why does Antony brandish a will? Of course Caesar would have a will. Something strange here . . .) comes the allure of greed. But first, since nothing is rushed that should not be, he implicitly compares the wounds to mouths ("the commons" would "kiss dead Caesar's wounds" (wounds as mouths, a recurring and powerful image which will bear much fruitful meaning later on), divinizes Caesar (who had "sacred blood"), and sanctifies him, describing his hair as a saintly relic (for which the commons would beg and leave as a "rich legacy" to be mentioned in "their [own!] wills"). He then joins the beloved to the crowd, who "are not wood . . . not stones, but men," by professing that they are Caesar's heirs!

The circle of Antony, Caesar and the mob draws close. And yet, Antony proclaims, he would not inflame the crowd: does he not have a bargain to keep? The conspirators are honorable, an epithet already fraught with ambiguity (if not outright irony) owing to the reasonableness of Antony, the apotheosis of Caesar to divine status, and, of course, the now-long-gone notion of Caesar's ambition. So Antony proceeds to . . . not read the will! Here organization disposition is all. He will use a rising pattern, winding up the audience as he approaches both climax and dénouement. Greed gets attention (a "takeaway," as marketers put it) but is not the stuff of strong passion. The time has come for drama at a high pitch.

"Set it Before Their Eyes"[13]: *Disposition.* Having reminded the crowd that they are not stones—an image that now is the seed of *a fortiori*[14] rea-

---

13 *Rhetoric*, II.20-22; also *Institutes*, 8.3.61-71.
14 Literally "with yet stronger [more probable] reason." *A fortiori* is a comparative mode of reasoning from relative probability; for example (as we shall see), if lifeless

soning to come later—Antony flatters the crowd by taking the precaution of asking their permission to descend to the body, to "show you him that made the will." But not yet. First he must associate the conspirators concretely with the horror-to-come. So Antony, without yet uncovering the body, shows the crowd Caesar's mantle, a special mantle worn by Caesar on one of his particularly heroic days; indeed, Antony remembers seeing—talk about friends!—the great man don the garment on that very day. (Who now will stop to do some fact-checking?) And so the ring of association—Rome (and its "friends"), Caesar, triumph, and Antony—is tightened. That other circle, too, is tightened; it consists of blood-encrusted, gaping rents in the garment and the name that goes with each (*e.g.* "see the rent the envious Casca made").

Of course, he saves the foulest for last and associates it with Brutus. Emboldened by the arousal of greed and by the incipient arousal of pity and horror, Antony now risks all and aims at full-blown wrath. "Brutus, as you know, was Caesar's angel," the friend of all friends, and so "this was the most unkindest cut of all," an act, not of political principle but of personal betrayal. After all, Caesar's blood was like someone at rest in his own home, expecting a friend and getting instead an "unkindly" knock. That is why ingratitude, not plunging knives, kills Caesar, "ingratitude, more strong than traitors' arms."

Traitors' arms: finally, an accusation. And if you were a conspirator standing by what could you do about this violation of Antony's agreement with you? But Antony does not pound the theme; rather he remains disciplined and patient. He amplifies its personal aspect with a wondrously sustained instance of periodic construction (when the point of a sentence is saved for the end, after a long cumulation of both meaning and rhythm): "Then burst his mighty heart [that's right: Caesar dies of a broken heart—but we're not done],/ And, in his mantle [how?] muffling up his face,/ [where?] Even at the base of Pompey's statue [*that* Pompey, the great adversary defeated by Caesar? How did it look?]/ Which all the while ran blood [alright: *what happened?*] great Caesar fell." "*Great.*" "*Caesar.*" "*Fell.*" A sentence that could have been a one-act play—"then burst his mighty heart and great Caesar fell"—becomes a self-contained, full-fledged, five-act tragedy.

"Set it Before Their Eyes": Pathos. The emotion builds, heading toward its release. With Caesar, says Antony, "Then I, and you, and all of us"—there's that circle again—"fell down,/ Whilst bloody treason flourished over us." There is that accusation again, treason to go with the al-

stones would rise in mutiny, what must living men do?

ready-planted *traitors,* which at the end of the paragraph will be repeated; and any part of the cat not yet out of the bag will have emerged. Now the crowd, like Antony earlier, takes the earlier hint and weeps, so Antony plays his ace, unrelentingly stirring to the highest pitch both pity and hor- ror: "Kind souls, what weep you when you but behold/ Our [*our!*] Caesar's vesture wounded?" You think the *wrapping* is obscene? Hah! "Look you here,/ Here is himself, marred as you see with traitors." If there is anything more horrible than the sight of a bloodied, butchered human corpse, it is the bloody, butchered human corpse of a great man, a benefactor, who has been ripped to shreds *by his dearest friend.*

It is time for a call to action, on which Antony will spend one more oral paragraph. Thereafter the oration will continue—after all, *he has not yet read the will*—but that is a coda designed to reinforce passion with greed, for Antony knows that strong passion comes and goes, but mostly it goes, whereas self-interest abides. For now he will launch into a great consolidation of proofs.

He begins by reinforcing the personal: "good friends, sweet friends," with a reference to the conspirators' "private [!] griefs"; and with that, mere implication has become full-blown irony. Between the two comes an iteration of both *honourable* and *mutiny,* the former as an ironic affir- mation, the latter spoken as though reluctantly, an option devoutly not to be wished. And *of course* Antony is both sincere and trustworthy, his ethos high, since he is "no orator, as Brutus is;/ But (as you know me all) a plain blunt man." That is, we all know, do we not, one of those tricks rhetoricians play? Antony, rather, will not "steal away your hearts," for he "has neither wit, nor words, nor worth"—notice (again) the cumu- lation (the polysyndeton of "nor"), at first alliterative, always rapid, be- yond dispute—"Action, nor utterance, nor the power of speech"—to do what?—why, "to stir men's blood." (Its stirring, let alone its spilling, is not on Antony's hands.) No; Antony speaks "right on," tells the crowd "that which you yourselves do know," as with the finest enthymemes, shows them "sweet Caesar's wounds," which are "poor poor dumb mouths," and "bid them speak for me." (Do we recall that very same oral imagery from his vow of vengeance when alone with the dead Caesar? We should.) He "sets it before their eyes."

And soon enough their ears. For if he were a rhetorician like Brutus, a crafty man who knew the tricks, then he would "ruffle up your spirits, and put a tongue"—can you hear the pandemonium?—"in every wound [all those mouths] of Caesar." And what then would happen, if Antony were Brutus and knew the tricks? Do recall Antony telling the crowd that they are *not* stones and recall the number of times *mutiny* has appeared. Now put them together for this master stroke of *a fortiori* reasoning: he "should put a tongue/ in every wound of Caesar, [to do what?] that should move/ The stones of Rome to rise and mutiny." That is what stones would do: no need to say what men must do. Then, after fourteen lines of reading the will (virtually an afterthought—Antony has to call back the mob and remind them of it), he has only to say, to himself, "Now let it work: Mischief [a wonderful personification], thou art afoot,/ Take thou what course thou wilt." And right there is the most telling of last words: another invocation of will. Antony has conversed publicly with his listeners, only to turn privately to his closest friend, Mischief, to whom he confides the truth.

3.

There we have him, Antony at his highest point, seeming the very embodiment of the great Julius's own volition. And here too we see the Bard, at his highest command of rhetorical thinking, the consummation of two thousand years of its intellectual history on which he had gone to school. "New" rhetorics—Geoffroi's newer than his predecessors', in the eighteenth century newer rhetorics than those of the sixteenth, in the nineteenth newer still, and since World War Two the newest of all, and all always modern—these keep coming; no matter its name the art is ever renascent. However, though cherry-picked insights from new, newer and newest rhetorics (from Kenneth Burke's dramatistic criticism, to Derrida's deconstructionism, with all varieties of cultural criticism in between) can sharpen *our* understanding of Shakespeare, none, I think, would have sharpened *his* of Antony.

Moreover, our Will knew, and Antony would learn, that there are severe limitations to the power of rhetoric, especially when it meets *force majeure* and a willful bloodline. When Quintilian told us that the orator is "the morally good man skilled in speaking," he did not mean mischief-makers! Nor, in this respect, was Shakespeare thinking of Quintilian. But he may have been thinking of Cicero, who in his *De inventione* had taught Will that wisdom without eloquence is flacid, but that eloquence without wisdom is dangerous. Alas, Cicero himself would learn that even wisdom *with* eloquence might not be enough. At the end of the day, he was murdered—his head and hands cut off and publicly displayed—for his final speeches, a series of attacks on Antony known as the Philippics; murdered, that is, because of his one true love, Dame Rhetoric.

TWELVE

YET MUCH MORE THAN "MERE"
Rhetoric Descendant

Thought and speech are inseparable from each other. . . . Call to mind . . . the Greek word which expresses this special prerogative of man over the feeble intelligence of the inferior animals. It is called Logos: what does Logos mean? It stands both for reason and for speech. . . . It means both at once: why? because really they cannot be divided—because they are in a true sense one. When we can separate light and illumination . . . the convex and the concave of a curve, then it will be possible for thought to tread speech under foot.

— Cardinal Newman, *The Idea of a University*

O NE ANCIENT GREEK speaker wanted to orate about public policy but could not keep the attention of his listeners. So he said, "There once were two travelers on their way down from Athens." These two men get into a nasty quarrel about a donkey, almost coming to blows. At that point in the tale, the speaker walked off the stage, only to have the audience call him back to finish the story. Instead he said, "Oh men of Athens, when I tell you the things which concern the salvation of your city you fall asleep. Yet when I tell you the story of two men and an ass, you are all ears!" His listeners needed a connection, and they needed this man to make it now.

That old Greek was right, of course. Rhetoric goes far beyond supplying immediate gratification. Regard two witnesses to *the efficacy of rhetoric in the making of culture*. The economist and philosopher Deirdre N. McCloskey (in *Bourgeois Design*) tells us that rhetoric, not capitalist innovation, led to the revolution of wealth in Europe two hundred years ago (and elsewhere more recently): people talking about themselves to each other in terms more promising, self-assured and entitled than had ever been the case. Their rhetoric changed their culture, which now came with expectations respecting comfort and wealth, and comfort and wealth followed. The lifelong diplomat Charles Hill, in *Grand Strategies: Literature, Statecraft, and World Order*, teaches us how Homer, Las Casas, Henry Adams, Nietzsche, Pope John Paul II, and some seventy other figures have through their rhetoric shaped the governance, relationships, social change, common practices, and the values of nation-states and their populations.

1.

That is the work of Queen of the Liberal Arts, and she had her court. Sister Miriam Joseph, in *The Trivium: The Liberal Arts of Logic, Grammar and Rhetoric* (originally intended as a *high school* textbook), describes it. She tells us that "in true liberal education . . . the essential activity of the student is to relate the facts learned into a unified, organic whole, to assimilate them as . . . the rose assimilates food from the soil and increases in size, vitality, and beauty." She is speaking particularly of the trivium (grammar, logic, and rhetoric). In one form or another this curriculum goes back at least to ancient Rome. (What Dorothy L. Sayers has called "The Lost Tools of Learning," a commanding system whereby people are "liberalized"—*i.e.* prepared intellectually to live their humanity fully and freely.)

As a formal academic discipline, rhetoric is the oldest of these three liberal arts. (At least, the textbooks by two Sicilians, Corax and Tisias, are the earliest on which we have any commentary.) Of course, like any queen rhetoric has been attacked, defended, and interpreted. Fenelon, in one of his *Dialogues of the Dead*, offers this between Demosthenes, the great speaker, and Cicero, the great theorist of rhetoric (though no mean lawyer). Demosthenes is the speaker:

"You turned your hearers' attention to your own person; I directed it solely to the subject on which I spoke. Your were admired by them; they forgot about me while they concentrated only on the resolution I sought them to reach. You provided them intellectual entertainment; I smote, I hurled, I dashed in pieces like a thunderbolt. When they had listened to you they cried: 'How finely he spoke!' When they had heard me they cried: 'Arise – to arms against Philip!'"

But in his *Preface to Paradise Lost* C. S. Lewis's offers a higher perspective:

> I do not think and no great civilization has ever thought that the art of the rhetorician is necessarily vile. It is in itself noble [and aims] at doing something to an audience. [It does so] by using language to control what already exists in our minds. . . . [wishing] to produce some practical resolve. . . . and it does this by calling passion to the aid of reason. The proper use is lawful and necessary because, as Aristotle points out, intellect of itself moves nothing: the transition from thinking to doing . . . needs to be assisted by appropriate states of feeling. Because the end of rhetoric is in the world of action the objects it deals with appear foreshortened and much of their reality is omitted. Very roughly, we might almost say that in Rhetoric imagination is present for the sake of passion and therefore in the long run for the sake of action.

This synthesizing and instrumental aspect of rhetoric—a practical engagement of the most important human faculties at once directed toward a particular end under particular circumstances—is why, for example, through that Age commonly known as Dark (before the rise of universities), this liberal art survived in monasteries and in courts, for example Charlemagne's in the ninth century (thanks to scholar-advisors like Alcuin.)

Yet if it survives today it is by stealth, as Speech Communication, so-called, or Basic Composition. To paraphrase C. S. Lewis from his *Abolition of Man*, we demand the function even though, lamentably, we have amputated the organ. No wonder that most of us heard (and chanted? some variation on the theme, "you aren't a teenager—you just don't understand." The collective noun may, of course, designate any group thought by the speaker to occupy ineffable status—we are the mystery; and the claim may vary among "don't," "can't," and "won't" (for the clueless listener's stance) and "understand," "see," and "know" (for the listener's sorry epistemological state of consciousness). The combinations certainly do not mean the same, and each may be true under certain circumstances.

As commonly uttered, however, the thought is usually false. Actually it is the *speaker* who [does/can/will] *not* [invite /permit/direct] the *listener* to [understand/see/know]. The status of the designated group is not, after all, ineffable, notwithstanding the sincerity of the speaker, whose actual purpose may be merely to ventilate emotion rather than to assert objective truth, but whose inarticulacy is palpable.

This tendency toward communicative skepticism is common both to public and private conversation and has the effect, not only of isolating persons (and thus communities), but of demoting speaker and listener alike to a posturing subperson. What is mistakenly labeled "autonomy"— the "freedom to be you and me," to feel strongly, to exhibit those feelings, and to expect others to trust them as much as you do—necessarily subverts political sovereignty, as implied by E. D. Hirsch's reasonable premise that underlies our national system of education in the first place. In his *Cultural Literacy* he tells us "that people in a democracy can be entrusted to decide all matters of importance for themselves because they can deliberate and communicate with one another . . . the [ground] for Martin Luther King's [vision] as well as for Thomas Jefferson's."

The implication is inescapable, and whatever we call this belief, it is not an expression of ideology. After discussing the traditional allusiveness, formal correctness, and eloquence of The Black Panther revolutionary newspaper, Hirsch concludes, "to be a conservative in the means of communication is the road to effectiveness in modern life, in whatever direction one wishes to be effective." Between the polity and the individual should hover a robust higher liberal learning, not what we now have, which is flaccid when not downright amorphous. The sorry irony is that this decline of rhetoric has accompanied and partly resulted from the rise of "rhetoric" as a devil-term and the demise of this queen of the liberal arts—the first and best rationale for ordered communication—as the hub of education.

C. S. Lewis has given us one take on rhetoric; here is another. It is a skill, largely verbal, social in application, instrumental, probabilistic, and occasional (that is, tied to the circumstances of particular occasions); its goal is persuasion and it encompasses theory, method, practice and product. Its art lies in the proper adjustment between speaker, audience, and subject matter. It is a permanent and ineluctable feature of everyone's interior landscape, "the *faculty*," as Aristotle put it, "of observing in the particular case the available means of persuasion." He could easily have begun his great book on the subject with the words "all humans by nature love to, and must, rhetorize." In short, rhetoric largely defines the species; to maximize this faculty is to maximize our humanity. It is at our core. Shorter still: *rhetoric is the antidote to discursive entropy.*

2.

But here is a symptomatic thought from Petrarch, the great human-ist who lived a generation after Dante. He was thoroughly schooled in rhetoric, wrote poems based on rhetorical principles, and was a prolific letter-writer. Is he here too typically cynical, and, if so, is it this cynicism that elicits attacks upon rhetoric?

> The first thought of a letter writer must be the person he is writing to; then he will know what to say, how to say it, and all the rest. We should write one way to a strong man, another to a sluggard; one way to a green youth, another to an elder who has fulfilled his life. . . . there is no more similitude of minds than of faces . . . [and even] one mind is not to be fed on the same literary style. So the writer has a double task: to envision the person he is writing to, and then the state of mind in which the recipient will read what he proposes to write. . . . I have been forced into many contradictions with myself.

Socrates knew this nearly twenty-five hundred years ago when he (and Plato) contended with the Sophists. Their regimen was intended for aristocratic youth who would provide civil leadership, and it was tough. Students would show up at daylight and behold a master whose visage was "grim and fierce" (according to Xenophon) and whose tools included a leather strap and a striking cane (as well as a covering for his bald head.) The Sophists softened this tradition for older students and introduced writing, specifically the writing of speeches. These teachers were traveling pedagogues who took fees in exchange for their instruction.

Even today, much controversy rages over the good or ill done by the Sophists. Quite reflexively we tend to follow Socrates, who seems to have despised them for their putative relativism, their amorality, and for their enormous influence: we still label questionable reasoning "sophistry." Here is a descriptive exchange from Robert Pirsig's *Zen and the Art of Motorcycle Maintenance*:

> "Did I ever talk about an individual named Phaedrus?"
> "No."
> "Who was he?" Gennie asks.
> "He was an ancient Greek . . . a rhetorician . . . a 'composition

major' of his time. He was one of those present when reason was being invented."

"You've never talked about that, I don't think."

"That must come later. The rhetoricians of ancient Greece were the first teachers in the history of the Western world. Plato vilified them in all his works to grind an axe of his own and since what we know about them is almost entirely from Plato they're unique in that they've stood condemned throughout history without ever having their side of the story told."

Indeed, many regard their teaching as fertile ground for theories of liberating rhetoric, decision-making, and the building of character that emerges from having to make hard choices.

Now, any list of Sophists is highly variable but would ordinarily include Protagoras (he of "man is the measure of all things"), Gorgias, Prodicus and Hippias, and perhaps Thrasymachus, Critias, and Antiphon. But here we have a complication: the great (pre-Platonic) comic playwright Aristophanes, in his *Clouds*, lampoons Socrates as a Sophist!

Socrates picked on the sophists primarily because the one subject the teaching of which was sure to earn a Sophist a good living was rhetoric (which could teach both virtue and eloquence when taught well, for example by Isocrates). They used older literature, including poetry and speeches, as the basis of exercises, thus transmitting Greek culture. But they also encouraged speculative thinking. It was the hyper-versatile Hippias who emphasized the difference between nature and convention and encouraged his students to enhance themselves simply by altering their choice of convention—as the terrifying Callicles (another Sophist) proclaims as his project in Plato's *Gorgias* when he implicitly threatens Socrates with death for his verbal and mental trickery. (He would make good on that threat.) And it was Protagoras who would say, "In respect to the gods, I am unable to know either that they are or that they are not, for there are many obstacles to such knowledge, above all the obscurity of the matter and the life of man, in that it is so short."

We should not be surprised that Socrates was accused of corrupting the youth of Athens, who might, owing to Socrates, think themselves wiser than the laws and who fail in proper respect of their seniors. The great rhetorical scholar Everett Lee Hunt reminds us that, "the popular distrust of the Sophists was not so much that, as rhetoricians, they were different from Socrates and Plato, but that, as philosophers, they were so much like them."

It is instructive to re-visit one Sophist in particular, the aforenamed Isocrates, nearly a generation younger than Socrates. The latter was intensely curious about the newcomer who wrote speeches for others but who did not found a school or himself give public speeches. Apparently the older man was both impressed and flummoxed. (Noteworthy is the regard in which Isocrates held Socrates: it was not high, for to the younger man, the older did indeed seem to be an idle philosophical speculator, not unlike those Sophists who disregarded truth for the mere sake of the game.) Like the Sophists, Isocrates taught rhetoric; unlike them he did not teach it only as a technique for gaining immediate advantage.

Rather he counseled thorough knowledge: of subject, audience, and of his instrument—of their "fitness for the occasion." Though he charged for his services, he was not among the filthy rich Sophists who milked the aristocracy in exchange for instructing their progeny. The effects of his training, he argued, were increased wisdom, civic participation, and the development of sound leadership; in short, he taught that rhetorical training develops character. In his *Antidosis*, he writes:

> But I do hold that people can become better and worthier if they conceive an ambition to speak well, if they become possessed of the desire to be able to persuade their hearers. . . . It follows, then, that the power to speak well and think right will reward the man who approaches the art of discourse with love of wisdom and love of honour.

Those great professors from the Cornell School had read their Isocrates.

In his late dialogue *Phaedrus*, Plato attempts to redeem rhetoric from the near-total condemnation of it in his *Gorgias*, but it remains a close, demanding call. The speaker must know "the truth of the several particulars of which he is writing" and to "define them as they are," and then "to divide them until they can no longer be divided." Later Socrates displays his gifts for imagery, his intellectual scope and his poetic (he would say religious) vision: one must be a lover of words, he says, but must love souls more, for after one's own soul, nothing matters more than the soul of the beloved.

> . . . and until in like manner he is able to discern the nature of the soul, and discover the different modes of discourse which are adapted to different natures, and to arrange and dispose them in such a way that the simple form of speech may be addressed to the simpler nature, and the complex and composite

to the more complex nature—until he has accomplished all this, he will be unable to handle arguments according to rules of art. . . .

Those requirements leave one breathless. In fact, they seem to me to be downright Isocratean, and that is no coincidence.

Socrates notes that Isocrates and the young Phaedrus are contemporaries and friends. "How shall we describe [Isocrates]?" asks Socrates. Phaedrus simply calls him "the fair" and asks what message Socrates might care to send to him. "He has a genius which soars," answers Socrates, continuing, "he will marvelously improve as he grows older, and . . . all former rhetoricians will be as children in comparison to him." And then he grants the ultimate compliment: "*there is in him a divine inspiration*." Many readers are struck by the intimacy of this dialogue: two people fully present to each other, no onlookers, much self-revelation.

Of course, conversation was Socrates' meat. He didn't "publish," not even by the means available to Greeks of his day; in fact, he wrote almost nothing. What he did, though, was converse. My favorite passage in all Plato's renderings of the master comes near the very end of *The Apology*, after Socrates has been condemned to death by the Council of Five Hundred (by a mere thirty votes). He says we should not fear death because we don't know what it promises; but as for himself, he hopes for . . more conversation, with Odysseus, Sisyphus, "or numberless others"! He knew what one scholar has re-taught us. Very early in his *Comparative Rhetoric*, George A. Kennedy declares that rhetoric has "a place in nature. . . . an essence or reality . . . that is a form of mental and emotional energy." In other words, even if Socrates could help himself, he would not: too much good rhetoric to look forward to in the next life!

3.

Where is rhetoric now? Entropy in higher learning has been much documented of late. Put aside the behemoth of fiscal depravity: moral and intellectual relativism, the want of intellectual authority properly exercised (a confusion of *magisterium* with *imperium*), trivial utilitarianism, radical subjectivism, and emotional hedonism have not only brought standards of structure and rigor into disarray, but have worn out the very idea of "standards," except as a platitude. Educationalists now favor "outcomes." That is, we are no longer asked what we teach, or even why, but what will be the use of it. (And woe be to the professor who answers along the lines of, "to prepare my students to live the life of free people, rather than as slaves to their bellies.") An aspect of rhetoric is instrumental, so I am unchallenged by the demand. Rhetoric, though, is much more than an instrument of practical action.

In that masterpiece of social criticism, *The Culture of Narcissism,* Christopher Lasch wrote:

> . . . no aspect of contemporary thought has proved immune to educationalization. The university has boiled all experience down into "courses" of study—a culinary image appropriate to the underlying ideal of enlightened consumption. . . . Doing so, however, compounds its intellectual failures—notwithstanding its claim to prepare students for life.

Under such circumstances how can pluralism—*unfragmented* diversity—flourish? Wayne Booth (in *Now Don't Try to Reason with Me*) argues that we are a nonpublic because standards of reasoned discourse have virtually disappeared and that we have not noticed. "Every man in this newly leveled egalopolis is entitled to his own brand of nonsense, and woe to the elitist who demands evidence." And the philosopher and sociologist of religion Martin Marty (in "A Task for Pluralists: Promote Cohesion") argues similarly: fragmentation militates against pluralism, which has no chance in the absence of "cohesive sentiment" based upon shareable conversation, including the ability *"to argue more intelligently"* than we presently do, the teaching of which is a task perfectly suited to rhetoric.

This suitability is especially so because of its first canon, *invention,* that is, the discovery and arrangement of arguments. Formally the study of it begins with six works by Aristotle grouped together under the rubric *Organon.* Cicero wrote the influential and still-useful *de Topica* and *De inventione.* Peter Ramus writes his *Dialectic* in Paris in 1576. Not long before The Great War, Cornell University—with men like Winans, Wichelns, Howell, Gilman, Wallace, and Bryant—revived the tradition, after it had ossified into mere elocution, by re-uniting conceptual and stylistic rhetoric.

Such a rhetorical recovery is especially desirable because rhetoric reintroduces the person, and thus accountability, since the prototype of all human communication is direct oral communication: that old-time same-time face-to-face religion. "Personal presence is itself symbolic," Carroll C. Arnold (a formidable contemporary rhetorician) reminds us in "Oral Rhetoric, Rhetoric, and Literature." It represents the speaker's entire "physical and psychological organization. . . . A self that is not an abstraction but has a body supportively authorizing each signification."

This reintroduced self brings with it an inherent organizing ability. Richard McKeon (in *Rhetoric: Essays in Invention and Discovery*) calls it architectonic: capable of "structuring all principles and products of knowing, doing, and making. If rhetoric is to be used to contribute to the formation of . . . the modern world, it should function . . . in the resolution of new problems and architectonically in the formation of new [genuinely pluralistic] communities." Chaim Perelman, in his *The New Rhetoric*, argues that because "rhetoric covers the vast field of nonformalized thought we can . . . speak of the 'realm of rhetoric' . . . the once and future queen of the human [arts]."

If the environment of liberal learning was once centrally nourished by this art, then higher learning ought to be where rhetoric once again abides, especially since the liberal arts are the arts of language, opinion, and action and thus "provide the laws of thought and expression, induction and deduction, community and communication" (McKeon again). Perhaps this has been put most succinctly by Donald C. Bryant, one of the greatest twentieth century rhetoricians, in "Rhetoric: Its Function and Scope": "Rhetoric is the organon of the liberal studies, the formulation of the principles through which the educated person . . . attains effectiveness in society. A complete rhetoric is a structure for the wholeness of the effective person, the aim of general education." And it is that sort of education that underlies all knowledge, provides the means of communication and bases of community to all people, especially in a democracy conceived of as using reason to come to agreement by way of rational discussion.

It can be no coincidence that, as rhetoric has declined as a discipline, the meretricious practice of rhetoric has inclined sharply. We do indeed live in a "rhetorical age, if we mean by that . . . an age in which men try to change each other's minds without giving good reasons," says Booth. He continues:

> I know of no past culture where power was so persistently thought of as power to manipulate men's minds . . . where the truth of propositions was so persistently judged by whether this or that group accepts them . . . where, finally, educational goals and methods were so persistently reduced to the notion of conditioning or of imposing already formed ideas or practices upon infinitely malleable material.

Thus ought we to welcome a revival of interest in rhetoric, for without such formal instruction, whole precincts of human action—ethics, psychology, politics, and pedagogy—are disconnected from lives as they are actually lived. Booth again:

> to engage with one's fellow men in acts of mutual persuasion is . . . noble . . . when it becomes mutual inquiry. Indeed none of the corruptions found in our rhetorical time would even be possible in a society which had not also laid itself open to the great virtues of moral and intellectual suasion when properly used. (*Now Don't Try . . .*)

In short, any "great conversation" is required for truly dysentropic pluralism, and that requires rhetorical learning, in the academy to be sure, but anywhere else it might fit.

4.

Near the end of *Zen and the Art of Motorcycle Maintenance*, Pirsig reminds us of an Ancient Greek distinction between mythos, the sum total of pre-logos narrative, song and custom, on the one hand, and, on the other, yet another meaning of logos, "the sum total of our rational understanding of the world." We have inherited that powerful distinction, a liberation of logos that is also a sort of amputation. But what we must recall, Pirsig teaches, is that *mythos* gives rise to *logos*, so that to reject our *mythos* is to be "insane." Our rationality "is shaped" by our *mythos,* just as a tree is shaped by its roots and the soil into which they thrust themselves. "What keeps the world from reverting to the Neanderthal with each generation" he says, "is the continuing, ongoing *mythos*, transformed into *logos* but still *mythos,* the huge body of common knowledge that unites our minds as cells are united in the body of man."

And then there is love. The goddess Peitho (literally, "I believe" in Greek) is the goddess of rhetoric, and she is most often found in the company of Aphrodite herself. In his *Convivio* Dante routinely Christianizes the pair, confirming that together they occupy the third of the heavenly spheres. Moreover, Walker Percy, the novelist writing as a semiotician, brings Love and Word down to earth in his *Message in the Bottle*:

> [E]xistentialists have taught us that what man is cannot be grasped by the science of man. The case is rather that man's science is one of the things that man does, a mode of existence. Another mode is speech. Man is not merely a higher organism

responding to and controlling his environment. He is . . . that being in the world whose calling it is to find a name for Being, to give testimony to it, and to provide for it a clearing.

—as Richard Weaver has it, "the central idea is that all speech . . . is a form of eros."

He continues, "so rhetoric at its truest seeks to perfect persons by showing them better versions of themselves . . . links extending up toward the ideal" without any feeling for which puts a man "truly outside the communion of minds." He then suggests what I take to be the goal, not merely of Higher but of the Highest Education: "Rhetoric appears, finally, as a means by which the impulse of the soul to be ever moving is redeemed. . . . With that truth the rhetorician will always be brought face to face as soon as he ventures beyond the consideration of mere artifice and device."

There is our goal: to cultivate *arête*—excellence—in the best people possible and to help them to maximize their humanity. An elitist goal: the training of people capable and willing, not only of giving and of demanding "good reasons," but of establishing whole regions of rhetoric, that is, of cultures—recalling McCloskey and Hill—for that is what *Mythos* is. In that light we ought to restore the view of rhetoric—the manifestation of our share of the *Logos* in our continuing conversations—as the medium of cultural transmission, abiding from age to age, from way back when to the here and now and on to the there and then.

THIRTEEN

C. S. LEWIS'S QUANTUM CHURCH
An Uneasy Meditation

QUANTUM THEORY tells us that an electron may be both a particle and a wave (or a "probability distribution"), and that it is unknowable in several of its aspects. For example, at any given moment we simply do not know where it is, as opposed to where it probably is. That is why it may seem to be in two places at once: there is an equal probability of it being in both places. The particle does not exactly travel from one orbit about its nucleus to another; it does not even jump. It simply disappears from here and reappears . . . there. More vexing still, the theory tells us that merely observing the phenomenon changes it. The particle actually cannot be said to be in a particular orbit until we make the measurement, which influences the quantity measured. And finally (for our purposes) we are told that Uncertainty reigns: we may not know both location and momentum of a particle simultaneously.[1]

When he was thirty-four years old and not quite two years a Christian, Lewis published his first book that was not poetry. Tellingly, this book is also Lewis' first published Christian work. More tellingly still, it took him all of two weeks to write: it was nothing less than an effusion—a complex eruption wrought tightly of imagination, reason and purpose. And it is Lewis' rhetorical Template.

---

1 Any number of sources popularly describe Quantum Theory, the most recent being Jeremy Bernstein, *Quantum Leaps* (Cambridge: Harvard UP, 2009). Generally useful is Robert M. Hazen and James Trefil, *Science Matters: Achieving Scientific Literacy* (New York: Anchor Books, 1990) 65-74. Of great usefulness for my statement here was my colleague Samuel Borenstein, sometime of CERN and Brookhaven and Professor of Physics at York College (CUNY).

The Pilgrim's Regress[2] is a Dream Vision (a prototypically medieval form), as is his *The Great Divorce*, arriving nearly a dozen years later. It is autobiographical, a mode Lewis would virtually never abandon: we recall parts of the Narniad (*e.g.* Digory having a deathly ill mother), *Surprised by Joy, Till We Have Faces, A Grief Observed*, even *Letters to Malcolm*, any number of poems (some from the *Regress* itself), and very many letters. Of course the *Regress* is polemical, and philosophically so (Lewis first trained in and taught philosophy). He takes on Fascism, Freud, Communism, T. S. Eliot, Irving Babbitt, Hedonism, the English class structure . . . there seems no end to his targets. The same was true throughout his life, from literary to social and cultural controversies. And then there is *Sehnsucht*, which from the *Regress* on remained what Lewis himself called the heart of the story of his spiritual life. Moreover, throughout both book and life there is that rich interaction of Reason and Imagination. Lewis' argumentative power and dexterity are incarnated vividly, and Lewis Dialecticus is born-in-full. In short, and most tellingly of all, in one way or another *Pilgrim's Regress* tells us who he was from the beginning and therefore presages the lineaments of nearly everything else he would write: mood, motifs, themes and forms.

Lewis' depiction of the Church in this paradigmatic effulgence is no exception. Alas, he did not trouble himself greatly over a conception of "church." And yet—right from the beginning—there she is, unostentatious, but no mere scenic touch. Mother Kirk rocks away at the very edge of the Canyon (at the depths of which lies baptism), dispensing her guidance.[3] She both precedes and occasions John's encounter with the Man. Though modest, she is dispositive—commanding, magisterial, utterly reliable. For example, she saves John by instructing him to take off his clothes, to dive deeply (explaining how one dives), and to find a narrow, frightening tunnel which, if negotiated, will bring him across the river. He obeys. In short, the success of John's sort of journey depends upon his meeting and heeding Mother Kirk. Furthermore, John will do himself no good by searching for another Mother Kirk; she is not one among several to be sampled. And yet she—Lewis' conception of the Church—remains ambiguous, like an electron in Quantum theory, marked by uncertainty and the cause of uncertainty in others. Wherefore this Mother Kirk?

She simply flummoxes some scholars, like Alan Jacobs in his *The*

---

2 C. S. Lewis, *The Pilgrim's Regress: An Allegorical Apology for Christianity, Reason and Romanticism* (Grand Rapids: Wm. B. Eerdmans Publishing Company, 1992).
3 *Ibid.*, 69-75.

Narnian: the Life and Imagination of C. S. Lewis.[4] Jacobs writes, "[C]learly Lewis meant for [Mother Kirk] to represent orthodox Christianity in any or all of its forms'; but he offers no argument for that "clearly," and his "orthodoxy" is undefined. Perhaps unconvinced himself, he repeats the claim on the very next page, but this time with a difference (emphasis mine): "the *general* Christian orthodoxy represented by Mother Kirk." Here, *specific* orthodoxies go unmentioned, as though Jacobs expects his readers to know what he means. He regards Mother Kirk as a first effort by Lewis to forge a "transdenominational orthodoxy" (there is that word again, again tilted). I make no comment on the number of denominations to be transcended but do note that any transcendence contradicts Jacobs' final conclusion that, on etymological grounds, Mother Kirk is (as Lewis had been taught to be, Jacobs implies) really Presbyterian.

Doris Myers is another scholar who accepts the challenge, though she reads it quite differently than does Jacobs. Early in her book, *C. S. Lewis in Context,*[5] she writes of *Regress*, "in fact, [Lewis] has such a fine eye for twentieth-century follies that *The Pilgrim's Regress*, rather than the Cambridge Inaugural Address, should have been entitled '*De Descriptione Temporum.*'" In that light, she does not equivocate on the meaning of Mother Kirk. Myers astutely notes her dress, the resolute span and pace of her stride (she will not hurry to keep up with John: the Spirit of the Age is not hers to pursue), her reasonableness and her wisdom. Although Myers allows that Lewis's "tribute to the Virgin Mary falls short of majesty," she does acknowledge the tribute. Withal, Myers, noting that Kirk "ought to suggest . . . [a] perhaps Protestant church," concludes that when all the elements "are combined it is easy to conclude that Mother Kirk symbolizes Roman Catholicism rather than 'Mere Christianity.'"

With his *Apostle to the Skeptics* in the late forties,[6] Chad Walsh was the first major commentator on Lewis. Thirty years later he gave us *The Literary Legacy of C. S. Lewis.*[7] In his attempt to address the question of Mother Kirk's identity, he anticipates Myers by citing another scholar, whose conclusion about Mother Kirk is (I think) as satisfying as Lewis permits. "Gunnar Urang's excellent short treatment of the book," writes

4 Alan Jacobs, *The Narnian: the Life and Imagination of C. S. Lewis* (San Francisco: HarperSanFrancisco, 2005), 158.

5 Doris Myers, *C. S. Lewis in Context* (Kent: Kent State UP, 1994), *passim* 15-23.

6 Chad Walsh, *C. S. Lewis: Apostle to the Skeptics* (New York: The Macmillan Company, 1949).

7 Chad Walsh, *The Literary Legacy of C. S. Lewis* (New York: Harcourt Brace Jovanovich, 1979).

Walsh, "explains [the differences between Bunyan's book and Lewis']." He then quotes Urang's *Shadows of Heaven*:

> Bunyan's concern is with the sense of moral guilt and helpless-
> ness and the need for forgiveness and power; and the means
> for this are all religious, consisting of the Bible, preaching and
> teaching, prayer, and Christian companionship. C. S. Lewis,
> however, stands in the Catholic tradition. Created nature can
> enlist the interest of the natural man in a way that is not nec-
> essarily idolatrous but potentially gracious. Supernatural grace
> must supervene, however, to reveal the true meaning of the
> desire and to reorient it.[8]

In light of Jacobs, Myers and Urang, I offer a mental experiment. Mother Kirk's uniqueness and indispensability are among the reasons (along with the American publisher of *Pilgrim's Regress* being Sheed and Ward, a Catholic house[9]) that some reviewers assumed the author was a Catholic. I pose the following unasked (I hope not rude) question: How, and how differently, would Protestant (and Eastern) admirers of Lewis regard him had he (say, in the late forties) gone to Rome but his work remained unchanged even in its jots and tittles? I wonder if the reader will agree with my answer. I believe Lewis' apologetic standing and influ-ence would have declined pronouncedly. Book-sales would be lower, the amount of secondary scholarship paltry, documentaries mostly unmade. His adversaries would be fewer and less passionate, his great influence hav-ing dissipated. A Catholic Lewis—let alone a Lewis Catholic convert—would have prompted a divide symmetrical to that both embodied and provoked by Mother Kirk.

In his *C. S. Lewis and the Catholic Church*[10] Joseph Pearce cites a revealing exchange. Two weeks after Lewis' death, Fr. Guy Brinkworth discussed in *The Tablet* an exchange of letters with Lewis from the nine-teen-forties. "In the letters I received from him," wrote Brinkworth, "he time and time again asked specifically for prayers that God might give him 'the light and grace to make the final gesture.' He even went so far as to ask

---

8 Gunnar Urang, *Shadows of Heaven: Religion and Fantasy in the Writing of C. S. Lewis, Charles Williams, and J. R. R. Tolkien* (London: Student Christian Movement Press, 1971), 8.

9 *The Downside Review*, 54 (January, 1936), 138-39.

10 Joseph Pearce, *C. S. Lewis and the Catholic Church* (Francisco: Ignatius Press, 2003), 148.

in a postscript to one of his letters for 'prayers that the prejudices instilled in me by an Ulster nurse might be overcome.'" Books by Lyle Dorsett (*Seeking the Secret Place: the Spiritual Formation of C. S. Lewis*[11]) and Christopher Derrick (*C. S. Lewis and the Church of Rome*[12]), as well as a number of biographies, document Lewis's Catholic beliefs and practices: meatless Fridays; belief in the efficacy of, and regularly practiced, auricular confession; belief in the Real Presence and the taking of Holy Communion frequently within the Anglican Church; belief in the Apostolic Succession and in the efficacy of prayers for the dead. He believed in the ordained priesthood of Canterbury, of Rome, and of the East, and firmly opposed the ordination of women to the priesthood. Most of these beliefs and practices separately are not within lightyears of Protestantism; as a cluster they are in a galaxy far, far away.

Most revealing, though, of Lewis' Catholic dispensation is his disregard of Article XXII of the Thirty-Nine Articles of the Anglican confession. It reads:

XXII. Of Purgatory. The Romish Doctrine concerning Purgatory, Pardons, Worshipping and Adoration, as well of Images as of Relics, and also Invocation of Saints, is a fond thing, vainly invented, and grounded upon no warranty of Scripture, but rather repugnant to the Word of God.

On 1 April 1952, Lewis writes of his late and beloved friend, the novelist, critic, poet and lay theologian Charles Williams, "I do miss him. But what strikes me even more is the sense that he is already helping me more from where he is than he would do on earth."[13] *From where he is.* Lewis does not say *Heaven.* In other words, a soul bound for sainthood (all the souls in Heaven are saints) is . . . intervening (just as the dead Jack intervened when he appeared in the sitting room of J.B. Phillips to lift the latter's spirits[14]). The Communion of Saints not only compels us to pray for the dead but permits the dead to help us. We see this belief in *Letters*

11 Lyle Dorsett, *Seeking the Secret Place: the Spiritual Formation of C. S. Lewis* (Grand Rapids: Brazos. Press, 2004).

12 Christopher Derrick, *C. S. Lewis and the Church of Rome* (San Francisco: Ignatius Press, 1981). Also see John Randolph Willis, S.J., *Pleasures Forevermore: The Theology of C. S. Lewis* (Chicago: Loyola UP, 1983).

13 Walter Hooper, ed., *C. S. Lewis: Collected Letters* (London: HarperCollins, vol. I-III, 2000, 2004, 2006). All references to Lewis letters are from Hooper's edition.

14 J. B. Phillips, *Ring of Truth, a Translator's Testimony* (New York: The Macmillan Co., 1967), 117.

to Malcolm, of course, as "Lenten lands." But we see it, too, in T*he Screw-tape Letters* (Letter XXXI). Not only is the Patient not finally saved by his baptism alone, but after his death (saved indeed, but by a close call—the patient was subject to temptation until the very end, when death, as is so often the case in Lewis, intervened) he is due a good "scrubbing."

The possibility, then, of Lewis having become a Catholic was palpable. In fact, maybe the question should be, Why didn't he? Surely the inventory above shows that he could not have been, say, a Baptist, or even a Presbyterian. I know there is a small bookshelf of answers to the question. Mine is this: for reasons having nothing to do with intelligence or rationality—but everything to do with the interanimation of certain shortcomings of character ("prejudices instilled") and temperament (more anon), and, as Lewis saw it (correctly, I think), the constraints of his vocation—*he simply could not*. Mother Kirk was as troubling to Lewis as she is to us.

Lewis scarcely touches upon the Catholic Question. A passage published during his lifetime in *Surprised by Joy*[15] is brief but suggestive, revealing a conventional (and largely unrelenting) anti-Catholic Ulster upbringing to last a lifetime. Notwithstanding Lewis' many sympathetic words for Catholicism and his close friendship with Catholics, his great friend Tolkien, among others, saw the bigotry in the middle-aged Lewis.[16] It marked his character. In his biography of Lewis, A.N. Wilson reminds us that his nanny Lizzie would say, "'Now mind out there, Master Jacks . . . and keep your feet out of he puddles. Look at it there, all full of dirty wee popes.'. . . A 'wee pope' in Lizzie's vocabulary meant anything dirty or distasteful. 'Pope' was thereafter after associated with dirty puddles."[17]

A more ample and disinterested discussion of Protestant and Catholic differences than the one in *Surprised by Joy* is the essay "Christian Reunion" (unpublished during his lifetime). Here Lewis is eminently even-handed, clearing away anachronistic under-brush ("whatever the barrier . . . it is no longer a barrier of candles: whatever the fog, is not a fog of incense"), describing straw men on both sides (dismissing the Faith-Works controversy in a single paragraph!), and summarizing the view each has of the other in terms difficult to quarrel with. For a Catholic, being a Protestant is rather like agreeing, not with a debater but with a debating society; the difficulty of Catholicism for a Protestant is the requirement that he "accept in ad-

---

15 C. S. Lewis, *Surprised by Joy: the Shape of My Early Life* (New York: Harcourt, Brace & World, 1955), 216.

16 JRRT to Christopher Tolkien, 6 Oct. 44 , in *The Letters of J. R. R. Tolkien*, ed. Humphrey Carpenter (Boston: Houghton Mifflin, 1981), 96.

17 A. N. Wilson, *C. S. Lewis: A Biography* (New York: Fawcett Columbine, 1990), 9.

vance any doctrine. . . . It is like being asked to agree not only to what a man has said but to what he's going to say."[18]

> To you the real vice of Protestantism is the formless drift which seems unable to retain the Catholic truths, which loses them one by one and ends in 'modernism' which cannot be classified as Christian by any tolerable stretch of the word. To us the terrible thing about Rome is the recklessness (as we hold) with which she has added to the *depositum fidei*. . . . You see in Protestantism the Faith dying out in a desert: we see in Rome the Faith smothered in a jungle.

Any facile dismissal of the entanglement of culture (candles and incense) and theology strikes me as disingenuous: Lewis knew better. How children are schooled in their faith—including opposition to, and the characterizing of, competing options—is often dispositive; barriers are built, tics affixed, loyalties established. Lewis' reference to his own upbringing admits as much, but is as casual and as quick—as trivializing—as are the dismissive few lines of the essay. In both the essay and the autobiography Lewis confesses a truth (both general and personal) but will not dwell upon it. He would regard it as inconsiderable. But it is a ruse: a truth hiding in plain sight.

Withal in the essay, Lewis has gamely described the chasm, saying further, "I know no way of bridging this gulf." He has brought clarity, if not resolution: a standard Lewisian practice. There are, however, four items of interest in the essay lying beyond its central pool of light. The first is Lewis' self-identification; in referring to Protestants and Protestantism he uses the pronouns "we" and "our." Second, he identifies the single, major gravamen dividing Protestants and Catholics as "the seat and nature of doctrinal Authority." Third, he is protesting against the Catholic tendency of adding on (he doesn't like agreeing with what "a man is going to say"). And finally this: "My only function as *Christian writer* [my emphasis] is to preach 'Mere Christianity.' Any success that has been given to me has, I believe, been due to my strict observance of those limits. By attempting to do otherwise I should only add one more recruit . . . to the ranks of controversialists. After that I should be no more use to anyone." (As late as 11 February 1960, he wrote in a letter to Michael Edwards: "I have never said anything in print [on 'interdenominational' questions] except that I

---

18 "Christian Reunion," in *C. S. Lewis, 'Christian Reunion' and Other Essays*, ed. Walter Hooper (London: Collins Fount Paperbacks, 1990).

am not offering guidance on it. . . . Whatever utility I have as a defender of 'mere' Christianity would be lost if I did, and I should become only one more participant in the dogfight.")

Each of these four items warrants a distinct discussion beyond the scope of this essay, but I will presume to ask two questions relating to them. Was his dear friend Neville Coghill correct? He saw in Lewis "an indefeasible core of Protestant certainties, the certainties of a simple, unchanging, entrenched ethic that knows how to distinguish, unarguably, between Right and Wrong, Natural and Unnatural, High and Low, Black and White, with a committed force, an ethic on which his ramified and seemingly conciliatory structures of argument are invisibly based; but the strength that they derive from this hard core deprived him of certain kinds of sympathy and perception."[19] The second question is this: for Lewis, does the Catholic tendency of adding on go substantially beyond Marian doctrine and the practices it inspires (these dating back far more than one thousand years)? Given his own addings-on to Anglicanism (and Anglicanism's own addings-on, or subtractions from, itself), it seems apparent that it is the authoritative (*i.e.* compulsory) adding on that troubled Lewis. Kenneth Mason, in his pamphlet *Anglicanism: A Canterbury Essay,* writes: "If anyone asks, what is the final authority in matter of doctrine in Anglicanism? The reply must be, that there is no final authority. . . ." As for "differences of opinion . . . [The English temperament] would rather see the matter left unresolved, with dogmas held undogmatically."[20]

That Anglican resistance to final authority inheres in Lewis' temperament. That is, he was something of an Anarchist—not a self-absorbed or narcissistic or vain and preeningly supercilious intellectual, but a ferociously independent Self: his temperament tended toward the radical freedom. We need only note how often his data for an argument is his own experience or inner landscape, and how characters such as he (*e.g.* Orual in *Till We Have Faces*) struggle with their own spiritually feral autonomy. He needed to obey and he knew it. Thus (to use the characters from *Pilgrim's Regress*) there was about Broad something that satisfied an intellectual requirement—liberty—and something in Angular that spoke to his spirit—Sacramentalism. Having both at once would satisfy both of those needs. He could be both a loyal subject (believing in the monarchy) and a man who, though he knew he should and thought he did, could not quite

19 'The Approach to English', in Jocelyn Gibb, ed., *Light on C. S. Lewis* (New York: Harcourt, Brace & World, 1965), 60.

20 Kenneth Mason, Anglicanism: A Canterbury Essay (Oxford: The Sisters of the Love of God, 1987), 21.

surrender that Little End Room (as Lewis described his juvenile refuge in *Surprised by Joy*[21]) all his own, free of authoritatively dispositive belief.

Here that second instance of an unpublished discussion comes to the point. Between April and June of 1945, Lyman Stebbins, the founder-to-be of Catholics United for the Faith, wrote two letters to Lewis. The exchange merits a close look. The first letter asked for reasons not to convert to Catholicism. In a letter on 8 May, 1945, Lewis uncharacteristically replied: "In a word, the whole set-up of modern Romanism seems to me to be as much as a provincial or local variation from the central, ancient tradition as any particular Protestant sect is." Lewis goes on to invoke the inability of Catholic theology to trace some of its doctrines to "within 1000 years of [Christ's] time," and the importance of fidelity to Scripture. "The great point is that in one sense there's no such thing as Anglicanism. What we are committed to believing is whatever can be proved from Scripture. On that subject there is room for endless progress"—an odd word for Lewis to use, given his untrusting view of the concept and his reliance upon regress for more than just the title of a book.

Stebbins replied at length on 16 June, 1945. First he calls into question Lewis's question-begging tendency:

> It seems to me that the whole idea of seeking an interpretation of a text from some outside authority or authorities presupposes that no one specific interpretation can be proved from the text itself. The question, 'Where shall I find a true interpretation of a doubtful text?' is not answered by 'read the text' or by 'believe the texts which are not in doubt.' And yet, 'we are committed to believing whatever can be proved from Scripture' seems to me just such an answer to just such a question.

Stebbins then takes on the Unanimity Argument (presciently, it seems):

> If we adopt the principle that unanimity is the mark of the area of doctrine which must be believed, does not recent history as well as our own reason tell us that that area will shrink and shrink? It is true that the remaining area would always be

---

21 Lewis, *Surprised by Joy*, 10, 172, 210. Later (117) in *Regress* Lewis lampoons Mr. Broad by having him comment on Mother Kirk as follows: "I love and honour her . . . but . . . we are none of us infallible. If I sometimes . . . must differ from her at present, it is because I honour all the more the idea that she stands for. . . ." Lewis seems to suggest that the church is infallible, just not the Catholic church.

where we would feel most confident; the question is how long it would be big enough to sustain life.

Next he addresses an apparent contradiction in Lewis' thinking.

> You imply that you would reject an interpretation if it could not be traced back to within 1,000 years of Christ's time. Yet, on the subject of what can be proved from Scripture, you say there is room for endless progress. I do not see how these two principles can be reconciled. Suppose we were to progress one step tomorrow—really progress. Would another generation be wise in rejecting the step because it could not be traced back to within 1,900 years of His time? If progress is both good and possible, then we cannot reject a group which claims to have progressed in interpretation, on that very ground. We must be able to convict them of a contradiction.[22]

As far as we know, there is no rejoinder from Lewis; he simply had no patience with a discussion of the subject.

In his *C. S. Lewis and the Church of Rome*, Christopher Derrick reports a strange incident. At one point, Warren, while in Ireland, seriously considered taking instruction in Catholicism. Upon hearing of this, Jack rushed to Ireland to argue Warren out of his decision. There he entered into debate with a local priest and, according to George Sayer (Lewis's pupil, friend, and biographer, who heard the tale from Warren), got much the worse of it. Perhaps it ran as did his exchange with Stebbins. Jack apparently simply vetoed Warren's decision.[23] Character, maturing from its juvenile imprint, held sway.

What we do know, of course, is that Lewis settled on being "churched," even though he might have settled differently. "To me," he writes in *Surprised by Joy*, "religion ought to have been a matter of good men praying alone, and meeting by twos and threes to talk of spiritual matters."[24] In the event, he chose a church that brought him as close to that model as possible without, he must have thought, allowing the (dangerously) wanton

---

22 The whole of Stebbins' share of his correspondence with Lewis is at https://www.cuf.org/About/Stebbins/StebbinsWritings/cslewis.asp

23 Derrick, *C. S. Lewis and the Church of Rome*, 40.

24 Quoted by Alan Bede Griffiths, O.S.B., in 'The Adventure of Faith', from *Remembering C. S. Lewis: Recollections of Those Who Knew Him*, ed. James Como (San Francisco: Ignatius Press, 2005), 88.

freedom towards which he remained disposed. He assented to the Fathers, the Creeds, and perhaps the first five or six Councils, as well as sages, devotional writers (*e.g.* St. Francis de Sales), mystics (*e.g.* Boehme) and believing religious thinkers (*e.g.* G.K. Chesterton). The ferociously independent Lewis, certainly catholic, was also always . . . sifting.

Just here we arrive at Lewis' actual Authority. Richard Hooker and his *Laws of Ecclesiastical Polity* tamed (so to speak) the influence of the Great Knock, William T. Kirkpatrick, Lewis' atheistic, dialectically unforgiving tutor-cum-mentor. Hooker emphasizes Tradition (never over, but certainly equal with, Scripture), respects Catholics (even beyond controversial prudence), and defends Natural Law; he is the great defender of "the light of Reason," in Lewis' opinion Hooker's most valuable contribution. Surely second to this contribution is Hooker's manner, which, says Lewis, "marks a revolution in the art of controversy." His style is neither colloquial nor merely decorative, "yet often rendered in the 'voice of the people'. . . . And much of his argument," Lewis appreciates, "is on behalf of moderation in controversy." He concludes, "everywhere in his writing there is a sense of 'the beautiful variety of all things.'"[25] Tradition (or a segment thereof), moderation of thinking, and mildness of manner (leavening Kirkpatrick's severity) would become the ingredients of Lewis' apologetic recipe.

His private practices and beliefs aside, the very discussion of division—"Christian Reunion" being a unique (and, remember, unpublished) exception—would subvert the lesson learned from Hooker and militate against Lewis's usefulness as an apologist for Mere Christianity; that is, it would adulterate his credibility, or *ethos*. From Aristotle to Quintilian and beyond, "ethical proof" ranks first among the rhetorician's tools of persuasion (the very heart of rhetoric), ahead of emotional and logical proof in its effectiveness. Lewis's focus on Mere Christianity was unrelenting, and he would allow no compromise of a reader's view of his *intelligence* (expertise, or intellectual authority), *goodwill* (the speaker's taking to heart the best interests of his audience), and *honesty* (the ability to tell the truth as well as he knows it)—the three components of *ethos*.[26]

Vocational interests—that is, rhetorical prudence, prevails: ". . . after that I should be no more use to anyone." He would be Hooker's man all

---

25 C. S. Lewis, *English Literature in the Sixteenth Century, Excluding Drama* (Oxford: The Clarendon Press, Oxford UP, 1954), 451-463.

26 Book Two of Aristotle's *On Rhetoric* is the fountainhead of thinking on ethical (that is, personal) proof. The best summary of classical rhetoric by far is that by George A. Kennedy in the superior one-volume *Encyclopedia of Rhetoric*, ed. Thomas O. Sloane (Oxford: UP, 2001), 92-115.

the way. Almost never has adhering to a conventional baseline elicited controversial attention; rather, it is inconspicuous, a haven beyond attention and therefore beyond reproach. Nothing made more sense for Lewis than remaining in the monarchical-cum-latitudinous place that was and ever-more-so is the Anglican Church. (It gets, so to speak, the fame without the blame.) This claim also answers the question: Could Lewis have been unchurched? As explicitly as conversion, such a stance would have invited attention and controversy: Lewis might have been of use to some, but it would have been no refuge. Withal his primary audience was not the atheist but the skeptic. This profoundly rhetorical man took few risks with the starting lines of his persuasiveness, moderation and trustworthiness. The Anglican church proffered no risk. He could say, and mean, "the great point is that in one sense there's no such thing as Anglicanism."

If Lewis had discerned a denominational truth and eschewed it, he would have been in grave danger, and he would have known it. We must conclude he had no such discernment. I believe Coghill was right about Lewis' Protestant fundament, views (Coghill's and Lewis's) which seem to me shared, axiomatically, by Protestant scholars.[27]

Others, not so constrained as Lewis, leaped over the Tiber. In doing so they have paid some price of course, but many knew they would, and would do it all over again. Unlike the electron's phantom aspect, the traveler at a divide has very few options, and they exclude disappearing from here and reappearing over there. But, owing to a mix of anti-authoritarian temperament, religious bigotry, intellectual reserve, and (especially) vocational-commitment-cum-rhetorical-astuteness, Lewis comes close. Mother Kirk could be Presbyterian—and also Catholic; she is unadorned, ancient, and deliberate; and she merely *suggests*. Yet her suggestions are infallible: *she* is not Anglican. But Anglicanism did leave Lewis the Prayer Book and most of the Thirty-Nine Articles. It allowed for Reason (to a point), Scripture, a version of Tradition, and Faith. But it disallowed that single, dispositive authority. In other words, it provides for Lewis' "room for endless progress," as well as for Mr. Mason's "matters . . . unresolved." Thus this quantum electron, in his multi-orbit habitation, is too elusive to pin down—as elusive as Mother Kirk, and from the very beginning.

---

27 Angus J.L. Menuge, *C. S. Lewis: Lightbearer in the Shadowlands, the Evangelistic Vision of C. S. Lewis* (Wheaton: Crossway Books, 1997).

FOURTEEN

THE MARRIAGE OF TRUE MINDS
C. S. Lewis's Lost "Aeneid," a Review

A T. REYES' EDITION of Lewis's partial translation of Virgil's epic is of more value than meets the eye—but first some perspective. Fewer than sixty of its 220 pages carry C. S. Lewis' translation of the *Aeneid*, with a commensurate number carrying the original text from the Loeb edition (not Lewis' primary text). Whereas we have all that Lewis translated of the epic, we have only 15 percent of the twelve books of the poem itself: all of Book I, much of Book II, about half of Book VI, and snippets thereafter (including prose summaries by Lewis). So even though he was at work on this translation for half his life, until his death in 1963, the work is both abbreviated and unfinished.

Machinery includes a foreword, a preface, and the editor's introduction (as well as manuscript pages, maps of Aeneas' journeys, a convenient glossary, and a name index). The first, by Walter Hooper (Lewis' renowned literary steward and editor), describes the provenance of the manuscripts and their rescue from a bonfire. The preface, by the classicist D. O. Ross, discusses the translation proper, especially in light of Lewis' thinking on Renaissance humanism (he was not a fan), and does so as to suggest that he had just read the great classical critic D. S. Carne-Ross on translation.

A. T. Reyes' introduction lays out what there is of Lewis' engagement with the *Aeneid* and with Virgil (vocations and their price looming large), his religious importance to Lewis, and Lewis on translation generally: he loved the poem as no other and re-read it more than he did any other book. He did believe that "all translations ruin Virgil"; but, in light of his belief in the success of the *Aeneid* as a Secondary Epic (so-called in his *Preface to Paradise Lost)*, he could not have agreed with Carne-Ross that "no epic 'succeeds' after Homer."

While discussing Robert Fitzgerald's 1981 *Aeneid* in his *Classics and Translation*, Carne-Ross is silent on Lewis, even though the older Lewis anticipated much that the younger man has to say; but Carne-Ross does pose the telling question whereby to assess a translation: Does it work "for whatever creative and enlightening relations between [itself] and the original"? Here refractions from the critic and translator Bernard Hoepffner's essay "Proxy Literature" (*TLS*, May 27, 2011) are helpful. Translation is "language creation," he says, that should "alter the complexion of [its] language for its own good." Moreover, "the target language should somehow be violated" so that readers will "feel the otherness of the source language and culture as well as the otherness of the [original] author." A translation, then, ought to infuse the original work and its culture into our mind and our culture, enriching our literary tradition with a variegation—not a mere novelty—that refreshes both. Lewis would have meant his translation as just such a renovative infusion.

Given that what we have is largely unfinished, the best we can manage in our assessment of Lewis' translation are line comparisons. Consider the following passage (out loud, of course) from Robert Fitzgerald's translation:

> Saturnian Juno, burning for it all,
> Buffeted on the waste of sea those Trojans Left by the Greeks
> and pitiless Achilles, Keeping them far from Latium. For years
> They wandered as their destiny drove them on From one sea to
> the next: so hard and huge
> A task it was to found the Roman people.

Now here is Lewis's:

> Therefore she bars from Latian soil for many a year
> The Trojan few, the leavings of Achilles' spear, Leading them
> far, for-wandered, over alien
> foam —So long was fate in labour with the birth of Rome.

Fitzgerald is sea-faringly rhythmic, I think, and Lewis economical and dramatic. Which is better poetry? "Those Trojans left" (Fitzgerald) lacks the evocation of savaged waste that we hear in "the leavings of Achilles' spear" (Lewis); "Their Destiny drove them on" (Fitzgerald) pales against the urgency and graphic menace of the personified "fate in labour" (Lewis). Lewis was an accomplished narrative poet in his own right (and, along with narrative poetry generally, woefully neglected as such). He had command of both his matter and his meter. This passage from his narrative poem Launcelot is in the same meter as his *Aeneid*:

> and when That door was opened, fragrance such as
> dying men Imagine in immortal countries, blown about
> Heaven's meadows from the tree of life, came floating out.

Why did Lewis leave scarcely more than the draft of a fragment? Other long poems of his are unfinished, but in this case it may be because, as he said, "all translations ruin Virgil" and Virgil meant too much to him to fail at. Is Hooper correct when he tells us that, "of all the literary remains of C. S. Lewis published since his death, this "—even unfinished—"is the one that would have pleased him most"?

Whatever the impediment, had he completed the work he would have drawn many more readers to Virgil and made the point that "the poem would still be as good as anyone ever said it was" (Carne-Ross again). Withal, the actual book affords us a glimpse of how one rich, enormously sympathetic, and religion-charged literary imagination engaged another, religion-charged, though greater, literary imagination; that, and it recovers for us a well-spring of Lewis' mind and spirit.

FIFTEEN

Thorton Wilder's "Alcestiad," or A Life in the Sun ... and C. S. Lewis

Thornton Wilder (1897-1975) may be our quintessential American Man of Letters: man-of-the-theatre, novelist, critic, scholar (in his day, no one knew more about Lope de Vega—or *Finnegan's Wake!*), polyglot, cosmopolite of international renown—an American in Paris who alone among his generation certainly was not Lost—and soldier. (Wilder volunteered for service in W.W.II when already in his forties, went through basic training, and served admirably enough to be both promoted and decorated.) And yet he is close to forgotten by the reading public. Sure, *The Bridge of San Luis Rey* (Pulitzer Prize for fiction, 1928, with films in both 1944 and 2004) may still be read in some high schools, and, sure, *Our Town* (Pulitzer Prize for drama, 1938) is a hit whenever produced (which is often) in venues, large and small even as far away as Peru. And, yes, Wilder would win a third Pulitzer, for *The Skin of Our Teeth* (drama, 1942). Moreover, in the thirties he was worth a vituperative Marxist attack and in the sixties was worthy of the Presidential Medal of Freedom. Yet how many culturally literate readers can even name anything other than *Our Town* and *The Bridge of San Luis Rey*? No writer has won Pulitzers for both fiction and drama and sustained fifty-year careers, Wilder's running from the mid-twenties (*The Cabala*, 1926) to the early seventies (*Theophilus North*, 1973).

His masterwork, *The Eighth Day* (his penultimate novel and winner of the National Book Award, 1968), explores *agape* in history and among members of a family. The narrator tell us that "it is doubtful whether hope . . . can sustain itself without an impulse injected by love." Later, when explaining that a woman's love for her children is her "boundless, ineffable thanks to God," he tells us, "that's what destiny is. Our lives are a seamless robe, rather like the "complex mazelike design" in a rug admired by a young man looking for answers. "Turn it over," he is instructed, and when he does so he sees the "mass of knots and of frayed and dangling threads," which is the aspect that Eternity—never far away in Wilder—presents to us in Time. That is why this book, in its themes of design and provident love, and especially in its obliquity, typifies Wilder's work.

Thus prizes and longevity are not the most telling points about his work. Rather that point is this: for all of those decades there abides a piercing sensibility marked by a fusion of reverence, gratitude, wonder, *Sehnsucht* (that stab of longing to which C. S. Lewis attributes his Christian awakening) and the numinous. Only once did he abandon his obliquity and attempt to make these explicit, and so, alas, as theatre Wilder could not find a way to make *The Alcestiad* work.[1]

As a child, he first heard of Alcestis and her husband Admetus from Bulfinch and, in one way or another, worried it—implicitly in *The Woman of Andros* (1930), explicitly in *The Ides of March* (1948)—until he could no longer not treat it formally. After a long gestation and many interruptions, *The Alcestiad, or A Life in the Sun* premiered in Edinburgh on August 22, 1955, and remains Wilder's only flop. (Even Lincoln Konkle, who in his superb *Thornton Wilder and the Puritan Narrative Tradition* [2006] treats the dramatic literature at length, slights it.)

There are good reasons. Wilder was never happy with its dramaturgy, nor with his friend Montgomery Clift's behavior (Clift was picky and pulled out), nor with Irene Worth, whose attack of opening-night nerves slowed down the pace, nor with Tyrone Guthrie's direction. In his review Kenneth Tynan, who had been thrilled by Wilder, called him "a schoolmaster who would like to be a poet" and the play "a dramatic nullity." Wilder himself thought that his "intellectual passion" had been "dulled and dimmed" and that he had allowed "the old TNW [his initials]-pathos the human tug" to enter too largely; he had allowed it "to get out of hand." That may be true—of the play, on stage—but it is not true of the piece as literature, on the page.

The tale is simple enough. When Apollo's son, the doctor Aesculapius, restores a dead man to life, Pluto is offended. Jupiter, at the request of

---

1 The play, along with Wilder's "Notes on The Alcestiad," is in *Thornton Wilder: Collected Plays & Writings on Theater* from The Library of America, ed. J.D. McClatchy.

his underworld brother-king, kills the doctor, which act provokes Apollo to kill Cyclopes, the maker of Jupiter's thunderbolts. Apollo's punishment is to serve a mortal, King Admetus, as a common herdsman, the same as any other laborer. Admetus competes for Alcestis, she of other-worldly beauty and divine delicacy, winning his bride only through the help of Apollo, even though Alcestis longs only to know and to serve that same god. Then, when Admetus' death is fated, he learns that he will be spared if someone else volunteers to die in his place. But not even his very aged parents will do so. Only Alcestis will, and does. Hercules, however, fond of Alcestis for her beauty and virtue (Antigone, Penelope, Leda, Helen, and Clytemnestra, each of whom he knows, he calls "Dirt. Trash," compared to Alcestis), revered by all, and a dear friend to Admetus, travels to the underworld and, with very great effort retrieves Alcestis, restoring her to Admetus. Wilder's greatest alteration is to deny Admetus any knowledge that a surrogate will save his life—or that his wife is that surrogate.

Antedating the play, however, is *The Ides of March*, a riveting epistolary novel about the events and characters surrounding that fateful day in 44 B.C. There Wilder gives us Catullus' version of the myth, or a part of it, since we are told, at a crucial point, that "the narrative breaks off." "And I?" Alcestis asks, "what am I to do? What I am doing now? My interest is to inquire into the nature of the Gods—whether they exist and in what ways we may find Them. You may well imagine—" Exactly here, then, is the kernel of Wilder's interest. In his *Notes on the Alcestiad* he tells us that stories about the gods have lasted precisely because "they are ambiguous and puzzling."

> We are told that Apollo loved Admetus and Alcestis. If so, how strangely he exhibited it. It must make for considerable discomfort to have the god of the sun, of healing and song, housed among one's farm workers. And why should a divine love impose on a devoted couple the decision as to which should die for the other?

That could be Pamphilus, the narrator of *The Woman of Andros* (1930), speaking, as he speculates similarly:

> It seemed to him that the whole world did not consist of rocks and trees and water nor were human beings garments and flesh, but all burned, like the hillside of olive trees, with the perpetual flames of love,—a sad love that was half hope, often rebuked

and waiting to be reassured of its truth. . . . as though it were waiting for a voice to come from the skies, declaring that therein lay the secret of the world.

That secret is tortuously difficult to suggest. Wilder (in the *Notes*) recalled "some meditations" on Kierkegaard, and this "extreme difficulty" and "incommensurability" is right out of S.K., whose "The Parable of a King and a Maiden" Wilder had long pondered. In it the king wonders if the maiden would love him if he were a common person, a dilemma (S.K. affirms) that is precisely God's own. "The poet's task," says S.K., "will be to find a solution . . . the God's anxiety be set at rest . . . his sorrow banished. For the divine love is that unfathomable love. . . ." The unfathomable nature of love is that "it is indeed less terrible to fall to the ground when the mountains tremble at the voice of the God, than to sit at table with him as an equal. And yet," S.K. concludes, "it is the God's concern precisely to have it so." Wilder's conclusion (in his *Notes*) is that "Alcestis, through many a blunder, learned how to listen and interpret the things that Apollo was so urgently trying to say to her." In his *Thornton Wilder*, Rex Burbank quotes Thornton:

> [*The Alcestiad*] is a wildly romantic story of gods and men, of death and hell, of resurrection, of great loves and great trials, of usurpation and revenge. On another level, however, it is a comedy . . . about the extreme difficulty of any dialogue between heaven and earth, about the misunderstandings that result from the 'incommensurability' of things human and divine.

As late as January of 1955 Wilder is still wondering how to work out "the donnee of the numinous," and in August of the same year he is almost grieving: "I am ashamed of this lukewarm imitative dilettante religiosity. Pfui!" But this pessimism is as much existential as it is dramatic, providing a context for a question he placed by letter to his great friend and one of his favorite actresses Ruth Gordon: "What does man do with his despair?" Isabel Wilder, Thornton's sister and until her death a keeper of both the books and the flame, opines that her brother was a traveler and a socializer because of his "deep loneliness," that "he could not allay an unsatiable need," and that "he had no sturdy last resource against the occasional conviction 'I don't belong.'" But in his notes, he wrote that, like S.K., "an eternal truth has come into being in me . . . precisely like any other individual human being." He would write of Alcestis, "Apollo leads her to his

Evergreen Grove where she still wanders, a symbol, a myth, a truth for us all: one who escaped from darkness, to her herself a light on the horizon comprehensible to the spirit of Christian humanism."

At the magnificent beginning of *The Woman of Andros*, the narrator tells us, "the land that was soon to be called Holy prepared in the dark its wonderful burden," and in conversation (with George Wagner, 1953), Wilder says, "I am a Protestant and a practicing Christian." Nevertheless Wilder allowed that "as writers we have only one duty, namely to pose the question correctly. It is not the task of literature," he continued, "to answer the question. But only a religious person will ask the question correctly." He concluded, "someone with religious faith can only write with the inspiration of faith."

Take, for instance, the early debate between Apollo and Death. (Does not the very designation quicken one's soul?) Here is Death: "[Shrilly] Leave these human beings alone. Stay up on Mount Olympus, where you belong, and enjoy yourselves. . . . You made these creatures and then you fell in love with them. You've thrown the whole world into confusion." And here is Apollo's response: "They have begun to understand me. At first they were like beasts—more savage, more fearful. . . . Then two things broke on their minds and they lifted their heads: my father's thunder, which raised their fears to awe; and my sunlight, for which they gave thanks." In response to which, Death: "All this loving . . . It's hard to tell which is the unhappier—you or these wretched creatures. When you try to come into their lives you're like a giant in a small room: with every movement you break something." And later, Alcestis to her maid: "the thing that I love more than Admetus is . . . . Is Apollo. . . . I wish to live in the real." No wonder that, at the very end, Apollo tells Alcestis, "The grave means an end. You will not have that ending. You are the first of a great number that will not have that ending. Still another step, Alcestis."

The Old and New Testaments, with a dash of church history, in a nutshell.

And just so are there those who, rankled by the benedictions that Wilder conveys, facilely dismiss him as a mere sentimentalist. In response I call upon Amos Wilder, Thornton's brother, from his *Thornton Wilder and His Public*:

> . . . sometimes talent or virtuosity is combined with something more, some further stature or scope or power of conception, and this is both rare and disturbing. . . . For those excited by talent or contemporaneity all such untimely or timeless works

will appear austere or insipid. All about us—yesterday, today, tomorrow—there is an unrecognized court in the hearts of men and women which sifts the arts of an age and . . . . breaks through our modern fates.

In that light I again invoke the name of C. S. Lewis, who shares enough literary and biographical affinities with Wilder for the two to be both professional and spiritual brothers. His greatest work (he thought) and his one true novel is *Till We Have Faces*, also published in 1955, also based upon a Greek myth (Cupid and Psyche, from *The Golden Ass*), and also posing a question about the gods.

Its first-person narrator, Orual, is the vexed and vexing sister of a transcendent beauty, Psyche, who will be sacrificed to the presumed Brute of the mountain, a Brute who, it turns out, is no brute at all but a resplendent god. Here is Psyche, attempting to persuade her sister to worry not over her impending sacrifice:

How can I be the ransom for all Glome unless I die? And if I am to go to the god, of course it must be through death. . . . . [Some masters] have taught that death opens a door out of a little, dark room (that's all the life we have known before it) into a great real place where the true sun shines. . . . The sweetest thing in all my life has been the longing—to reach the Mountain, to find the place where all the beauty comes from. . . . my country, the place where I ought to have been. . . . The longing for home.

I offer, then, a piece of personal advice: read these two works in tandem. If you do, you will, I think, see that in evoking the numinous—and the *agape* that often emanates from it—Wilder's work vindicates its author's long devotion to his tale—and that he and Lewis make siblings of us all.

SIXTEEN

His Fugitive Voice
After Fifty Years

*May the God of hope bring you such joy and peace in your faith
that the power of the Holy Spirit will remove all bounds to hope.*
— Rom 15.13

*A man's life of any worth is a continual allegory—and very few
eyes can see the mystery of life—a life like the Scriptures, figurative.*
— John Keats, in a letter to his brother George, May 3, 1819.

FIVE DECADES BEYOND C. S. Lewis's death on November 22, 1963, the fashion in some precincts is to describe the man as "quirky," as though the folds, edges and concealments of his character and of his mind are only lately evident, or that owing to some set of cryptic psychotics he was, really, a tweedy eccentric. This revisionism is unfortunate, and not because he didn't have his quirks. He did. In the late thirties, for example, he contrived—for a chuckle, and as a joke on Oxford University no less—to have his friend Adam Fox, who was barely a poet, elected Professor of Poetry. Very few of Lewis's colleagues thought it was funny. Later in life, when his old dog Mr. Papworth would not eat standing still or if anyone were watching, the by-now-famous man could be seen twice a day walking down his lane tossing dog food over his shoulder as the dog followed along gobbling it up. Those were quirks, and there were some others, too, like his ability to quote any page from memory if someone gave him a few lines from it and yet (as we see in the manuscript of *The*

Screwtape Letters) not confidently to spell "rivet"; or the co-existence of his irrational fear (not as bad as his brother Warnie's) that he might run out of money—that, along with an enormous personal generosity, giving out-of-pocket to any vagabond who came his way ("I don't care if he's going to drink it up, Tollers [Tolkien]; that's exactly what I was going to do with it") and continuously out of his bank account—to the tune of nearly seventy per cent of his income. But all of this is standard fare for readers who have looked into the life.

In that light, I will not be offering anything brand new—no code-breaking or any chronological novelties. After all, Dr. Johnson is right: people need to be reminded more often than instructed. Nor will I argue my own hobby horses, that Lewis' life falls into nine semi-neat stages, or was dramatically changed by five pivotal deaths (although I will touch upon three of those). In fact, I will hardly argue at all—hardly. Instead I will attempt a portrait of the Lewis who is unnoticed in plain sight, whom I have pondered for some time, and whose nature is useful in its ability to help us understand the master, his work, and the relationship between the two. I realize that my fondness for my own themes—*resistance* and *escape*: I fundamentally share the impulse behind both—may have distorted my view. For its tendency to make us see its manifestation everywhere we look, Lewis himself has warned us against just such enthusiasms.[1]

I have called the current views of Lewis unfortunate, though not because they are simply false. I say unfortunate because they are simplistic reductions, and this is especially unfortunate because the really useful revision would go much farther. Here is the Lewis whom I see: *no mere eccentric but, intellectually and temperamentally and radically so, a proto-anarchist, a not-so-undercover counter-cultural resistance fighter, and especially a rebel whose final cause was escape*—first against and from a sorrowful childhood; then from social convention, university rules and paternal oversight and overreach; thereafter from many settled assumptions of his own profession; then grandly, persistently, from his *Zeitgeist* generally; even from some friends; and finally from *Zeit* itself. Moreover, and along the way as he aged, he sought to flee, not only from guilt but from his own gifts. In short, this fugitive motif was the bass riff that ran under all the rich and varied fugues of his life and work and that knits them of-a-piece, finally making of him a towering, multi-faceted figure—and a Christian apologist

---

1 On October 24, 1960, Lewis answers Alistair Fowler's praise for Ellrodt's enthusiasm in his *Neo-Platonism in the Poetry of Edmund Spenser*: "reading your account of the book I am divided between a great greed to see it and the little haunting fear 'is he beginning to see pictures in the fire?'"

straight from Galilee. I begin with . . . reminders.

Just as his many geniuses give his widely varied works their distinctive qualities, so for him to have traveled so many literary roads is itself astonishing. Consider . . . He was a published (if minor) poet of great metrical and narrative skill; a philosopher (that is, academically trained as such, whose first university appointment included philosophy, and whose admonitory *Abolition of Man*, for example, is proving frighteningly prescient); a first-person novelist the equal of Nabokov in technical proficiency and psychological depth; a writer of speculative fiction dense with ideas and of fantasy with some peers but no betters; a religious thinker whose sermons and essays have settled much epistemological hash, undone many a strawman, and clarified opaque doctrine; a fearsome public debater and engaged public figure; a vital social presence; a Christian apologist who wrote and roved and broadcast and who still invites attack as well as aspirants to be the "next C. S. Lewis"; and an assiduous book reviewer and unrelenting letter-writer. In short, we know him—through his several voices—as much more than the supple apologist, the avuncular adviser, and the compelling fabulist. Such are his works and his work.

The man behind those is at least as variegated. We have come to know the unsettled boy who (unlike his brother at the very same schools) simply could not fit in; the brilliant student and legendary scholar, lecturer and demanding tutor at Oxford; the badly wounded combat veteran who would argue against pacifism; the animal-lover and that bountiful alms-giver who opened his home to evacuees during World War Two and tutored the needful among of them; the intrepid walker and talker; the constant imbiber of tea with a fondness for alcohol and tobacco; the prodigious reader and writer; the Famous Man and so that dutiful correspondent; and the valued friend whose conversation, joyfully dogged encouragement, and sheer presence was of great delight to all whom he befriended.

His lifelong friend Owen Barfield has reminded us that he was, as much as anything else, "a very funny man"; and his pupil, friend and the sometime-Inkling John Wain has described him as "all the time delightfully aware of [his] identity and out to get, and to give, as much fun as possible with it." Nor can we forget the devoted brother and, finally, husband; and of course the prayerful, reverent and humble Christian who, though unrelenting in the practice of his apologetic vocation and quite conscious of his popularity and effectiveness, would never assert beyond his knowledge nor abuse his influence.

All of this has made of Lewis (or a version of him, officially we might say) someone overlooked, or underestimated, by even the most astute literary critics and journalists: a top-shelf literary figure. Regard: 1/ As a prose stylist his gifts of wit, analogy, imagery, epigrammatic economy, rhythmical dexterity, and rhetorical adroitness should place him in any canon worthy of study by anyone who pretends to know—let alone to teach—the literature of English speaking peoples. 2/ His many voices have produced a trenchant body of work that includes hallmarks of its many types, remains relevant, and invites commentary. 3/ His personal influence upon very many millions of people is deep, significant and abiding. And 4/ his personality and life continue to arouse interest. And to think I'm still sometimes asked, "Why all the fuss?"

Well, all that of course, but why this continuing interest? One reason, I believe, is that he was a man with a private and social life marked by striking anomalies. In fact he was what so many of his readers do not expect and therefore have overlooked: personally as well as professionally, at least among men, *he was very much his own man.* And it is this independence—in the tweedy, conventional, and conventionally Anglican Oxford don who had barely traveled and whose circles were few and small—that often confuses even the people who do notice its ubiquity in his life and work.

Even though it should startle or confuse no one. From the beginning—we must begin with a childhood which, though lovely at its start, would be roiled soon enough—from that beginning he was his own boy, too. He wanted company on his terms or, better yet, to be left alone (even though he would learn that God would not comply). As a very young child he named himself—Jacksie (after a slain pet dog), and Jack he would remain. He was a smart aleck, answering, when queried about his self-professed prejudice against the French, that if he knew why he was prejudiced then it wouldn't be a prejudice, "would it!" More than anything he treasured his time in The Little End Room of his family's huge house, away from his overbearing father, reading and writing his stories of dressed and talking animals. That would become the redoubt of his one-boy resistance movement.

He would need it. Three months before his tenth birthday came the death of his mother, Flora: "a continent sinking like Atlantis." Now, the literature on the effects of early parental loss is dispositive.[2] It tells us that coming to terms with such a loss may be delayed (*e.g.* until we see a version

---

2 See Sol Altschul, ed., *Childhood Bereavement and Its Aftermath.* Emotion and Behavior Monographs: Monograph No. 8. Madison, Conn.: International Universities Press, Inc., 1981.

it in *The Magician's Nephew*, more than forty years after the fact); school phobias will likely ensue; the pre-adolescent child (especially a boy who has lost a mother) will delay long-term romantic love (Lewis wouldn't find "the romance that passed [him] by in [his] teens" until his fifties, when he married Joy Davidman Gresham); nightmares are frequent (in Lewis's case about spiders); and conversions are common, including conversions away from religious faith. By the time of his Confirmation this grandchild of clergymen and child of serious and observant Christians—it was not, as he would claim, a nominally Christian household—was both signing himself "philomastix" (an adolescent sexual reference: "lover of the whip") in letters to his first friend Arthur Greeves and calling himself a "blaspheming atheist." (Blaspheming he certainly was: an atheist he was not, in spite of what he said: we must handle with care assertions that great people make about themselves.) Perhaps this stage of his flight was owing to typical teenage foolishness, not to the sorrowful boyhood from which any sane youngster would flee, and he would himself say that it took him as long to gain inhibitions as it took his contemporaries to lose them.

This time he was right. The survivor of early parental loss may search for a relationship analogous to the one lost. Practically stepping out of the textbook, he would set up a household with his slain army buddy's mother, Janie King Moore—a mother-surrogate whom he would refer to as his own mother and who would, in the twenties when Lewis was that "blaspheming atheist," become his lover. Of course the whole ménage was rebellious, not just against Christian and conventional morality, but against conventional *immorality* as well—and against University regulations that required college residency. Worst of all, it was contrary to the sorry tale he was fobbing off on his confused and confusing father (who had not visited his wounded son but was his sole support: Lewis' diary from the twenties reveals that his trousers were so worn he thought them on the verge of indecency, and he could afford only one razor blade).

Mrs. Moore was some twenty-five years older than Lewis, and he would care for her until her death in January of 1951. The erotic aspect of their liaison would lead to a haunting guilt lasting at least until his early fifties (more about that anon). Even when not erotic, though, his relationship with Mrs. Moore was the first concrete example of the *Weiberherrschaft* to which he was disposed.[3] He had fled from one little end room in search of

---

3 That there was an erotic relationship of some kind is now a commonplace in Lewis scholarship, though the evidence is, of course, circumstantial, the most telling of those circumstances being Lewis' absolute refusal to discuss Mrs. Moore, even in his autobiography—or even with his brother. Christopher Derrick, Lewis' pupil and, later, his

another, where being "left alone" took the form of a self-indentured servitude to a woman, putative atheism, and lies. Well: no one promised that the route back home from behind enemy lines would be direct, or easy.

During the following decades—from young adulthood and even beyond his conversion—his closest friends intuited an unfinished, subcutaneous layer in Lewis. The philosopher Owen Barfield, his dear "second friend" and solicitor, would describe some of his work as "pastiche" and thought his post-conversion life was marked prominently by "voulu"; his devoted brother – his dearest friend – said of his conversion that it was not a conversion as much as a recovery from "a long mental illness." In the opinion of some who would know, he was a wonderful friend but given to new, unbounded enthusiasms even at the cost of compromising old friendships. Will we ever adequately understand *l'affair* Davidman or Lewis' secrecy surrounding that marriage? I think it likely that, at least at its beginnings, we have the same *Weiberherrschaft* here that we saw in the case of Janie King Moore. And there was the Ulsterman who had a strain of anti-Catholic bigotry but who once was suspected of having "poped," in part because of certain Catholic dispositions (*e.g.* frequent auricular confession, belief in the Real Presence and frequent taking of the Eucharist, prayers for the dead, belief in Purgatory), because *Pilgrim's Regress* had been published by Sheed and Ward (a leading Catholic house), and because of his early popularity among Catholics. In the event, the possibility of his— or Warnie's—crossing the Tiber horrified him. These were neither quirks nor eccentricities but signs of a severe independence and an inner conflict pockmarked by a self-professed bigotry.

As his own man, the mature public Lewis—as scholar, critic, and what these days we call a public intellectual—*this* Lewis would have assumed himself so situated as to indulge his rebel spirit and thus to resist his *Zeitgeist*, and not at all undercover but defiantly. His first book as a Christian was the militant allegory *Pilgrim's Regress* (1933). Written in two weeks, it subverts most of the tides of his time (fascism, communism, Freudianism, materialism, spiritualism) and features, of all heroes, an escaping pilgrim who instead of progressing actually regresses: a thrown gauntlet if ever there was one. And—of course—there would be more to come. For example, in "The Dangers of National Repentance" (1940) he is admonitory: "You can indulge in the popular vice of detraction without restraint, and yet feel all the time that you are practicing contrition"—as contrarian then as it is now. By then he had already converted to Christi-

---

friend, argues for the presence of *Weiberherrschaft* in Lewis in his *C. S. Lewis and the Church of Rome*.

anity—again, let us remember—*against* the stylish Oxford tide, and would defend it against all comers at meetings of the famous Socratic Club. And who else but Lewis—Eliot? John Dewey? Chesterton?—would write, *in 1933 yet*, the following? By the way, this too swam against the tide:

> Nothing can fully excuse the iniquity of Hitler's persecution of the Jews. . . . Did you see that he said 'The Jews have made no contribution to . . . culture and in crushing them I am doing the work of the Lord'? Now [Lewis continues] as the whole idea of 'the will of the Lord' is precisely what the world owes to the Jews, the blaspheming tyrant has . . . in a single sentence . . . shown that he is as contemptible for his stupidity as he is detestable for his cruelty.

Or consider this, from "Religion and Rocketry" (1958), than which there is no more astute, trenchant, or profoundly Christian critique of the impact of Christian evangelizing upon the heathen: "The missionary's holy desire to save souls has not always been kept quite distinct from the arrogant desire, the busybody's itch, to (as he calls it) 'civilize' the (as he calls them) 'natives.'" In the late and largely neglected "The Seeing Eye" (1963), published first in America as "Onward, Christian Spaceman," he expands upon the theme, contemplating the possibility of humanity meeting an alien rational species:

> I observe how the white man has hitherto treated the black, and how, even among civilized men, the stronger have treated the weaker. . . . I do not doubt that the same story will be repeated. We shall enslave, deceive, exploit or exterminate.

(An aside: I suspect that this opinion was prominent among his reasons for turning down the offer of a CBE from the great Churchill, an avid imperialist.[4])

Even as this "untamed lion" (as he called his great Aslan in *Narnia*) forged his escape through the spirit of the age he relished the resistance fighter's stance, in his 1954 Cambridge University inaugural lecture famously referring to himself as a dinosaur, and he was. He had tackled Eliot's mega-influential snobbishness and modernism (he could not look at the night sky and see "a patient etherized upon a table") and would do the

---

4 Also see Weston's imperialist manifesto delivered at the end of *Out of the Silent Planet*.

same with F. R. Leavis's in "High and Low Brows" and with his defenses of the infra dig Walter Scott, Rudyard Kipling, William Morris and George MacDonald. No one was safe: in our school-ridden Age of Methodology he eschewed all schools. Moreover, here and there (especially in book reviews) he would toss off epochal and contrarian ideas—the Renaissance never happened, Aristotle's *Poetics* is a ruinous book, tragedy is a "phantom concept"—and not bother to elaborate upon, let alone to defend, them. In his dispositive *Oxford History of English Literature in the Sixteenth Century* he designates a five-decade period of that literature "Drab," claiming— could C. S. Lewis be this tone-deaf?—that the word is merely descriptive of the normative style of the period, not at all judgmental.[5]

In his counter-cultural rebelliousness he took few prisoners of any sort, allowing no unexamined assumptions, literary, religious or otherwise, and pricking the balloons of jargon wantonly. Even in the sermon "Membership," pronouncedly not lit. crit., he could not help himself, writing of the psychological concept *du jour*, "I mean the pestilent notion (one sees it in literary criticism) that each of us starts with a treasure called 'Personality' locked up inside him, and that to expand and express this . . . is the main end of life." Elsewhere he would remind us that "feelings"— *our treasured feelings!*—"come and go, but mostly they go." (Imagine for a moment him telling this, say, to Dr. Phil or Oprah.) And just in case you thought he was a tame *Christian* lion, he would oppose anti-obscenity and -sodomy laws, avow that it was better for people to live in sin rather than violate their marital vows, and opine that a truly Christian society would surely be a socialist one.[6]

Here Lewis's treatment of culture *per se*—his radical, that is, his *uprooting*, of its claims—enters our portrait. The concept now seems to have achieved hegemony and demands for itself exactly the diffidence that Lewis could never afford it. Note his . . . cheekiness . . . in nearly trivializing (is that too strong a word?) an existential threat to Western Culture in "Learning in Wartime," a sermon preached at the Church of St. Mary the Virgin on December 22, 1939:

The war creates no absolutely new situation: it simply aggra-

---

5 He seems similarly disingenuous when expressing his frustration at those who believed there was a real Malcolm receiving those letters on prayer. At first reading, should I really have known better?

6 See especially "Sex in Literature" (1962). Not incidentally, he was a Christian apologist whose conception even of church is the theological equivalent of a quantum particle in Heisenberg's uncertain universe.

vates the permanent human situation so that we can no longer ignore it. . . . Human culture has always had to exist under the shadow of something infinitely more important than itself. . . I reject at once an idea . . . that cultural activities are in their own right spiritual and meritorious.

As we shall see, two years later Uncle Screwtape would confirm this very perspective to the pathetic Wormwood. Maybe more to the point is "Christianity and Literature" (also 1939). There Lewis argues that a striking contrast exists between the basic principles of modern literary criticism and those of the New Testament: "creative," "spontaneous," and "freedom" rule the former; whereas "convention," "rules," and "discipleship" inform the latter: not an argument against culture *per se*, but certainly the sort of skepticism that broke, and breaks, ranks. And in "Christianity and Culture" (1940) Lewis goes farther still in his questioning of the uses of culture.

He finds that the strictly natural level of creation, including culture, "is held on sufferance" within a Christian, supernatural, perspective, and that the New Testament is "decidedly cold to culture," warning, as it does, against any kind of superiority. He reminds us of Newman's thinking that "culture does not produce Christians but it may produce Christian gentlemen," warns us that "good taste" is not a spiritual value, and concludes that though culture-sellers (like Lewis himself, he says) may include Christians, they should serve mostly as an antidote! And finally there is "On Living in an Atomic Age" (1948). Such an age, Lewis tells us, is no different than "an age of Viking raids, plague, or death-by-auto accident." He says, "such threats may break our bodies (microbes can do that) but they need not dominate our minds." After all, everything—including all civilizations—will end in oblivion, and their durations will have been infinitesimal compared to the "oceans of dead time" both before and after. He ends with a characteristic, and unsparing, reversal:

We must resolutely train ourselves that survival of man on this earth . . . must be only by honorable and merciful means. . . .Those who care for something else more than civilization are the only people by whom civilization is likely to be preserved.[7]

---

7 Lewis's most belligerent anti-cultural statement is "Lillies that Fester" (1955), in which he explicitly urges "rebellion," claiming "there is no time to spare." Here, though, the attack is not on culture *per se* but on its self-conscious consumption and the harms that result from that.

I trust that Lewis has made my point, which is simply this: his long and unrelenting resistance yields a commanding perspective that is not only *not* cultural, not only *not* trans-cultural, not only not *merely* counter-cultural, but almost *anti*-cultural; in a word it is *supra*-cultural—and in being that seems quite orthodox *if you share the eternal perspective.* That is, from beyond the culture—beyond that combination of language, literature, the visual arts, customs, mores, and unexamined assumptions of all kinds that make up a culture—or from above it, *he helps us see culture as a sort of insanity, a fetish and worse, an idol.* Has his Great Divorce ever been greater? Surely Lewis's sharp-shooter's application of the phrase "enemy-occupied territory" to Western culture must come to mind. Of course, from *inside* the culture, it is Lewis who must seem crazy: if not quite as febrile as Jeremiah out there in the wilderness, surely close enough? And so his genius—the application of his transcending individuality—is to present us with a choice: in or out? We, with Lewis, might escape, leaving the *Zeitgeist* behind.

Enter here two of the most widely-read and influential works of Christian apologetics in the language, the nearly-contemporaneous *Screwtape Letters* and *Mere Christianity:* the first a masterpiece of satire and psychological insight, the second a marvel of concision and direct address, both intensely counter-cultural. Consider this, from *Uncle Screwtape's* fifth letter: ". . . the European humans have started another of their wars. . . . Of course a war is entertaining. . . . But what *permanent* [my emphasis] good does it do us unless we make use of it for bringing souls to Our Father Below?" Or this, from the fifteenth letter: "The humans live in time but our Enemy destines them to eternity. He therefore . . . wants them to attend chiefly to two things, to eternity itself, and to that point of time which they call the Present. . . . Our business is to get them away from the eternal, and from the present. . . . far better to make them live in the future [which is] of all things, the thing least like eternity."

Having undone the *Zeitgeist*, Lewis here opens a salient that is the point of the spear in an assault on *Zeit* itself. And in its stance against culture and against time, *Mere Christianity* is no different. Near the end, in his chapter "Nice People or New Men," Lewis asks, "What will all that chatter and hearsay count (will you even be able to re-member it?) when the anaesthetic fog which we call 'nature' or 'the real world' [or 'culture'] fades away and the Presence in which you have always stood becomes palpable, immediate, and unavoidable?" Any attentive and willing reader of *The Chronicles of Narnia* certainly understands: that wardrobe door opens, first to another timeline, space, nature and culture but finally to timelessness.

And Ransom, too, in his second adventure understands: is there a greater escape from our time and culture than his trip to un-fallen Perelandra? It can be no wonder that Lewis referred to time as that "gaping wound."

In its daring, its urgency, and its compelling expression, such an array invites wonder. How much more wonder, then, must we feel over Lewis's ambiguous—in fact hostile—stance towards his own rhetorical gifts? I've suggested that he would flee from these as he did from those other regnant claimants upon him—his boyhood, convention of varying sorts, the Spirit of the Age, and time itself. For he found the Classical lineaments and post-Classical emphases of rhetoric (the "Queen of the Arts," let us remember) entirely uncongenial, even disturbing. His notebooks offer virtually no use of rhetoric that is not derogatory; and in his literary history he writes, "rhetoric is the greatest barrier between us and our ancestors. If the Middle Ages had erred in their devotion to that art, the *renascentia*, far from curing, confirmed the error." Acknowledging that they praised "beauties" at best opaque to us, he asserts, "this change of taste makes an invisible wall between us and them. Probably all our literary histories, *certainly that on which I am engaged*, are *vitiated* by our lack of sympathy on this point [emphasis added]." (I note that his copy of Aristotle's *Rhetoric* is utterly unannotated, rare among Lewis' books. It seems he may as well not have read it.)

Withal he was as troubled by his own susceptibility to the practice of rhetoric as he was impatient with the art behind it. "I don't know if I'm weaker than other people, but it is a positive revelation to me how while the speech lasts it is impossible not to waver just a little," he wrote, after hearing a speech by Hitler (the night before he conceived the idea for *The Screwtape Letters*). Even more telling is the conversation between Augray the *sorn* and Ransom in chapter six of *Out of the Silent Planet*. There Augray chides the hrossa for their inflated love of beautiful words. You see, the *hrossa* sent Ransom on his way by an excessively long and dangerous route. "It is just like a *hross*," Augray laments. "If you died on the *harandra* they would have made a poem . . . and all this would seem to them just as good as if they had used a little forethought." But perhaps most telling with respect to his distrust of rhetoric are the instances when he brings his own fictional talk to a halt.

During the debate on Perelandra, the wrong side has the better argument; Ransom "wins" only because he acts non-rhetorically—by punching the Un-man in his mouth. The only passenger on *The Great Divorce* bus to Heaven who stays is the one who stops rhetorizing and exclaims, "Damn and blast you! Go on can't you? Get it over," and presently shuts up. In

The Silver Chair Puddleglum's affirmation follows his determining action: With his naked webbed-foot he stamps on the fire that is complicit in the witch's verbal spell. And at the end of *Till We Have Faces* the queen writes, of what had been her lucid and, at least Part One of it, rather convincing complaint (in fact a rhetorically formal Greek *apologia*), "only words, words; to be led out to battle with other words."

His old, ambivalent view of the art is intimately tied to his equally ambivalent view of one's self and the Christian demand that it be transcended. In the private venue of lyric poetry this alarm surfaces explicitly in "As the Ruin Falls":

> All this is flashy rhetoric about loving you.
> I never had a selfless thought since I was born.
> I am mercenary and self-seeking through and through:
> I want God, you, all friends, merely to serve my turn.
>
> Peace, re-assurance, pleasure, are the goals I seek
> I cannot crawl one inch outside my proper skin:
> I talk of love – a scholar's parrot may talk Greek –
> But, self-imprisoned, always end where I begin.

And what he finds particularly discomfiting is not only the effect of rhetoric upon his credulity but its hold upon his self, for that hold symptomizes an inability to let go of his old, needy theatrical ego. Listen to this *cri de coeur*, written late and also un-published in his lifetime:

> From all my lame defeats and oh! much more
> From all the victories that I seemed to score;
> From cleverness shot forth on Thy behalf
> At which, while angels weep, the audience laugh;
> From all my proofs of Thy divinity,
> Thou, who wouldst give no sign, deliver me.
> . . . .
> Lord of the narrow gate and the needle's eye,
> Take from me all my trumpery lest I die.

I find such rejection of one's own gifts and of the voice it gives rise to profoundly, almost intolerably, heartbreaking. Yet the more deeply we look into Lewis the more personally unsettled—really, the more imprisoned—he seems, especially in the late forties and very early fifties. Surely this period was Lewis' Dark Night of the Soul, the first of three quick steps that take him into his fifties.

We see the first stage, this darkness, most clearly in his Latin letters to Don Giovanni Calabria, more intimate, even, than those to Arthur Greeves as an adolescent.[8] On January 14, 1949, he confesses to being troubled in his home life and to suffering from accidia, lukewarmness almost to the point of despair. He allows that he may never write another book worth reading—and expresses gratitude for that, since his popularity has given rise to pride. Better that he fall silent. This is happening as Mrs. Moore's mental health is worsening, along with her moods and her character, and before she is hospitalized. On January 12, 1950, he writes to his friend Sister Penelope, "Pray for me; I am suffering incessant temptations to uncharitable thoughts at present; one of those black moods in which nearly all one's friends seem to be selfish or even false." Then, no fewer than three years later (December 26, 1951), he reveals that only recently (eight months earlier, on St. Mark's day, April 25th) does he finally come to believe that his sins have been forgiven. And note: this is *four years after* having written an essay on forgiveness (not published during his lifetime) in which he asserts that it is itself grievously sinful not to accept forgiveness if one has confessed one's sins, repented of them, and done penance for them. As Lewis's conversion occurred shortly after the death of his father, this great relief comes to him only after the death of Mrs. Moore.

Thus begins the second, very brief, step. What remission the unencumbered fugitive must have felt, foreshadowed twenty years earlier but now the real thing. For just here we see that change in Lewis's work (sowed earlier and ripening gradually) that some have so securely, and so implausibly, attributed to a presumed defeat by Elizabeth Anscombe at the Socratic Club (and not-so-by-the-way: he never stopped making the argument that she supposedly rebutted, that naturalism is self-refuting). After a harrowing descent, followed by this transitional remission, we will have fruition.[9]

---

8 This abysmal state could have been triggered by any number of events, probably many in combination. Warnie's alcoholism may have had its part, and certainly the worsening of Lewis' household circumstances was prominent: he says as much. But I suspect the complicity of yet another death, that in May of 1945 of his great friend Charles Williams, whose presence Lewis continued to feel strongly even after-the-fact.

9 Perhaps Joy Gresham, though only after a while and for all her own affliction and the complication of her children, relaxed Lewis, provided a zone not unlike his original redoubt but more capacious, and thus afforded him the comfort and reassurance that would be the conditions for an amplified vision, a *Zeit* flight, so to speak, into his fifties. It seems the marriage became, and quickly, a genuine love affair, the real thing, and Warren thought Joy, of whom he was very fond, one of the best things ever to

His work becomes more eschatological, and before our very eyes blossoms into the third step.

Of course, the full and formal expression of Lewis's vision of longing, hope, and heaven comes in 1941, in his magnificent sermon "The Weight of Glory,"[10] the first full flowering of his apologetic signature. It is there that he famously tells us, "I believe in Christianity the way I believe the sun has risen, not only because I see it, but because by it, I see everything else."[11] But it is, I believe, in the early fifties that we see the irruption of what I think of as Lewis's full-blown eschatological stage, the Oil of Gladness pouring Himself forth into the now fully-receptive soul, beckoning him, not away from boyhood, social and professional convention, the *Zeitgeist*, and the like—that he had achieved—but from our "gaping wound" itself and towards the only Geist who counts. "The World's Last Night" appears in 1951, debunking the myth of evolutionary progress, arguing (again) that naturalism is self-refuting, and reminding us that we must "dress our souls not for the electric lights of the present world but for the daylight of the next. The good dress is the one that will face that light. For that light will last longer." *Narnia* too is pouring out, and notably, at the very end of the last book he saw through the press, *Letters to Malcolm, Chiefly on Prayer*, Lewis suggests much more of that "everything else" he had referred to "The Weight of Glory," certainly much more than most of us routinely see:

> Then the new earth and sky, the same yet not the same as these, will rise in us as we have risen in Christ. And once again, after who knows what aeons of the silence and the dark, the birds will sing and the water flow, and lights and shadows move across the hills. . . . Guesses of course, only guesses. If they are not true, something better will be.

It's as though he were training a telescope on Eternity, bringing us closer and closer as he leaves space-time and its cultures and mores and assumptions and sorrows behind. He shows us the Only Real Thing: then

---

happen to his brother: telling testimony from the man who despised Mrs. Moore.

10 Strong adumbrations are in *Pilgrim's Regress* and even in *The Problem of Pain* (1940).

11 Whenever this vision arises, no matter if the mode be narrative, expository, argumentative, or imaginative—and often these modes tumble forth as though all at once—his rhetoric tends to move from the possible to the probable, then to the promising, thereafter to the pleasurable, penultimately to desire, and finally to the hope for Heaven.

and there, not here and now. It is why he could say, and mean, "anything not eternal is eternally out of date."

Yet, while guiding us through his joy-filled escape route to hope, then Heaven, he also turns his telescope around to show us the small world we would be leaving. He had done this in *Screwtape*, of course, and in *The Last Battle*. More complexly he did it in his great masterwork *Till We Have Faces*. Orual learned the lesson that Lewis also teaches in "The World's Last Night": ". . . a man should 'sit loose' to his own individual life, should remember how short, precarious, temporary, and provisional a thing it is, and should never give all his heart to anything which will end when his life ends. . . . the whole life of humanity in this world is also precarious, temporary, and provisional." However, my own favorite look back upon our small snare-of-a-world comes (again) from that minor masterpiece "The Seeing Eye." Avoiding Christ, Lewis tells us, has become very easy in our time: "avoid silence, avoid solitude, avoid any train of thought that leads off the beaten track. Concentrate on money, sex, status, health and (above all) on your own grievances. Keep the radio on. Live in a crowd. Use plenty of sedation. . . . You'll find advertisements helpful: especially those with a sexy or a snobbish appeal."

So as the fifties unfolded, Lewis became more and more withdrawn from the life he had led: from some of his friends, from Oxford, from bachelorhood, and from the sorts of things he had been writing. He became less of a controversialist (though his book-reviewing remained crisp and severe) and more meditative (as in "The Apologist's Evening Prayer"). Even in his professional work his old militancy was mitigated. Take *An Experiment in Criticism* (1961). For its premonitory (reader-oriented) thinking, this anti-high brow (*i.e.* anti-Leavis) corrective should be a touchstone for the literary professoriate. But who ever heard of a work of theory *that* short, *that* readable? *this moving?* Consider its stirring peroration:

> My own eyes are not enough for me, I will see through those of others. Reality, even seen through the eyes of many, is not enough. I will see what others have invented. . . . I regret that the brutes cannot write books. Very gladly would I learn what face things present to a mouse or a bee. . . . Literary experience heals the wound, without undermining the privilege, of individuality. . . . as in worship, in love, in moral action, and in knowing, I transcend myself; and am never more myself than when I do.

Has any literature student here, or anywhere, ever read any criticism or theory as appealing as that? Maybe in Foucault, or Derrida, or Leavis? Lewis made it look just too easy, too understandable, too *uncomplicated*: it just couldn't be serious. He certainly did not toss it off, but it is leavened: unbelligerent, pellucid and convincing, without the pastiche Barfield saw in Lewis's contribution to *The Personal Heresy* some thirty years earlier.[12]

We might say that, like another fugitive, his heroine of *The Queen of Drum*, Lewis is finally making it to Elfland. But we can go back farther than that poem. His earliest hero, Dymer, was escaping too, and was killed for the rebellion he caused in the Perfect City—but not before he lay with the perfect bride and begot a monster who, after killing his father, became a god dwelling in "white lands long-lost Saturnian years." In fact Lewis, I believe, wrote four autobiographical works in addition to *Surprised by Joy*: *Dymer, The Pilgrim's Regress, Till We Have Faces*, and *A Grief Observed*, but the first of these was *Dymer*. It is he, the eponymous fugitive-hero, who lived in Lewis to the very end.

So there we have my rendering of Lewis the fugitive and his voice. But what of Lewis himself, the radical subversive who would say that the only people who condemn escape are jailers? Alas, by now we must wonder if the *personae* of such a figure are at all reliable avatars of the actual person. Any great writer's reputation is complicated, tenuous, and somehow false: a dicey matter even for the writer. Ann Rigney, making some sense of a reputation in *The Peculiar Legacies of Walter Scott*, tells us that to have legs a reputation requires "productive remembering": that is, portability, re-mediation (or non-print versions of the work), and diffusion. For Lewis it would prove a long, hard haul. Over the past seventy-five years or so Lewis's reputation simmered, then boiled to the brim, then simmered again, then boiled again, though not so high as it did the first boil, then, some fifty years ago, went cold, only to resume a slow, then to a very quick, boil.

Any number of events were influential: studies of Lewis dating from the late forties, then a blossoming of scholarship dating from the sixties onwards (thanks to the diligence of Clyde Kilby at Wheaton College and what is now the Wade Center), ever more Lewis works (thanks to the unrelenting editorial devotion of Walter Hooper), the founding of Lewis societies (here the New York C. S. Lewis Society was pivotal), the translation of Lewis's life and work into non-print media (not only the early

---

12 A portion of Lewis's work, especially his professional academic work, does not fit the paradigm I'm sketching here. But the preponderance of it—including his Experiment—does. Nevertheless, in light of those "pictures in the fire," we should remember that portraits, like lives, are not geometry proofs.

TV movies, the biopic, and the blockbuster movie, but the unlikely: *The Question of God* on PBS, and *Freud's Last Session*, Off-Broadway), the lamentable merchandising of Lewis-related products and pseudo-Lewis books, and the many internet conversations replete with a social network of sites and blogs. In short, the reputation, or some aspect of it, seems to have boiled over. Now Lewis gets thoughtful and approving print attention beyond *Narnia*, every now and then his name being dropped quite casually as an intellectual benchmark to be reckoned with. In short, he has achieved diffusion, or at least a version of him has, and from that there is no escaping—at least for the foreseeable future. But who knows?

More than fifty years ago there was this, largely unnoticed in Lewis commentary. You will, I believe, find it surprising, I mean beyond that it appeared in the first place. In May of 1959 "Christian Spaceman—C. S. Lewis," by the influential critic and book-reviewer Edmund Fuller, appeared in the high-brow, culturally eclectic hard-cover magazine *Horizon*, an event, for its length and analytical richness, but also for its prophetic insights. For example, in introducing Americans to the Deep Space (Ransom) Trilogy, Fuller makes the following tangential observation, so utterly surprising to us more than fifty years later:

> I rate high among Lewis's accomplishments a work generally less well known, as yet, than the trilogy [this is 1959, remember], but for which I predict a growing reputation and a long life. This is the series of seven books for children which compose *The Chronicles of Narnia*.

He then gives a wonderfully inviting, concise summary and interpretation of the *Chronicles*. But he ends his essay with an appreciation: "I am grateful to Lewis for some of my richest experiences of mind and heart," leaving us with choice imagery from Deep Heaven (not *Narnia*) and writing, "am I to say these are not real? I count them among the great symbolic visions of ultimate reality which reveal to us that we are more—and are part of more—than the data of our senses can record." In our Narnia-saturated habitation, we see that Dr. Johnson is right: we need to be reminded more often than instructed.

Here, then, are two final reminders. Twenty years ago Christopher Hewetson, the vicar of what for three decades had been C. S. Lewis' church in Headington Quarry, Oxford, seemed to sum up the English attitude towards the great man perfectly. He told his congregation that, yes, perhaps the time had come to improve their "connection with C.S. Lewis." After all, Mr. Hewetson continued, "when I came here three and a half years ago . . . [t]here was a certain 'yes but'. I found it difficult to get a well-known preacher to preach at the dedication of the Narnia window. *Since then his rating has increased.* [my emphasis] . . . He was a very committed Christian. . . . We must be proud of our connection with him. . . ." But this good man was wrong. By the time of the vicar's condescension, Lewis had already been the most famous Christian apologist writing in English for most of the century, his voice among the most recognizable on the BBC during the war, his picture on the cover of *Time* magazine, his books selling in the millions. This year The Cambridge University Press is bringing back five Lewis titles that have been out of print (including *The Allegory of Love*, originally from the Oxford University Press), and there is a statue of Lewis in Westminster Abbey.

The second reminder gets it right, pointing from the *personae* to the man himself. Not too long before Mr. Hewetson made his plea, Peter Bayley, the distinguished scholar who also had been Lewis's pupil, really did strike the resonant chime about the man he saw buried twenty-five years earlier:

My last memory is of his funeral on a very cold and frosty but brilliantly sunny morning. There was one candle on the coffin as it was carried out into the churchyard. It seemed . . . a symbol of the man and his integrity and his absoluteness and his faith that the flame burned so steadily, even in the open air, and seemed so bright, even in the bright sun.

So long his own man, Lewis had labored hard both intellectually and spiritually to give himself away. Toward the end of his life he seems to have succeeded and now, finally, was home, free. Though too convivial to be a Jeremiah, this resistance fighter had "fought the good fight, ran the race, and kept the faith," and "to the ruddy end," as he might put it. That Little End Room turned out to be no smaller than all Eternity.

And—in my rendering, at least—he has left us that fugitive voice (which I first encountered nearly fifty years ago). It speaks now, making and marking a way out of this "enemy-occupied territory." For his imaginative effusions remain as radical as nature itself; his reason and reasoning as dependable as the multiplication tables; and his spirit as beckoning, as liberated, and as liberating as the open arms of the Cross at which he worshipped.

SEVENTEEN

DIGGING (into "old") MOVIES
Let's Talk

IF YOU ARE AMONG those who think an old movie is one that didn't come out in the last ten years, that movies older than that aren't worth your time, that the experience of seeing a movie on the big screen is the same as watching it on your television or your computer (or on your telephone!); or if you cannot abide movies not in color, or that have sub-titles, or you cannot fathom the intellectual, social, and imaginative richness of being able to aptly quote lines from movies, to see connections among many movies, to discern a director's signature in his work, or—especially—to appreciate the difference between you liking a movie and a movie being a bad piece of work even though you enjoyed it—if any of this applies to you or is you, then stop reading. Right now. You, as Wayne in his World would put it, are not worthy.

Some of us still go to the movies, frequently and often alone, and look forward to talking about them with others. We also enjoy reading movie reviews, including reviews of movies we probably will not see. (I will not be talked out of seeing a movie by a negative review but can be talked *into* seeing one even if only, as part of a negative review, there is one favored element, like a performance that might grab me.) Yet many people enjoy great movies have little patience for movie *criticism*, which usually provides more cinematic and historical context than a review. And that's too bad: movies may not be urgent, and most of them aspire to nothing higher than a pop culture buzz and healthy box office, but they are art, often even high art, while also being successful.

188

Moreover, criticism digs, technically and with commentary, into the formal elements of movies, such as shot composition and length, transitions between shots, movement within a shot, aspects of both visual and aural design, and script (of course). For example, the unrelenting gloom and doom music—too loud and relentless at that—of *Out of the Furnace* almost ruins the movie, in spite of strengths like Woody Harrelson's inventive intensity: it's okay to cue my emotions but not to dictate them (those rising violins at the end of *The Woman in Gold*: there oughta be a law). The critic notices details, of pacing and mood, of an actor's small movements and the like, because details make movies. (Carefully watch Brad Pitt, a superb actor, in his small, almost micro-movements, in *Moneyball*, for example his eye contact or lack thereof.) And there those details are, hiding in plain sight, to be replayed and stopped cold as necessary. Then comes *Meaning*. Why is Paul Newman's "Butch Cassidy" not able to see the face of his pursuer but somehow intuits who it might be? There, right there, is the whole movie.

Here, then, are three examples of film criticism, each all-to-brief, merely suggestive of a great deal more that could be said, on movies from 1971, one of them made in black and white. Why 1971? Because interesting art never gets old, and I'm told 1971 was a very interesting year for movies (though no year could come close to 1939). Besides, if you're under fifty, they are supposed to be too old to matter, and yet they do.

First, though, the big picture, what in movie-making is called an establishing shot. The reviewing clan and I both thought highly of *The Hospital*. I was moved, provoked and challenged. And those effects have not gone away; both the movie and my memory of it hold up. On the other hand, we (reviewers and I) disagreed on *The Nightcomers* (a prequel to Henry James' ghost story *The Turn of the Screw* and its fine movie version, *The Innocents*), to which I give a thumbs up. If you still really need to know what made Brando the greatest of his generation, here you shall see. (And if you care to appreciate what makes a character truly frightening—although the very recent *Babadook* really is the scariest movie of all time, as even William Friedkin says, and he directed the second scariest, *The Exorcist*—if you want to know a scary person pay attention to *The Nightcomers*. My movie-savvy friend Sylvette, who to this day remains in love with Brando, had to stop watching.) Finally reviewers and I disagreed on *The Last Picture Show*—seminal this, epoch-making that, courageous (courageous!) something else—to which I give a yawn, in spite of Ben Johnson's deeply moving performance. (He would win a Best Supporting Actor Oscar for his work in this movie, as would Cloris Leachman; but her searing work and fetching derriere are not enough to overcome Cy-bill Shepherd's stick figure, with or without its frontal nudity.) You see? Movies are the only public mass medium of art that can provoke wide and passionate conversation. And, brother, can it get personal.

THE HOSPITAL

The Hospital is about middle-age and the middle class; about dropping out and copping out; about order and chaos; and about impotence. But ultimately it is about what our response should be to these, singly and in combination. Written by Paddy Chayefsky (winner of three Oscars for Best Original Screenplay, including this one), directed by Arthur Hiller, and stolen by George C. Scott (Best Actor Oscar for his *Patton*), *The Hospital* leaves you wondering but not guessing and, almost in spite of itself, finally leaves its threads woven into a very satisfying emotional tapestry. And all the spokes emerge from one superb metaphor. Sure, the hospital is a microcosmos, but within the scope of this movie it is also the only cosmos. Every question, every conflict, every posturing, whining, self-absorbed psyche, and every would-be do-gooder who thinks with the heart rather than the head—all of these and more are as true of the world as of the hospital we see in this movie.

The plot is thick. George Scott, as the Director of Medicine at a great New York hospital, does battle with himself and with some force (for some time unidentified) apparently bent upon sabotaging the hospital. His son a twenty-three-year-old, bomb-throwing Maoist, his daughter an ignorant tramp (at seventeen she already has had two abortions in two years), and his marriage a dismal failure, the Director contemplates the sole logical alternative to his sexual, psychical, and emotional impotence: suicide. Ironically, only the mysterious force, intruding from far outside of the Director's world, manages to save him.

That force comes in the from of an ex-doctor (Barnard Hughes) who, having experienced a mystical conversion, has abandoned his practice in order to become a Methodist missionary to Apache Indians in Mexico. He enters the hospital for a routine check-up in perfect health, but gross (though not uncommon) negligence reduces him to a comatose state within one week. When a fellow-patient, dead as a result of incredible (though not uncommon) ignorance, appears to him as God the doctor-missionary resolves to punish the guilty parties, three doctors and a nurse. His modus operandus, as he gleefully admits to the Director, is simply to reduce the staff-members to the status of patients in their own hospital.

Our hero, having decided to end all with a dose of potassium, is saved by the missionary's daughter (Diana Rigg), herself an ex-bomb-throwing radical, who accompanied her father to the mountains and now believes "in everything." After hearing his moving analysis of his own impotence (including a declaration that, in spite of having overcome great odds to achieve genuine fame, he no longer cares about medicine), she accuses him of indulgent self-pity, leaves, returns just before the fatal injection, and sustains a violent and thrice-perpetrated sexual assault. So happy are they both with his newly-resurrected flesh and spirit that the following morning they declare their mutual love.

The difficulty is that the Director, in order to enjoy this love, must abandon the hospital in favor of the Mexican Apaches. He is indeed torn, but, precisely when he has decided to leave, the hospital director quits his post in the face of a militant onslaught. Throughout the movie angry protestors and self-styled revolutionaries have been massing, disruptively and menacingly, outside the hospital (though within its ambit). They don't like the hospital's plans for expansion, or for employment, or . . . it really doesn't matter. Here we glimpse much about the confused Sixties: the villain Ivy is one of the radicals, a gifted young intern. And what the protestors do not know is that some Higher Power *within* the walls is setting right the actual evils that subvert the good work the hospital can do—*without* destroying the hospital. In the event, and true to his middle-class, middle-aged beliefs, the Director of Medicine declares to his Love that "someone has to be responsible" and—cognizant of his newly re-discovered potency—returns to work, now as its General Director.

The hospital trope proves irresistible. Is this not the world? Is this not life? But the central, unifying element is Scott's character; that is, Scott, who ranges from vexation to resignation to puzzlement and on to decisiveness and finally triumph. The problem—and a problem it very well may be—is one of response: Is the audience to take the film as a satire (on hospitals)? Or as a serious inquiry into the crisis of Middle-Age Menopause? As a Study of The Times? Or (as the presence of the microcosmic trope would indicate) as a lesson on the World? Choose all of them; you won't go wrong.

The film (a crisp ninety-eight minutes) begins in a semi-documentary fashion, with voice-over narration accompanying a travel-shot of the old patient. The very funny point about an empty bed, followed by the discovery of a dead intern, is then made in a conventional manner; indeed, throughout the entire film no use is made of an unusual lens or camera angle. A very sudden cut reveals the titles, over a close, still-shot of the missionary standing alone, watching. The unexpected, loud, up-beat, and heavily-rhythmic music screams to the audience "comedy-satire!" But already we don't trust it, and the Director's disturbed and sincere response to the fact of the dead intern belies the musical message.

All transitions are straight cuts except for one, a focus-out to a flashback (when the missionary describes his vision of God); but a traveling camera forces the audience to concentrate upon Scott with great intensity, and this concentration sounds the keynote of the entire film. Though the camera tilts only to follow some movement, it pursues, parallels, and pans almost mercilessly: where most directors would cut, Hiller simply moves his camera. Thus the average shot-length is an extraordinary 16.7 seconds, and the median average (I feel certain) would be closer to 25 seconds. The result of such length must be concentration, upon character and upon particular events.

The pacing, from frenetic to still, always fits, and camera movement is central to it. A very effective device, used sparingly, is for the camera, traveling in pursuit of a character (usually the Director), to be suddenly closed out, usually behind the glass window of a closing door; after such an event Hiller always allows the shot to linger instead of immediately cutting—further concentration upon character. The camera is hand-held two or three times, the most effective of these being when it follows the Director before he is assaulted by the missionary. You are there.

This effect is heightened by a very rigid control of sound. Music occurs a mere four times, unheard of, for a total of no more than 2.5 minutes—at the beginning and end of the film, immediately after the Director has his orgasm, and immediately before the Director is assaulted by the missionary. (All figures are approximate, though very close. They are based upon two consecutive viewings and a good stop watch.) Ambient sound is non-existent, wild sound is almost non-existent, sound-effects are unobtrusive and strikingly rare. Voices seem amplified: another way of focusing attention upon character.

Three shots deserve special attention. The first of these is the "hallway shot," during which the Director scolds Mrs. Christie, the Chief Nurse. The camera moves in, out, and around, the shot lasting an extraordinary 2'13". The second, lasting 45 seconds (though it seems longer), is the "curtain shot;" we are given an image of the medicine man, and then the camera pans *and* travels (right), through a close-up of a curtain, to a terrified patient. (The excellence of this shot, and of the other, is mitigated by what seems to be inept splicing, for a slight jump and an alternation in lighting are noticeable in the two images.)

The third shot, the climactic one, is the greatest in the film. George

Scott, explaining and justifying his impotence, is magnificent. The shot lasts 1'45" and consists solely of a close-up of Scott, framed by darkness, speaking for the full 1'45". The camera moves very little, and, except for the monologue, there is no sound. The result is total sympathy for the character and, fortunately, great insight into a/ the character and, thus, b/ the entire film. Indeed, this is *the* indispensable shot.

It is best to close with some words in further praise of Scott. His "business" is . . . perfect (*e.g.* the manner in which he crushes out his cigarette before the suicide attempt); and he, especially in his treatment of jokes, is almost solely responsible for the scathing humor that exposes the malice, insouciance and self-absorption of—not a toxic world but of too many of its inhabitants. "Where do you train your nurses, Mrs. Christie, at Dachau?!" "Impotent is beautiful. Power to the impotent!" He could have been merely a self-conscious satirist; instead, he becomes a grim character with a grim but dark and angry humorous view of himself and of his world.

Do we laugh at our universe? Get back to work? Better understand the nature of maturity? Re-adjust our reverence for doctors? Hold in contempt the exhibitionists who complain and menace but bring nothing more to the table? Worship the Life Force expressed by the Almighty Orgasm? Believe in God? Watch Scott, respond as he responds, and we cannot go wrong. Without his Director we might all be tempted to throw in the towel. As for myself: Thanks to the great Scott (and Chayefsky and Hiller) I've re-dedicated myself to the proposition that the antidote to chaos of all kinds is grownups.

THE NIGHTCOMERS

In taking the nearly one-hundred-and-twenty-year-old dare posed by Henry James' minor masterpiece, *The Turn of the Screw*, writer Michael Hasting and producer-director Michael Winner have offered to the world an emotionally and intellectually satisfying hypothesis. Cold word, "hypothesis," for a work as exciting as this; but James was himself both thoughtful and provocative of thought, and the movie is, as a prequel, faithful to its literary progenitor. Committed to terrifying us, the movie pursues the original themes of guilt, pain, love, hate, subjugation, and (especially) spiritual corruption.

That terror is based upon a response to the puzzle of Flora's and Miles' motivation: whence the relationship of these two young innocents to Quint, the groundskeeper who presumably provides their frighteningly premature knowledge and instigates their terror-tactics against Miss Jessel, their nanny? Marlon Brando as Quint is the key. More than merely eerie settings and near-gothic, seductive cinematography (as well as clever editing, which sometimes teases, sometimes shocks) buttress Brando's cold menace, casual sadism, tender malignancy, and his insatiable appetite for all of these. He creeps up on us, baffles us, and then horrifies us.

From the outset, a contrast—indeed, hostility—is established between the house, especially its interior, and the out-of-doors. The opening sequence consists of a game of hide-and-seek played in the woods between Quint and the children. Clearly we are in Quint's domain; the rack-focusing between him and elements of the forest establish their close relationship, as does his familiarity with the lake, marsh, and paths. Most striking, however, is his apparent fondness for, and insight into, certain creatures native to the forest. A permanent association between them is established when, in a grotesque early scene, Quint provokes, then explains, the behavior of a frog as it puffs on a cigar to the point of its own explosion.

Cross-cutting interpolates interior shots into this first sequence, and the contrast is remarkable. Within reign civility and order: drapes, furniture, paintings, knick-knacks, and (especially) sunlight. The interior is markedly devoid of those forest creatures (frogs, worms, turtles) for which Quint feels an affinity. Significantly, not until the seduction of the children becomes apparent does the camera reveal, and in close-ups no less, worms on and within the very meat and lettuce eaten by the children. Is the potential for evil inherent in Goodness itself? Once the seduction is well underway, Quint himself enters the house (in spite of the protests and commands of Mrs. Gross, the housekeeper), bringing with him those repellent symbols of incivility, disorder, and of post-lapsarian primitiveness. The visual contrast and philosophical hostility between the interior and the outdoors (happily Winner chose to shoot on location in Cambridgeshire) is further conveyed by that sly editing and a sort of peering, even voyeuristic, camera-work. (One complaint: too often, and too regularly, sequences are punctuated with the tiring cliché of a long-shot, usually by night, of the house.)

Quint is a delicate character. Brutal and corrupting, he does not himself seem corrupt; nor does he seem to be aware of his influence upon the children. He does not violate goodness, he does not even choose to deliberately ignore it; the moral realm is simply invisible to him, exactly as it is to any forest creature. Trees, marshes, frogs, worms, and turtles know no morality, and neither does Peter Quint. He loves the children, and his frolicking with them in the woods arouses great sympathy; he is distinctly not unnaturally depraved. Thus, when he enters the house and sexually brutalizes Miss Jessel, we are stunned and repelled—until she asks why he persists in torturing her. "Don't be a hypocrite," he responds, "it gives you great pleasure too." The wild out-of-doors inside all of us.

The achievement of this balance is solely Brando's. His lilting Irish accent, bear-like frolicsomeness, winsome, funny, and pitiable facial expressions, delicate and precise gestures (*e.g.* when telling of his father's abandonment of him) are never overdrawn, always consistent, and always compelling. Only once does the normally-pragmatic camera intrude on his behalf; after he brutalizes Miss Jessel, they make passionate love, which the camera reveals through very slow dissolves and superimpositions. The effect is to convince us of Miss Jessel's compliant pleasure and therefore to belie the suffering and pleading tone of her question, "Why?", to Quint.

Stephanie Beacham as Miss Jessel, Verna Harvey as Flora, and Christopher Ellis as Miles are precise. The first is never anything more than a bad girl; coming, as she does, from the world of the house, her corruption is merely very naughty; using the children as go-betweens in her love-affair, she never realizes the effects of her behavior upon them. Symbolic of her character is the fainting-spell in the greenhouse the day after her night of love-making. Again the hand-held camera dramatizes the event and helps to convince us that Miss Jessel simply is not up to it, emotionally or otherwise. Towards the end of the movie, when Quint discovers her drowned and filthy body at the shore of the lake, a medium-shot, followed by a close-up, reveal her to be (and, presumably, to have been) strikingly similar to Flora's hollow-eyed, grotesque doll. A riveting shot.

The children begin as innocents but, not having had the opportunity to mature in the world of the house, quickly begin to lose any sense of morality. Intrigued by the woods and emotionally nourished by Quint, the children come to view life—and especially the love-affair—as a game, where rules can be invented and manipulated at will. Quint, for example, describes to Miles how he may, simply by imagining, cause an arrow to hit its mark. During the kite-flying scene Miles actually defies the law of gravity by soaring high above a ravine; quick-cuts, a traveling camera, and low and high angles make this scene one of the most inventive and captivating I have ever seen. It is unrelieved in its manner, in portraying Quint's frightened response, and in communicating a pervasive, preternatural tone.

Their happy inability to distinguish reality from illusion (their woodland frolics with Quint are always accompanied by music, which almost never accompanies interior scenes) prompt the children to conclude that, in order to stay and consummate their love, Quint and Miss Jessel must die. Having seen the violent love-play (and imitated it), and having formed some confused notions about the relationship of pain, love, and hate, the children cause Miss Jessel to drown and Miles, closing his eyes and imagining, shoots Quint with an arrow, first in the back and then in the top of his head. Our horror is in knowing that Quint dies confused and ignorant and that the children—aware but ignorant, children of the forest—will return to the house, to be in it but, frighteningly, never to be of it. If you don't know the originals (book or movie) but do know that they exist, then you know, you certainly know, what poor Miss Jessel's successor is in for.

And therein lies the achievement of *The Nightcomers*.

THE LAST PICTURE SHOW

It is in the title that director Peter Bogdanovich makes his promise, and a worthy promise it is. As a metaphor for enchantment and escape a picture show is strikingly precise and evocative, but when that general correspondence is coupled with a more particular one—the movie theater as a metaphor for a specific time and place—then you have a figure of almost mythic proportions, a metaphor operating on so many different levels and in so many different ways that its meaning becomes exquisitely burdensome. This movie is not up to that task.

The end of innocence is the end of illusion, whether it be experienced by boys and girls, small towns, or whole countries. The counterfeit romances, for example, of boys-to-men, Dwayne, Sonny, Jayce and the other's seem harmless enough while innocence prevails, but later, when unprotected by adolescence, those same romances are revealed as being full of despair and frustration; that is, the children grow up to become the new adults, people dishonest with their own emotions, enthralled by cheap, obvious illusions (this new-fangled television), and ignorant of the moral consequence of their actions (extra-marital sex or incomprehensible wars). Worse yet, each generation seems damned to repeat the same performance. Provocative, important, even profound.

But there is a problem. A narrative should be both story and study; it should move forward by telling and showing, and it should examine (people, places, epochs . . .). In *The Last Picture Show* scenarists Bogdanovich and Larry McMurtry (working from the latter's novel) seem not to know how to tell the story, and director Bogdanovich seems unwilling to do so. The depiction of time and place is irresistibly evocative, but too often the evocation serves nothing but itself; and the consequence of that relationship, when it treats of the past, is mere nostalgia, a good enough sentiment, but not the one to do the heavy lifting this movie needs.

The two main culprits are the absence of color and an excessive reliance upon the image of the movies, the popular entertainments of the day. Doubtless, color was avoided in order to add verisimilitude, to bring a documentary effect; many movies, especially serious ones, were not done in color in the early fifties. But we here and now no longer live in a cinematically colorless age, so the device seems heavy-handed. Though it works well in some shots (*e.g.* the medium and long shots of the inherently colorless town), we nevertheless wonder how another director might have used color to evoke the same effects, instead of merely banging us over the head with them. The songs and television shows of the period reinforce the sense of narrative falseness; they are used too often, and their use is heavy-handed; an opportunity to insert them is never missed. So we have a sort of documentary. A study. The times they are a-changin' all right; just not fast enough

We have two exceptions to this fatal judgment, set-design and wild sound. The sets, interior and exterior, are full of accurate and consistent details which establish tone as well as authenticity and which never intrude (as does the background music, for example). Just as authentic are the sounds of creaking doors, clambering dishes, coughing motors, and rustling wind, especially during the tank scene when old Sam—Ben Johnson—tells of a former love. And then there is a third element . . . Bogdanovich uses four dissolves during the movie, one so long that it is very nearly a superimposition. This transitional device, at least when used with such frequency, is not now current but was fairly common in the early fifties. This element falls into the same category as the use of black-and-white and by all rights should be judged similarly; but they are not ubiquitous, and, since we still see them from time-to-time, the dissolves work, suggesting a faded reality and its loss.

The time spent on establishing atmosphere would be well-spent if it did not impede the plot; unfortunately, it is not until we are more than one third of the way into the movie that we catch a glimpse of any plot at all. Instead of plot, we are offered images designed to establish not character but "mentalities." In the truck with his first girlfriend, Sonny removes her brassiere and, while kissing her, fondles her breasts; when be becomes too aggressive, she slaps his hand and complains that she does not care to become pregnant. The scene fulfills its imagistic purpose, but nothing leads to it and nothing derives from it. Too often do we see Ruth, the middle-aged, frustrated, despairing housewife (Cloris Leachman) simply *crying*: you want to shout, "we got it – move on." But an effective moment comes when a medium pan shot reveals the entire class as its instructor reads a passage from Keats' "The Nightingale"—moving and communicative. Yet its dislocation is such that it could have been done in a dozen ways, or not at all. When Sam, the symbol of love, benevolence and decency dies, we sense that, at last, here is a plot-complication, but, alas!, there is no plot to be complicated. Such lack of economy—establishing atmosphere and mentality before getting on with the plot—makes the movie seem longer than its 113 minutes. As for the key element of the plot: I won't do more than mention the utter improbability of the discovered letter: any self-respecting *deus* would be embarrassed to use it as his *machina*.

Sam—that is, Ben Johnson—is the centerpiece, the axel from which all spokes emanate. He is near-craggy, self-possessed and, above all, decent. Aware of his surroundings and stoically unhappy with them ("I've lived around that sort of trash my whole life" and "I remember how this land used to be—I owned it forty years ago"), he is alone in choosing dignity and honor as alternatives to despair and futility. As Sonny recognizes after his "wedding," innocence died with Sam. Ben Johnson makes full use of the character, especially in the "tank" scene when, while fishing with Sonny, he implies that each generation must make the same mistakes. His features, his beard, his wavy, ruffled hair, the turn of his head are, without words, supremely eloquent. Here is study worth the work.

There are some very good moments in *The Last Picture Show*. The final scenes (of the truck-interior and of the town) are movingly reminiscent of the opening scenes (generations do indeed repeat the errors of their predecessors), and the camera-work during the Johnny-Boy death-sequence could not be better: close *and* unobtrusive. But the lack of story-telling economy (reinforced by generally long takes) mars the movie, and the black-and-white, the background music, and all those TV special inserts belie the intention of a fundamentally pragmatic camera. The movie could have been great. Alas, too many seams are too apparent too often.

Form always matters, whether the viewer knows it or not, cares or not, or sees it or not. In the case of these movies, best, I think, to see all of them: a varied cluster of themes, styles, techniques, appeals, and levels of achievement in a mere three, all from more than forty years ago. But why stop? Well, no movie-lover can really ever stop. We're only resting here. It's why my list of Top Ten Greatest American Movies now has nearly sixty titles. Movies are our waking dreams, an intricately collaborative mass medium of conversation, of *study* and *story*, still big (no matter what Norma Desmond says!) and all-possessing, and hitting us best when we are in the dark, just like when we are asleep, at night, dreaming. You go figure. I'm going to the movies.

EIGHTEEN

THE MICK
In Memoriam

WHERE IMAGINATION GOES the rest of us must follow, so our interior landscape matters greatly. Take, for example, a boy (and more than a few girls) aged, say, eight to fourteen, at a time in history (the 'fifties) when football, basketball, and the opposite sex offered no competition: when a boy *played ball*, from early morning until after dark under whatever street-lamp there was. Hardball, softball, stickball (in-the-box and on-the-bounce), stoopball, slapball, catch-a-fly, and variations of these, by himself if necessary. Few were the moments when there was no spaldeen at hand, and a stickball bat of some sort. ("Spal-deen" was the term-of-art for a Spalding rubber ball, much preferred to a Pensy Pinky, let a alone the effete tennis ball.)

This boy tunes his imagination to an archetypal scene, Providentially composed. The greatest sports franchise in American history, playing our most deeply-rooted game, in our largest city, to our first mass television audience, proffers a successor to an icon (one Joe DiMaggio) of mythic proportions—a successor whose very name is somehow apt. The family name lends itself to wordplay—he sure did wear the mantle—and the first seems (but isn't) a familiar, and alliterative, nickname used among chums. It's as though Hollywood had changed it from something commonplace to something suitable to a marquee (like "Marilyn Monroe," resonating contemporaneously in the back-ground).

The boy had never seen the great DiMaggio play, nor of course those earlier legendary New York Yankees who were no less than so many Zeuses and Apollos (because in those older days gods walked the earth). But

199

he had Mickey Mantle, who even looked like another, slightly older boy, whose very grin seemed to say "c'mon, Jimmy, let's call for Eddie and Raymond and Russell and Demetria and play in-the-box, three-on-three! I got lots of time before I have to get to the Stadium." He had Mickey Mantle, who seemed able to walk on water, in fact run on water—even with two bad legs.

That boy—now grown, and realizing how easily that successor might have failed—knows that Mickey Charles Mantle, born October 20, 1931, in Spavinaw, Oklahoma, and elected to the Hall of Fame in 1974, in fact prevailed: twelve pennants and seven world championships; from 1953 to 1965 achievements that outstrip those of his superb contemporaries Aaron, May, and Frank Robinson, and rival those of DiMaggio himself; possessed of a ballplayer's two greatest assets, speed and power, combined beyond the limits of anyone who ever played, and with leonine grace, under enduring physical duress, often in surpassingly dramatic fashion; and all this, finally, with an absolute absence of preening. This is how Mickey Mantle became, simply, *The Mick*.

When I was fourteen I watched him pinch-hit yet another game-winning homerun, this in his first at-bat back from a prolonged injury, and, in the presence of my father, made the mistake of referring to The Mick as a "hero." My father demurred. "Ted Williams is a hero," he said, "Coleman, Bauer, and Houk are heroes. "The Mick"—whom my father in fact admired—"The Mick," he said, "has heart. Lots of heart. But he's not a hero." My father had been a medic in WWII, and the men he named, ballplayers all, were combat veterans, three of them decorated for valor. Thus the difference between a metaphor and the real thing. But to a boy, then and there, with life around him largely illusory, metaphor was real, and *that* reality (believe me in this) could be a very great refuge.

After his retirement The Mick once again became Mickey Mantle, not least because of what we learned about his off-the-field antics (which in the boy's day did not make it out of the locker room and would not have mattered to the boy anyway) and beset by more failings than anyone could have thought possible. But at the end, after his liver was replaced and just weeks before he succumbed to a ferocious cancer on August 13, 1995, he once again became The Mick, his heart and his power intact even within a body which he himself laughed at for its depletion. After all, that power had always resided in his heart, not his muscle.

Here in the second decade of the twenty-first century two books have told us how troubled a man and how great a ballplayer he was, Jane Leavy's *The Last Boy* and Allen Barra's *Mickey and Willie*. Both authors (reluctantly but not grudgingly and using the complex combination of statistics now known as Sabremetrics) come to the same conclusion about The Mick's greatness as a player: he simply owned the 'fifties and early 'sixties, even beyond his preternaturally gifted contemporary Willie Mays. (Barra argues persuasively that each deserved seven Most Valuable Player Awards.) But I will rest my judgment on the response to him of his teammates. They were both in awe of his talent and baseball knowledge (he could learn the opposition pitcher's pattern by the second inning and more than once predicted his own homerun while waiting his turn on deck) and of his tolerance for pain, and they loved him dearly for his good cheer and generosity, especially towards rookies, who were generally ignored if not berated. (Once The Mick put his arm around you or victimized you with a harmless prank you were in, and it didn't take long.) Many of those teammates' first sons were named Mickey.

As for me, in my mind's eye I still see that right-handed swing, the most beautiful—in its speed, grace and ferocity—in the history of the game. And I still see him, at the end of a long, ineluctably fleet dash into the great plains of left-center field of the old Yankee Stadium, lunging to his right to make a fully-extended, knee-high, back-handed catch of a laser-launched line drive to save Don Larsen's perfect game in the 1956 World Series, the only World Series perfect game in history. Ever. For me, and for millions just like me, that, folks, is really The Catch.

Not long before he died he filmed a message to his fans. Ravaged to the point of emaciation, and not only by time, he told them that he had let so many people down and, above all, to look at him and to know that, at the end of the day, here was no role model at all. Will not ten thousand lives or more be saved by organs the donation of which will have been inspired by him? And just as many lives on the verge of alcoholism brought back by his admonition not to do as he did? I wonder if my father would not have conceded that here, at last, was, if not heroism then certainly gallantry.

The great game goes on, as it always will, and just so does The Mick endure, in the imaginations and memories of those of us of a certain age, born and bred New Yorkers, in this twentieth year of his passing.

Where metaphor meets Reality may he continue to rest in peace.

NINETEEN

THE SALON
Restoring Conversation

Conversation: from *com+versare*, "to occupy oneself along with"; and from *conversus*, the past participle of *converter*, "to turn about."

The most fruitful and natural exercise of our mind, in my opinion, is discussion. I find it sweeter than any other action of our life; and that is the reason why, if I were right now forced to choose, I believe I would rather consent to lose my sight than my hearing or speech. . . .
– Michel de Montaigne (1533-92), "Of the Art of Conversing"

THE CENTRAL MODE of expression of any self is speech, the physical manifestation of our participation in the *logos*—the Word. We all intuit this centrality. It permeates the whole of our lives, work, and internal landscapes. All of our societies and clubs; all the words from print and electronic media; all the emailing, Facebook chatter and Twittering; every sermon and lesson taught in every classroom, lecture hall or laboratory; all the reading aloud and talking to ourselves, even if not aloud: none of these is anything but a surrogate for direct oral communication, the most concrete, palpable, frequent and important act of human being—speaking with others, same time, same place, face-to-face: *the interanimation of whole persons by way of speech.*

And so we converse. We "turn about" for many subsidiary reasons but really only for one big reason: recreation; that is, re-creation; making ourselves anew—intellectually, socially, emotionally and even spiritually. Or, as the English philosopher Michael Oakeshott (1901-1990) has it, conversation is "the invitation to disentangle oneself, for a while, from the urgencies of the here and now and to listen to the conversation in which human beings forever seek to understand themselves." In other words, understanding our Self—by way of and along with other Selves—is fun, and enjoyment intimately tied to two fundamental . . . not wants, but, rather, to two genuinely deep-seated needs: to be known by others and to know them.

Along the way we may persuade and be persuaded; we may instruct and we may learn; we may move and be moved; we may make decisions or not; we may be changed – trivially or fundamentally – or not; we may or may not live "the life of the mind." Mostly, though, we *recreate* in the presence, and with the participation, of *other people*. Of course there are variations: recreation takes many forms, as do people. But at the end of the day it is humanity—sentience, cognition, verbosity, affect, faces and voices—that we need. If we don't have other humans we create surrogates, like pets (even rodents or bugs, if, say, we're in solitary confinement), or plants (if we're half nuts), or even alter egos (much more than half, although I frequently talk to myself aloud). At the end of the day, I believe that *identity* is at the heart of healthy conversation. "Who are you? Would you like to know who I am? I would like both, but obliquely."

In his small, oddly definitive work on Charles Dickens, while discussing *The Pickwick Papers*, the great G. K. Chesterton pinpoints the recreational essence of conversation:

> To every man alive, one must hope, it has in some manner happened that he has talked with his more fascinating friends round a table on some night when all the numerous personalities unfolded themselves like great tropical flows. All fell into their parts as in some delightful impromptu play. Every man was a beautiful caricature of himself. The man who has known such nights will understand the exaggerations of *Pickwick*. . . . [Dickens] exaggerate[s] life in the direction of life. The spirit he at bottom celebrates is that of . . . friends . . . talking through the night.

– the quintessence of recreative fun.

Our engagement ought to be continual, whether at the dinner table, in the classroom or the public house, or the . . . *salon*. Aaah, the *salon!* Say it aloud, and if its very sound does not make your juices flow then you have been wasting your time. Notice the immediacy, vitality, and urgency implicit in this passage from "The Voice of Poetry in the Conversation of Mankind," again from Oakeshott: "Thoughts of different species take wing and play round one another, responding to each other's movements and provoking one another to fresh exertion." He continues, "nobody asks where they have come from or on what authority they are present; nobody cares what will become of them when they have played their part. There is no symposiarch or arbiter; not even a doorkeeper to examine credentials. Every entrant is taken at its face-value and everything is permitted which can get itself accepted into the flow of speculation. And voices which speak in conversation do not compose a hierarchy." Finally, "conversation is not an enterprise designed to yield an extrinsic profit, a contest where a winner gets a prize, nor is it an activity of exegesis; it is an unrehearsed intellectual adventure. It is with conversation as with gambling, its significance lies neither in winning nor in losing, but in wagering." In short, we need the action.

Yet not just any action will do. Montaigne tells us that "stupidity and senselessness are not curable by a bit of admonition. . . . Moreover, nothing vexes me so much in stupidity as the fact that it is better pleased with itself than any reason can reasonably be. It is unfortunate," he continues, with life-learned, homespun sense, "that wisdom forbids you to be satisfied with yourself and trust yourself, and always sends you away discontented and diffident, whereas opinionativeness and heedlessness fill their hosts with rejoicing and assurance." Occasionally conversation must become Conversation; *verbum* ought to sustain *ratio* ('reason', 'thought' or even "intellectual proportion") so that they may make us, individually and collectively, bigger on the inside than on the outside.

That is what happens to a reader while visiting with Montaigne. One comes to see that his extremely high regard for conversation is not excessive. Not only is it medicine for the soul and, as such, recreative, but it is the lifeblood of civil society as well as of culture generally, enhancing social cohesion, enabling our most intimate interactions, and even catalyzing international comity. For example, the contemporary German sociologist Jurgen Habermas links the rise of the coffee house with the vitality of open conversation, and attributes the "rise of a public space" outside the control of the state to those conversations. Thus free and peaceable talk practiced in public has become a cornerstone of democracy, which is one reason behind the many calls for a "national conversation" (no matter how cynical) on this or that.

Jacques Barzun (1907-2012), the great cultural historian and teacher, tells us what the result of rich conversation might be when describing his conception of intellect: "the capitalized and communal form of live intelligence . . . intelligence stored up and made into habits of discipline, signs and symbols of meaning, chains of reasoning and spurs to emotion—a shorthand and a wireless by which the mind can skip connectives, recognize ability, and communicate truth"—this from *The House of Intellect*, a book now nearly fifty years old. "Intellect," he continues, "is at once a body of common knowledge and the channels through which the right particle of it can be brought to bear quickly, without the effort of redemonstration, on the matter in hand. Intellect is community property that can be handed down." That's action; and it is speech action.

The finest recent look at this fundamental adhesive is a brief one from the anonymous author of "The Chattering Classes" in the *Economist* of December 23, 2006. She or he has high standards. We are told that "great brilliance, fantastic powers of recall and quick wit are clearly valuable in sustaining conversation at . . . cosmic levels. Charm may be helpful too." And cooperation is downright necessary. "This principle . . is one of the things that sets conversation apart from other superficially similar activities such as lectures, debates, arguments and meetings." Other features of healthy conversation are "the equal distribution of speaker rights; mutual respect among speakers; spontaneity and informality; and a non-businesslike ambience." And we are reminded of the essence of the salon when the author cites the great Dr. Johnson, defining conversation as *"talk beyond that which is necessary to the purposes of actual business."* Who could add to, or would take away, from that?

The author tells us that, for enthusiasts, "conversation is an art, one of the great pleasures of life, even the basis of civilised society." Clearly the author is acquainted with Mme. de Stael (1766-1817), perhaps the greatest of all the salon arbiters, who called conversation "a means of reciprocally and rapidly giving one another pleasure; of speaking just as quickly as one thinks; of spontaneously enjoying one's self; of being applauded without working . . . [a] sort of electricity that causes sparks to fly, and that relieves some people of the burden of their excess vivacity and awakens others from a state of painful apathy."

Conversations differ from culture to culture. "It might reasonably be said that Italians are more tolerant of interruption, Americans of contradiction and the English of formality. . . . In seventeenth century France, a man without conversation was liable to find himself devalued, whatever his other qualities." Newton may have been the greatest mathematician of the century, but the French would have expected him to be agreeable, too. Here again is Dr. Johnson, telling us "a Frenchman must always be talking, whether he knows anything of the matter or not; an Englishman is content when he has nothing to say." George Orwell confirms that observation, sort of: "in very many English homes the radio is literally never turned off. This is done with a definite purpose. The music prevents the conversation from becoming serious or even coherent."

Modern chatterers have a hard act to follow. Three men in particular exercised more influence on our conception of conversation than almost anyone else. The first of these, the most important, we will save for last. The other two flourished in an age when conversation as an art was coming into its own largely because leisure time was beginning to rise. These two are Stefano Guazzo and Baldassare Castiglione.

Stefano Guazzo's *Civil Conversation*, (1574, in English 1581-1586) was intended for the bourgeoisie. It is in the form of a dialogue between Guazzo and Annibal (who seems to be Guazzo's real mouthpiece), for Guazzo's thinking, which would become common, was that conversation can be taught only by demonstration. Yet as a dialogue it is odd: it has an extraordinarily high number of long speeches (especially its center-piece on solitude). Guazzo's objective is to reveal "the fruites that may bee reaped by conversation, and teaching howe to knowe good companie for yll. . . the manner of conversation, meete for all persons, which shall come in any companie."

Along the way, he (rather, Annibal) provides guideposts. For example, he complains about "they [who] do not thinke what they say, doing it to no other ende, but to shew theeir sharpe and good wit, not that they have conceived any such opinion in themselves. . . . and when they are able to mainteine Argument no longer by any reason, they inter into a chafe. . . ." Who among us has not met that person? (Or has been that person?) The learned also come in for a scolding, which is telling, given Guazzo's admiration for scholarship and its fruits: "the learned must not glory too much in their knowledge, but remember that the Eagle carieth away the prise with his force, the Peacocke with his feathers, the Nightingale with his Melody, and that nature shoulde have dealt injuriously with others, if shee had bestowed all her graces and perfections upon one only." Late in the day Guazzo notes a certain suasory tack to Annibal's talk and admonishes him: "if then your meaning be wee shoulde moove affections, and persuade mens mindes with the tongue, you can not chuse but you must have recourse to the preceptes of Rhethorike, which are not for every mans capacitie." Indeed. Annibal backs off, finally allowing that, "I perceive also, that in discourseing with you, with yur gentill and loving conditions, you have bound mee to manifest the inward affection of my heart, by outward signes and tokens of good will."

In his introduction to an English edition of Guazzo's book, Edward Sullivan assures us that Guazzo was a great believer in the "free power to criticise both the topic and the point of view from which it was presented," and he calls attention to some of Guazzo's advice: "not to be lolling asleepe"; not to "buskell them selves, reache, streach and yawn"; not to "pull out their knives or their sciser and doe nothing els but pare their nailes"; not to "pounch with the elbowe," and not, even for emphasis, to "chide at the table." Withal, and except for the knives and scissors, I wonder if anything Guazzo has to say is dated.

The second of the two is the more renowned Baldassare Castiglione and his *The Book of the Courtier* (1528, in English 1561). He certainly did not write for the bourgeoisie but, as his title indicates, for the social climber, a man whose fate (and, at the extreme, possibly his life) depended upon his conversational skills. It would be difficult to overestimate the importance of this book during the late sixteenth century. It depicts a four-night conversation in the salon of the Duchess Elisabetta Gonzaga and is an *exemplum* of "the trade and manner of courtiers . . . a brief rehearsal of the chief conditions and qualities in a Courtier," whose stock in trade prominently includes conversation.

The participants sit in a circle, with four main speakers taking turns. But they are frequently interrupted, so that real conversation emerges. Here is a sampling of Castiglione's pointers:

To be well born and of good stock
To be of a mean stature . . . well-made to his proportion
Not to be womanish in his sayings or doings
Not to praise himself unshamefully and out of reason
Not to crake and boast of his acts and good qualities
To shun affectation or curiosity about all things
To do his feats with a slight . . . and use a recklessness to cover art
Not carry about tales and trifling news
Not to be overseen in speaking words otherwhile that may offend where he mean it not
Not to be stubborn . . . nor to contrary and overthwart men

after a spiteful sort
Not to be a babbler or chatterer, nor lavish of his tongue
Not to use any fond sauciness or presumption
To confess his ignorance . . .
Not to become a jester or scoffer to put any man out of coun-
tenance
To have the virtues of the mind, as justice, manliness, wisdom,
temperance, staidness, noble courage, sober mood, etc.

And then there are the "Chief conditions and qualities in a waiting gen-
tlewoman":

To accompany sober and quiet manners and honesty with a
lively quickness of wit
Not to make wise to abhor company and talk, though somewhat of the wantonest, to arise and forsake them for it.
To be learned.
To use a somewhat more familiar conversation with men well
grown in years than with young men.

Castiglione has his character Canossa declare that he cannot teach
conversation, only show it, if he is to form "the perfect gentleman." Only
by example is *honestas* (simplicity, fair dealing, uprightness of character,
dignity of deportment), which is the core of *societas*, communicated to
others. In short, to learn conversation we must converse, and always with
sprezzatura—that crucial liveliness of an art that hides art.

Here enter our Number One. The first formal and influential elab-
orator upon the art of conversation was the Roman rhetorician, lawyer,
senator, essayist and public speaker, Marcus Tullius Cicero (106 B.C - 43
B.C). In his early *De oratore*—presented as a conversation—he links the
arts of conversation and oratory. Both are rhetorical arts, the former providing practice in winning the audience's goodwill, so necessary to the
latter. This winning, he tells us, is indeed based upon *honestas*, a restrained
candor that helps strengthen social bonds.

Later, in his *De officiis* (tellingly, *On Duties*, written in the fateful
year of 44B.C., he provides nine rules of "honest" (*i.e.* decorous and temperate) conversation: 1/ it should be undogmatic; 2/ it must have wit; 3/
each person should have a part: no monopolizing; 4/ tone should match
subject-matter; 5/ participants should not betray defects of character, and
the home, politics, the professions or learning are suitable subjects; 6/ talk

should not be allowed to drift, but neither should a given subject be rigidly adhered to; 7/ we must observe if the conversation is proceeding agreeably, and just as it has a beginning, so must it have an end; 8/ it should be free from mental excitement, or passion uncontrolled by reason—especially there should be no anger, inordinate desires, indolence or indifference; 9/ we must take care to show courtesy and consideration toward those with whom we converse.

In short, we must be tactful, easy and familiar, accommodating ourselves to others. He goes on to tell us that "the whole art of oratory . . . is concerned in some measure with the common practice, custom, and speech of mankind." Its concern is with the "changeable matter," exactly like those of private conversation—which, I repeat, is what *De oratore* is. This insight from Jennifer Richards' indispensable *Rhetoric and Courtliness in Early Modern Literature* is suitably succinct in its description of Cicero's valuation of conversation: " . . . we need to recognize the ongoing cultural significance of ideas of community and the common good with which any defense of self-interest or personal aspiration must negotiate." (Richards goes on to assure us that, for Cicero, there must be nothing perfunctory or insouciant in the *performance*—her superbly apt word—of conversation. Finally, according to Richards, Cicero saw Caesar as the quintessential *anti-social* interlocutor, and since he was a dictator, boilerplate oratory had to subsume conversation. He destroyed "private space" and controlled public space.

The summit of artful conversation—the application of the best of Cicero, Guazzo, and Castiglione— occurs in the seventeenth and eighteenth centuries, and it has very much to teach us. In her incomparable *The Age of Conversation*, Benedetta Craveri tells us of the French *salons*, run by commanding women of strong will and very high standards of conversational conduct. Throughout Europe they would be influential at all levels of culture for two centuries.

In them, the basic skills brought to the table were expected to include *politesse* (sincere good manners), *esprit* (wit), *galanterie* (gallantry), *complaisance* (obligingness), *enjouement* (cheerfulness) and *flatterie*. More specific techniques would be required as the conversation took flight. A comic mood would require displays of *raillerie* (playful teasing), *plaisanterie* (joking), *bons mots* (epigrams), *traits* and *pointes* (rhetorical figures involving "subtle, unexpected wit"), and perhaps *persiflage* (mocking under the guise of praising: Castiglione would be perplexed by that if not absolutely appalled). Here is Craveri's description of the ideal salon participant:

> Antoine Gombard, Chevalier die Mere . . . established his au-
> thority by giving shape to [salons]. . . . To him, success in *bonne*
> *compagnie* was based on conversation and depended on the
> ability to please and amuse others by the simple appeal of the .
> . . word. The art of *conversation* did not rely only on intuition
> and improvisation but also presupposed a sum of knowledge
> and expertise. . . which involved paying everyone the regard he
> was due. A regard for etiquette and for different social condi-
> tions . . . was an integral part of the *bienseances*. . . . Rather than
> indicating the homogeneity of social belonging, the aim was to
> value individual talent and involve everyone in *the pleasure of*
> *the game* [my emphasis].

Yet more—creation.

Craveri goes on to tell us that Honore d'Urfe, the archetypal socialite
and intimate of Mme. de Rambouillet, valued conversation as much as
Gombard, and for the same reasons, but may have understood it better:

> Of all these arts [literature, fine arts, music, dance, theater] it
> is the art of conversation—society's art *par excellence*—that we
> miss most and that most demands our admiration. . . . Devel-
> oped as an entertaining end in itself, as a game for shared pleas-
> ure, conversation obeyed strict laws that guaranteed harmony
> based on perfect equality. These were laws of clarity, measure,
> elegance, and regard for the self-respect of others. A talent for
> listening was more appreciated than one for speaking. Exqui-
> site courtesy restrained vehemence and prevented quarrels.

Madame de Stael, at the end of the eighteenth century, knew even better
than Gombard the powers of conversation, when she called it "an instrument that it is enjoyable to play and that, like music with some people and
strong liquor with others, raises the spirits." Powers aside, Craveri reminds
us of the nature of this instrument:

> A gentlemen's education aimed precisely at knowing how to
> master emotions, words, and gestures through different degrees
> of rhetoric. . . . In this process of dramatizing the self, conver-
> sation became crucial . . . tone of voice, gesture, bearing, and
> facial expression were as important as the spoken word. . . .
> [conversation] was also an education in the world—for many,

the only one available. Its usefulness was so obvious that even dictionaries praised it.

Said one *saloniere*, "conversation should be loved; it constitutes good society; friendships are formed and preserved through it"; and another: it "brings natural talents into play and polishes them. It purifies and sets the mind to rights and constitutes the great book of the world." In short, it teaches the "beauties of language" and forms taste and helps one acquire that eclectic, dazzling culture so necessary to life in society.

At the end of the *Ancien Regime*, de Stael opined that "the development of ideas has, for a century, been entirely directed by conversation"; it was "primarily a method of thought." One Mlle. de Scudery describes the ideal manner and matter of the art:

> And yet I hold that there is nothing that may not be included: [it] must be free and varied according to the time, the place, and the people present. . . . Furthermore I would like a certain joyous spirit to preside, which . . . would nevertheless inspire in the hearts of the whole Company a disposition to be amused by everything and bored by nothing; and I want great and small things to be spoken of, so long as they are spoken of elegantly . . . without there being the slightest constraint.

The range and continuity of concern respecting conversation, with its rhetorical inherency and its educational thrust, has marked our culture from longer ago even than Cicero. It marks every one of us. How could it not? Conversation broadly conceived has what philosophers call ontological status; that is, it's there, as part of a reality that cannot be denied, use it or abuse it as we might. Whether you think of the world as something like a rock, or maybe as something alive (like a tree), or just the expression of some cosmic Tourette's syndrome, conversation is the great muse of humanity—our Logos—flowing out of us. Within that context we can discern a number of characteristics.

1/ the dynamic of interaction tends to become more varied (riskier too, and perhaps more guarded – at first), usually more vital, more challenging, and more . . . fun, when a third party joins the conversation; spectators matter; 2/ we learn about ourselves on the fly, so to speak, by what we do and do not reveal, what interests and does not interest us in others, and to what degree we enjoy (or don't) learning about others by listening to them, if we have learned to listen at all; 3/ norms (*e.g.* of both interruption and filibustering) vary, but there are norms, and we should abide by them; 4/ the greater the intimacy the richer the conversation; 5/ some people are simply clueless, failing to follow the thread of a conversation, for example, or parading their narcissism, or simply not respecting the particular rhythm of a given conversation (*e.g.* by breaking in too soon) or by starting a side conversation about a special interest that overflows into, and therefore disrupts, the collective pleasure; 6/ suppleness matters: that is, the ability to abandon a thread, lend a ready response, or have just the *bon mot* or quip ready at the tongue; 7/ what seems a small point but isn't: we should physically arrange ourselves so as to maximize mutual exchanges, so that everyone hears everyone else and anyone may respond, confident that all participants have heard what's been going on.

Moreover, good conversation eschews the meretricious (just how much can we watch *Jersey Shore* or *The Housewives of ___*?). It invites but does not compel the intimacy that, to some degree, all rich conversation requires, lends itself to building community, and strives for fairness. Sure, there is a point beyond which the distance we need to listen to objectionable opinion or language closes: then we are tempted to passion. Always there are tricksters: people who shift ground, pretend to misunderstanding, feign offense when there should be none (either taken or given), or even claim ignorance when all along they've been parading a presumed authority. In short, the comity among people that invites healthy conversation is based on an assumed social contract; maintaining it requires vigilance and . . . good will.

At its best conversation requires *sophrosyne*, that self-control and soundness of mind that is the opposite of *hubris* (see Plato's *Charmides*). Yes, conversation is often a sort of negotiation (as Jennifer Richards suggests), if that means adjusting ourselves to others. Here I offer a personal case study (so to speak). I take special delight in recounting this episode because the key figure had (I'm told) a sizeable ego, was a perfectionists, and rose to fame in a businesses marked through-and-through by competition. The person was a personal icon of mine: the Hardest Working Man in Show Business and Soul Brother Number One, Mr. James Brown. It was in the KLM Rembrandt Room at JFK airport. He and I sat on a sofa, with his wife and manager nearby but remaining utterly unobtrusive. Mostly Mr. Brown (as he preferred) and I (to him, always "professor" or "professor Como") discussed two of our favorite subjects, boxing and baseball.

He showed me his pitching motion; I showed him my boxing stance (at the time I was training and sparring) and how Roberto Duran (in my judgment the greatest fighter since the retirement of Ray Robinson, who was the greatest, period) would throw that devastating overhand right. We traded anecdotes, with me doing most of the listening. Very early on we had gone from an interview to a conversation. Only toward the end of our ninety-minute chat did I bring up music. He explained Funk and the importance of the "one"—that first beat. He told me how much work it took to have "the tightest band in show business." He told me of his fondness for Elvis and of Sinatra's untold personal charities. (That was in response to my expressed distaste for a man I considered a bully.) He stressed, and more than once, the importance of a band being racially integrated; and he told me an inside item or two.

Then he asked me about my teaching. I allowed as how I used him as a model: "Follow James Brown's advice," I tell my classes, "tell yourself—'I feel good'! – and mean it." He was very touched by that and, although at first demurring, he shouted his famous line into my recorder and sent a greeting to my students. We ended with him paying me a high compliment. "Professor," he said, "I've never been more relaxed before a tour than I am now." And he turned to the other two and asked, "when have you heard me talk baseball and boxing as I have with this man?" They chuckled and shook their heads. "Thank you, professor, and God bless you." After all, his presence was not a function of theatricality.

I was struck by how frequently he asked me questions, including questions about music. He pondered my answers, engaged them, and amplified upon my thinking. In short, I mattered to him: the secret indeed, especially of healthy conversation. Later, when I reflected on our conversation, it occurred to me that Mr. Brown's presence was owing to how intensely he paid attention, above all to human beings, whether they were an audience in the dark or an unknown professor sitting next to him.

There is an art to paying attention, and that ability was the mark of a civilized man. "The baby cannot attend," Jacques Barzun tells us, and "the savage and the boor will not. It is the boorishness of inattention that makes pleasant discussion turn into stupid repetitive argument, and that doubles the errors and mishaps of daily life." Alas, Barzun believes that only six or seven people in a lifetime know and sustain the art. Nevertheless, it matters so greatly because its applicability matters. Barzun writes:

> Thinking means shuffling, relating, selecting the contents of one's mind so as to assimilate novelty, digest it, and to create order. It is doing to a fact or an idea what we do to a beefsteak when we distribute its parts throughout our body. We are . . . more competent to assimilate more of the same protein with-

out strain. . . . Digging into the laws of thought illuminates not controversy merely, but all conscious endeavor.

Moreover, he continues, in all good thinking and feeling we find the "three great ideas underlying both logic and mathematics: Generality, Form (something that can be handled when its type is recognized), and Variability. They appear in different guises when fit to different subjects, but they rule thinking about art as well as politics, business as well as science. They assure intellectual poise: the ability to resist mob judgment."

Since we must rhetorize in the first place—our *logos* does not rest— why not do so by conversing? I will let the great Barzun make my point. "Why am I so bent on conversation? " he asks. His answer is memorable:

> For pleasure first, pure selfishness, but also because conversation is a school for thinkers and should be a school for democrats. When one finds supposedly educated people arguing heatedly over matter of fact and shying away from matters of opinion; when one sees one's hosts getting nervous at a difference of views regarding politics or the latest play; when one is formally entertained with information games or queries cut of the paper . . . when intelligent youth is advised not to go against the accepted belief in any circle because it will startle, shock, and offend—it is time to recognize, first, that the temper of democratic culture is tested at every dinner table and in every living room—just as much as at school, in the pulpit, or on the platform. . . .despite our boasted freedom of opinion, we lack men and women whose minds have learned to move easily and fearlessly in the perilous jungle of ideas.

William James, that godfather of American psychology, tells us why those sparks might fly. Along the way he further answers Barzun's question respecting his devotion to conversation:

> When two minds of a high order, interested in kindred subjects, come together, their conversation is chiefly remarkable for the summariness of its allusions and the rapidity of its transitions . . . true feasts for gods to a listener who is educated enough to follow them at all. . . .

In that light, reader, who would be in your ideal *salon*? Sorry: mere "followers" on Twitter and "friends" on Facebook simply cannot count— which gets us to the *salon*. I leave the answer to Mme. de Stael:

> The feeling of satisfaction that characterizes an animated conversation does not so much consist of its subject matter. Neither the ideas nor the knowledge that may emerge within it are of primary interest. Rather, it is a certain manner in which some people have an effect on others; of reciprocally and rapidly giving one another pleasure; of speaking just as quickly as one thinks; of spontaneously enjoying oneself; of being applauded without working; of displaying one's wit through all the nuances of accent, gesture, and look, in order to produce at will a sort of electricity [!] that causes sparks to fly, and that relieves some people of the burden of their excess vivacity and awakens others from a state of painful apathy.

High standards indeed, yielding an image of an ideal (but not completely unreal) conversation. More down-to-earth, I think, is Jonathan Swift's conception in his poem "Conversation":

> Conversation is but carving!
> Give no more to every guest
> Than he's able to digest.
> Give him always of the prime
> And but little at a time.
> Carve to all but just enough,
> And that you may have your due,
> Let your neighbor carve for you.

Even so, when we converse we *cannot not perform*, cannot *not* blow things up a bit. There is no opting out. Do it badly, sporadically, thoughtlessly, indirectly, or by way of surrogates: but do it we must. The alternatives are sleep, coma, death, or removal to a desert cave. We run on *conversation*, on all kinds of it—personal, social, public, direct, mediated. We have no choice. We must remember just what was "in the beginning."

TWENTY

The Ongoing Salon
or, Conversation Abides

VERBAL EXCHANGES between people present to each other have
been depicted since the beginnings of narrative and dramatic literature. But the earliest of these depictions—from the Jewish Bible, Homer, and *Gilgamesh*, for example—depict them not as conversation as we
know it but as speeches. Job with his friends and Yahweh with Job certainly debated (sort of), but each speaks only oratorically, and at length. The
same is true of the exchanges in *The Iliad*, where talk is rarely anything but
oratory, and in Plato's dialogues, where we read either speeches or reciprocal interrogations. These days, of course, we've run out of patience with
oratory: almost anything smacking of it gives most people a rash. Still, we
need our conversations and always will—no matter how inhospitable the
culture.

1.

No longer are we instructed by rich and ample models. For example,
only people of a certain age will remember the entertainer Steve Allen. He
was a multi-talented man who, among his other achievements, established
the grammar of late-night television talk shows. A versatile entertainer,
Allen was also an (albeit minor) "public intellectual." He was a self-pro-
claimed liberal: in those days, a man of the moderate Left. His crowning
achievement, in my view, was a program unlike any before or since: *Meeting of the Minds*. The premise was a question: if noted historical figures
from vastly different times and places were to sit at the same table and

converse, what would their talk be like? So, on any given show, we would vicariously participate in talk between, say, Marie Antoinette, Henry VIII, Catherine the Great, and Newton. Fascinating: and Allen himself wrote most of the scripts.

In fact imaginary dialogues between historical figures (like books of instruction on the art, with their two-thousand-year history) are many, and often compelling. Walter Savage Landor (1775–1864) surely enjoyed himself in writing his *Imaginary Conversations*. His book has three sections: Dialogues of Literary Men, Dialogues of Famous Women, and Miscellaneous Dialogues. He pairs such historical figures as Melancthon and Calvin, Milton and Marvell, and Dante and Beatrice (whom he has telling Dante essentially to man up). My own favorite pair is in number XXI, with the fabulist la Fontaine and the epigrammist la Rochefoucauld. "Speaking of cats," says the former, I would have avoided all personality that might be offensive to them . . . by their tongues they are flatterers, like men." The latter responds that "dogs are not very modest," eliciting this comment from la Fontaine: "Never say that . . . they are the most modest people on earth!" Landor manages to convey the impression that, if the great contemporaries had conversed, this is what they would have said— about cats and dogs.

But the finest imagined conversations by far are those by the prolific Bernard Le Bovier de Fontenelle (1657-1757!) in his *Dialogue of the Dead*. (One George, Lord Lyttleton wrote a similar book, and with the same title, not long after: the great Dr. Johnson seems to have liked it.) Fontenelle's book has four parts, the first three with twelve dialogues each, the last with two. The parts are Ancients, Ancients and Moderns, Dialogues of the Moderns, and Two Additional Dialogues. Fontenelle's pairs include Homer and Aesop (with Homer insisting there are no mysteries in his works and Aesop insisting, no, there must be "allegories"), Apicius (a late Roman gourmet) and Galileo (who insists that new knowledge can be discovered but not new pleasures), and Cortez and Montezuma, the latter of which Fontenelle has winning a debate by favorably contrasting Aztec superstitions with "the Greek practice of recovering an eclipsed moon with hideous noise or trying to win the approval of the Holy Chicken." Wit marks almost all the dialogues, and some raise interesting questions that have the reader thinking along (*e.g.* Mary Queen of Scots and her advisor Riccio discussing if we can achieve happiness by reason alone).

In his day (already a lifetime ago), Steve Allen was far from alone in his zeal for meaty, enjoyable, wide-ranging conversation. David Susskind, a Broadway producer, had a program every Sunday night beginning at 9 p.m. and broadcast on Channel 9 in New York. (I mention the channel only because of its obscurity: almost no one watched the station except for its Million Dollar Movie, which showed the same movie every night, twice a night, for an entire week.) Susskind had a point-of-view (it was the same as Allen's) but, unlike Allen, really could not understand that there could be another side. (When referring to the notorious Sen. Joseph McCarthy, the great broadcaster Edward R. Murrow famously said, "sometimes there is no 'other side'!"—clever, but dangerous in its invitation to wanton, and mistaken, application; as it happens, Murrow was wrong.) Still, Susskind remained civil (if often sardonic) with his guests—writers, politicians, entertainers—who were on that other side; and Susskind (unlike the jejune simulacra these days) had no agenda. Indeed, the show had no formal closing time. He and his guests simply went on—often till past midnight—until they all ran out of things to say, at which point Susskind would bring the show to a close and channel 9 would go off the air with an American flag flying and the playing of the National Anthem.

Two programs were particularly strong. One of these was *Firing Line*, the longest-running public-service program in the history of broadcasting, invigorated by the giant of Conservative thought, of American political journalism, *and of civil conversation*, William F. Buckley, Jr. He did have antagonists as guests, and they were candidly so. (His very first guest was the perennial Socialist Party candidate for president, Norman Thomas.) The talk was chilly sometimes, but rarely belligerent. The second was *Tony Brown's Journal*. Without coming close to racism Brown, a black man, never abandoned either reason or African American causes. Noteworthy on radio were the two Barrys, Farber (from the Right) and Gray (from the Left), providing hours of nocturnal delights, as did Jean Shepherd, the finest raconteur in the history of broadcasting. Interesting talkers all, because they, like Susskind and Allen and the others, were interested—in almost everything, but especially interested in other human beings. (In the running was Jack Paar, but his smugness too often detracted from his congeniality and up-staged his guest.)

I've taken a woefully brief three paragraphs to recount these few abiding conversational pleasures, not only to tease the not-yet-geriatric reader with foregone joys, but to lament their scarcity, since what today passes for broadcast conversation is rarely more than exhibitionism, posturing, self-indulgence (*e.g.* Charlie Rose, Bill O'Reilly), tightly orchestrated "blocks," and polemic. My dismay was heightened when I had a luncheon conversation with an old high school friend, a congenial man who is now a high-ranking programming executive for a television network—an "insider" if ever there was one. When I opined that TV needs more real conversation—and provided exemplars from the past as models—he simply . . . scoffed.

2.

So these days we partake of only the diluted remnants of a great tradition. How great? Any number of people have written the script of actual conversations. These usually go under the rubric of "table talk." Does that designation ring a bell? The practice, especially the family practice of table-talk, has almost disappeared, at least in The United States. In Hispanic cultures, however, the tradition of *sobremesa*—"over-the-table"—still lives. If you Google "table talk" you will be astounded at the sheer number of entries that pop up: who has not published their *sobremesa*, real or imagined?

Alas, we no longer have anything like those of Oliver Wendell Holmes (1809-1894), with his *Autocrat at the Breakfast Table* (1858, consisting of songs, jokes, stories and conversation—not always actual—and selling ten thousand copies the first three days) and its sequel *Professor at the Breakfast Table* (1859). In the first we find "a weak flavor of genius in an essentially common person is detestable"; in the second, the refreshingly candid "women are more subject than men to atrophy of the heart." Took the words right out of my mouth. Yet my own judgment of both is largely negative: they become ponderous and largely undisciplined; Holmes seems overly fond of his own opinions, and the occasional snappy expression of them is too occasional. But those are one man's impressions one hundred and sixty years after the fact. In his day, and that day lasted fifty years, his reputation and influence as a conversationalist (and essayist, lecturer, and medical researcher), as well as a leader of what is known as the American Renaissance, was enormous.

Yet earlier in the nineteenth century there was a still greater conversationalist—an Olympian conversationalist, apparently—the great Romantic (revolutionary) poet, essayist and philosopher Samuel Taylor Coleridge (1772-1834).[1] His influence and achievements in all three modes is far beyond dispute, and the capaciousness of his reason and his learning was legendary. His published work, especially his "notebooks" that go on and on, fill long shelves in any library. Yet he was reputed to have published too little because he talked so much. Men unknown and known—Emerson, De Quincy, Lamb, Crabb Robinson—would make pilgrimages to his

---

1 Here my source is a strange and wonderful book, *Coleridge the Talker* (Cornell University Press, 1940), a compilation of more than seventy-five first-hand accounts and assessments of the man in conversation.

home, where he lived a more or less solitary life. Dozens of people would visit more than once, even over the course of fifteen years just to listen to Coleridge talk, since listening was just about all they could do.

And how he talked! For hours—analytically, judgmentally, reciting long passages from memory, often in German, Latin, and French. According to Thomas De Quincey, "what a tumult of anxiety prevailed to 'hear Mr. Coleridge', or even to talk with a man who had heard him. Had he lived to this day, not Paganini would have been so much sought after." It did not seem to matter that he would often make "a capital error," De Quincey continues, "of keeping his audience in a state of passiveness . . . by an eternal stream of talk which never once intermitted." It certainly did not matter to Henry Crabb Robinson: "[He] kept me on the stretch of attention and admiration from half past three till twelve o'clock"—nearly nine hours!—"On politics, metaphysics, poetry. . . . On Kant and Shakespeare he was astonishingly eloquent." Withal, his conversation "had the primary attraction of moving, luminous ideas." Moreover, "expounded face-to-face, these ideas had a clarity of meaning and a persuasive force which print could never reproduce, or even . . . approximate." People "with distinction in literature, politics, religion, science, and the arts" traveled to him, as John Sterling put it, "with keen and buoyant expectations, and returned with high and animating remembrances." There is no such talker alive today, and, in our technological age, we are the worse for it. "[This] mere surplus of his studies, his meditations, and his dreams provided intellectual nourishment for almost a whole generation." As his friend, the great Wordsworth put it, "he was the only *wonderful* man" he had ever known.

3.

My late friend, the admirable Fr. William Edy, when pastor of Christ Church, Tarrytown, would convene salons that often included people he'd never met but simply invited by telephone. In this way did I meet Pavel Litvinov, a prominent Soviet physicist and colleague of the great physicist and Soviet dissenter Sakharov (and grandson of Maxim Litvinov, who negotiated the Hitler-Stalin pact); and Martin Gardner, the polymath genius. Though my wife and I have conducted several *salons*, I've never done what Fr. Edy did: call a stranger out of the blue (though maybe now, in my retirement, the time has come).

My favorite ongoing *salon* very closely approximates a certain ideal. Every Wednesday at 5pm a group of colleagues meet for dinner until 6, when most must then get to class. Every year we add a cake on the occasion of the Marine Corps birthday, November 10; the baker is a former Marine. We are sure to pay homage to all those who have served in the military, after which we are treated to certain songs not widely sung outside the barracks, tents, and mess halls of Marines. Politically, intellectually, racially, chronologically, religiously and temperamentally we are a motley group. One woman has attended regularly, on the condition that we men do not alter our conversation, and we (mostly) did not.

Attendance is by informal invitation, but no innocent interloper has ever felt less than perfectly welcome; some have even returned. Our best conversations have been about religion, sex, politics, race, movies, TV, and each other. Disagreement is not unwelcome. We have often been given to impatience, but very rarely to anger; riotous laughter is the most common outburst. My reasons for recording this custom is twofold: such circles exist; such circles depend a good deal on trust. In their own charming way, they achieve intimacy.

Not long ago, owing to a sabbatical, I had been absent from the college but took great pleasure in knowing that my colleagues persisted in enjoying this tradition (of which I have been denominated the godfather, if not the father). Knowing that I would miss this collective badinage, my old friend the philosopher Howard Ruttenberg wrote minutes for each session. These nourished my spirit considerably during the leave semester, giving me a concrete sense of participation. For the sheer pleasure of it, I offer these snippets of Howard's minutes. Like our conversations they are in no particular order.

A bit later we were joined by Officer Milverton S. His keen sense of duty and willingness to risk himself in its pursuit, as well as his love of conversation, made him a fit addition for celebration of the 236th birthday of the United States Marines, and he has been invited back. Walter J. had baked a (delicious) cake for the celebration, as is his wont, showed us a card from his drill sergeant, and then read the Marine oath to us. . . . Milverton and Walter D. (both Jamaican) engaged in a lively exchange. . . . It had to do with Jamaica gang-violence—Milverton was a Jamaican police officer who Walter described as "individualistic and opportunistic." Milverton referred to Walter as "a mere footballer. . . ."

I arrived in the salon at about 5:15 to a table full of diners. Fortunately, sliced kielbasa was still on the table; otherwise, these minutes would have been crabby indeed. I found Jim [who was visiting this one evening] sitting on the north end, as was his custom (though he never knew it was north until now), with Hux chewing in silence to his right. (Later Como referred to Hux as "precious" when I alerted him to Sam's use of a plastic knife to cut in half a slice of kielbasa scarcely larger than a twenty-five cent piece.) Mitch and Eric chewed (though not as elegantly as Hux—and both had their own dinners, es-chewing, as opposed to chewing, the kielbasa.) I squeezed in on Eric's right, with Hux slicing kielbasa to my left. (Zeno, the disciple of that famous Polish philosopher Parmenides, claimed that if you slice kielbasa forever, nothing will be left . . . Walter D. had already added that he expects his last, dying word to be "kielbasa."[2]

I omit the bawdy humor, the absolutely funniest—and raunchiest—instance of which was told, and with conviction, by our female member. I hasten to add that the joke was academically relevant, having to do with speech, which I teach, and history, which she does, and sexual practices (another colleague's academic specialty) so, you see, the joke was really the result of legitimate interdisciplinary collaboration, a collaboration always sought by deans.

I partook of a memorable conversation in 1993, when my then-twenty-one-year-old son and I traveled to Oxford, England, to visit a closed movie set on the grounds of Magdalen College. It was the final day of shooting of the film *Shadowlands*, about the romance between C. S. Lewis (Anthony Hopkins) and Joy Davidman (Debra Winger). I would be writing on the film and had been invited to interview as many principles as possible. The experience was marvelous. I spoke with both the producer and the writer of the movie and was scheduled to meet for ten minutes with (now the late) Richard Attenborough, the director. Meanwhile we lunched (too lavishly) at the catered offering provided each day for the acting company and crew. Thereafter and for quite a while we sat on the lawn and watched the shoot from afar: there was Anthony Hopkins at a window, being filmed from the outside. (In the movie the scene would last fewer than two minutes; the shooting of it took hours.)

Then I was invited into the control room for a scene being shot next

---

2 I am pleased to say that only rarely do we engage that low form of conversation, gos-sip. For a rich and amusing treatment of that, see Joseph Epstein's *Gossip: The Untrivial Pursuit.*

door: Hopkins was in dialogue with a young actor whose timing was all off. "Dickie, Dickie, Dickie," I heard, "just a word please?" "Of course, Tony. I'm pushing too hard"—not true, I thought—"and we all need a break." I saw them chat briefly in the hallway; then (on a monitor) I saw Attenborough meander around the set, finding his way, as though randomly, to the young actor. They chatted briefly. Finally, Attenborough said something like, "oh, by the way, you might try opening the window before Tony speaks, so that when you turn back to him the job will already be done."

Here, I thought, is a very fine gentleman sparing this young actor's feelings. Just how fine I would find out presently. Some hours later Attenborough received me in the college quad. I mentioned that my son was along. Immediately he insisted that "young Jim" join us, and he did. To our great delight and utter surprise, Attenborough turned the encounter from an interview into a conversation—and he was very careful to include Jim; in fact, for a long stretch the conversation was with young Jim, who (already a cineaste of considerable knowledge) more than held his own, both with his expertise and with his relaxed deference. We touched upon Lewis, upon casting, upon directing Anthony Hopkins ("oh, you don't really direct Tony"), and upon the question, Why did he not take the Lewis part himself? "Because," he said, "Tony is better suited than I." I countered with a reminder of his superb acting in *The Great Escape* and, especially, in *The Guns of Batasi*, at which he simply smiled—"and it's very, very hard to direct oneself"—although, "yes, some, like Eastwood, can pull it off." In the event, the conversation did not last ten minutes but close to sixty. I, not he, finally mentioned the hour and that he must be very tired. "On the contrary," he said, "such talk is relaxing, don't you think?" When we parted with handshakes all around, he thanked us and said he hoped we would meet again "down the road." Am I too easily impressed by such graciousness and generosity? Maybe. Maybe that's because I see too little of it.[3]

As it happens there is a short coda to this event. Many months later I attended a private screening of the film. There were no more than fifty people in the audience, and the only principal there was Attenborough. I did

---

3 Several weeks thereafter I would have opportunities to speak with both Hopkins and Winger. Hopkins was attentive and responsive, willing to discuss the movie and Lewis and moviemaking, emphasizing especially how important it is to be gracious to co-workers, particularly young ones. Winger, on the other hand, was professionally vain, going on about her preparation for the role and her (often erroneous) knowledge of Lewis. When I presumed to correct her she responded, "so, we know a lot about C. S. Lewis, do we?" I answered with, "well, yes, actually, I do." I was alone in not being permitted to photograph her. And so ended my crush.

not much like the work—not least because at the end there was too much tear-jerking. (Those of you who know your reviewers will be stunned, as was I, to learn that the loudest bawler was none other than the utterly unsparing John Simon!) As we exited the screening room into the lobby, and very much by accident and inattention, I literally rubbed elbows with Attenborough. We both looked up, surprised, and he said, "why, Professor Como, how good to see you." I was struck dumb that he remembered me at all, let alone remembered me by name. And then the *coup de grace*: "and how is that very impressive son of yours, young Jim?" I was very shaken to learn that my friend—for that is what he seemed to me, now my late friend—lost his granddaughter in the Great Tsunami: he was utterly bereft, and I pray for both of them.

4.

All healthy salons depend upon the good will—even the good cheer—of the participants. Some people get it, others never will. They mistake re-*creation* for self-indulgent recreation: posturing, smugness, implicit *ad hominem* (*e.g.* "you say that only because you're a _____ [fill in the blank]), accusation (via an attribution of motive), the dismissive sneer, loudness, interruption, the filibuster—those, or they mistake it for attacks on their egos; they have no real interest in *knowing others and in being known by them*; their self-images, dammit, are fragile and fixed in amber, and these days we seem suspicious of each other's intentions.

Here, in that spirit, is one last, restorative thought: a familiar and resonant scene, qualitatively rich in its conversational promise because so uncontrived in its authenticity—brief, complete, utterly transparent, and fraught through-and-through with affection. For me it represents the highest ideal: conversational intimacy at its finest, fresh as the dawn. I wish I knew who wrote this piece of lovemaking but I don't: may the writer be blessed. It is the fitting conclusion to our conversation, the perfect final note. In its eloquence it puts the monumental undertaking of conversation and its importance to our mental, spiritual, social, and cultural good health in the irresistibly appealing setting of some good morning there and then. It is exquisitely human:

> Sing me a song of the jangle of spoons on coffee cups, subtle music to make my mouth water and my heart glad. I'll pass the cream to mingle with coffee and add a lump of sugar for each of us. You split the Danish pastry and keep talking. 'About what?' you ask. 'About those trivial things that make glad con-

versation in the morning, of course.'

Of course. . . .

Index

Y

Z

www.ingramcontent.com/pod-product-compliance
Lightning Source LLC
Chambersburg PA
CBHW021224090426
42740CB00006B/372